CHRISTIANITY AMONG OTHER RELIGIONS

Roch Kereszty, O. Cist.

CHRISTIANITY AMONG OTHER RELIGIONS

Apologetics in a Contemporary Context

Edited by Andrew C. Gregg

ST PAULS

Library of Congress Cataloging-in-Publication Data

Kereszty, Roch A.
  Christianity among other religions: apologetics in a contemporary
context / Roch A. Kereszty.
      p. cm.
  ISBN 0-8189-1227-8
  1. Apologetics. 2. Christianity and other religions. 3. Religions.
I. Gregg, Andrew C.   II. Title.
BT1103.K47 2006
261.2—dc22
                                    2005030365

Produced and designed in the United States of America by the
Fathers and Brothers of the Society of St. Paul,
2187 Victory Boulevard, Staten Island, New York 10314-6603,
as part of their communications apostolate.

ISBN 0-8189-1227-8
ISBN 978-0-8189-1227-6

Printing Information:

Current Printing - first digit   1   2   3   4   5   6   7   8   9   10

Year of Current Printing - first year shown

2006   2007   2008   2009   2010   2011   2012   2013   2014   2015

TABLE OF CONTENTS

Part III: Christianity, the Sacramental Presence of God's Saving Love in History

Part IV: The Christian View on the Relationship Between Christianity and Other Religions

Reader's Guide

ACKNOWLEDGMENTS

The chapters "Toward a Christian Theology of Inter-Religious Dialogue" and "Evangelization" are modified versions of my two articles published in *Communio* 29 (2002) and 21 (1994). They are re-published here with permission.

INTRODUCTION

The literature on world religions is immense and a number of apologetic works intend to show the credibility of the Catholic Christian faith. However, I have found no reliable study which combines these two themes by presenting a Christian apologetics in the context of other world religions. Yet, in today's pluralistic culture this appears a most urgent task. Many people, Christians and non-Christians alike, search for the meaning of life but feel confused by the labyrinthine multiplicity of religions. In this book I intend to show that Christianity is God's response (expressed in human words and in human history) to the (divinely inspired yet sin-distorted) universal human search for God. I trust that the credibility of the Christian faith and the need for both dialogue with and evangelization of the major world religions will emerge from a sympathetic evaluation and comparison.

However, before investigating individual religions, we need to examine the philosophical "mood" prevalent in Western culture. After its critical evaluation, we should explore the possibility and the limits of a philosophical inquiry into the ultimate questions on the origin and meaning of human life in this universe. Only after the meaningfulness of the religious quest in general and the need for a comparative approach among religions have been outlined, will I attempt a more detailed investigation of the major world religions.

I designed this book primarily for today's college student with some knowledge of Christian doctrine but little expertise in philosophy who faces the bewildering variety of religions in real life and in his college courses. Yet, my hope is that anyone seriously interested in the religious quest will profit from this book. If a reader has not yet been exposed to the basic mysteries of Christianity, I recommend the recently published *Compendium of the Catechism of the Catholic Church* as a supplemental reading to the present work.[1]

At the completion of this work I express my heartfelt gratitude to Mr. Andrew C. Gregg whose careful editorial work has refined the rough Hungarian-English style of my original manuscript and to Brother Joseph Van House, O.Cist. whose insights improved "Part I: A Philosophical Approach to Reality and Its Meaning." I also thank Professor Edeltraud Harzer of the University of Texas who assisted me with her critical review of my chapter on Hinduism. I am also indebted to Professor Mahmoud Ayoub of Temple University, to my friend Rabbi David Stern of Temple Emanu-El, Dallas and to my former student Prasanth Pattisapu. Our dialogue helped me immensely in my understanding of the world of Islam, Judaism and Hinduism.

---

[1] For a more scholarly study of the mystery of Christ along with a recommended bibliography for further readings see Josef Ratzinger, *Introduction to Christianity*. A new edition with a new introduction (San Francisco: Ignatius Press, 1990) and my *Jesus Christ: Fundamentals of Christology* (New York: Alba House, revised ed. 2002).

Biblical Abbreviations

OLD TESTAMENT

Genesis	Gn	Nehemiah	Ne	Baruch	Ba
Exodus	Ex	Tobit	Tb	Ezekiel	Ezk
Leviticus	Lv	Judith	Jdt	Daniel	Dn
Numbers	Nb	Esther	Est	Hosea	Ho
Deuteronomy	Dt	1 Maccabees	1 M	Joel	Jl
Joshua	Jos	2 Maccabees	2 M	Amos	Am
Judges	Jg	Job	Jb	Obadiah	Ob
Ruth	Rt	Psalms	Ps	Jonah	Jon
1 Samuel	1 S	Proverbs	Pr	Micah	Mi
2 Samuel	2 S	Ecclesiastes	Ec	Nahum	Na
1 Kings	1 K	Song of Songs	Sg	Habakkuk	Hab
2 Kings	2 K	Wisdom	Ws	Zephaniah	Zp
1 Chronicles	1 Ch	Sirach	Si	Haggai	Hg
2 Chronicles	2 Ch	Isaiah	Is	Malachi	Ml
Ezra	Ezr	Jeremiah	Jr	Zechariah	Zc
		Lamentations	Lm		

NEW TESTAMENT

Matthew	Mt	Ephesians	Eph	Hebrews	Heb
Mark	Mk	Philippians	Ph	James	Jm
Luke	Lk	Colossians	Col	1 Peter	1 P
John	Jn	1 Thessalonians	1 Th	2 Peter	2 P
Acts	Ac	2 Thessalonians	2 Th	1 John	1 Jn
Romans	Rm	1 Timothy	1 Tm	2 John	2 Jn
1 Corinthians	1 Cor	2 Timothy	2 Tm	3 John	3 Jn
2 Corinthians	2 Cor	Titus	Tt	Jude	Jude
Galatians	Gal	Philemon	Phm	Revelation	Rv

PART I

A Philosophical Approach to Reality and Its Meaning

The Western intellectual climate of our times is strongly influenced by both the Enlightenment and a sharply critical reaction to it. The presence of the Enlightenment mentality is evident in the widely held conviction that truth is limited to scientific knowledge. In other words, we can know only material realities and only to the extent that our hypotheses about their nature and behavior are verifiable by experiment.[1] According to this view, however, the progress of such knowledge is unlimited and holds the secret to the increase of general well-being and happiness.

The inconsistency of this approach comes to light if we ask why truth claims are limited to empirically verifiable conclusions. Such a limitation of truth claims is not empirically verifiable; it would be justified only if one could transcend the limits of empirical inquiry and come to discover that there is no reality beyond what is empirically given. Thus the very denial of possible knowledge beyond empirical inquiry runs into a contradiction. Moreover, the dangers of nuclear fission and human genetic engineering make it increasingly clear that natural science, left to its own resources, leads not to human progress but rather to human self-destruction.

The postmodern mentality has not only questioned the over-

---

[1] Evidently, this approach derives in one way or another from Kantian epistemology. See J. Ratzinger, *Truth and Tolerance. Christian Belief and World Religions* (San Francisco: Ignatius Press, 2004), 31, 126, 130-137.

confidence of Enlightenment rationalism and its naive faith in un-limited human progress, but has cast doubt on the very founda-tions of any objective knowledge of reality: what we claim as truth may be determined by our socio-economic condition (K. Marx), by our psyche's subconscious forces (S. Freud), or by our will to power or actual exercise of power (F. Nietzsche and M. Foucault). In fact, our language, what we say and what we write, can and should be deconstructed to a variety of conflicting meanings, none of which might refer to the real world (J. Derrida).

Perhaps the most widespread and often subconsciously op-erating epistemological approach is a sort of cultural relativism or perspectivism. It urges us to know and respect all cultures equally, yet it argues that the meaning system of a certain language, cul-ture, and religion is valid only within its own boundaries. One must look not for universal truth, but only for the practical validity of an epistemic system within its own cultural boundaries.

A more simplistic version of relativism permeates our daily life and our intellectual conversations. Simply put, "What is true for me is not true for you and vice versa. What matters is that I live authentically according to my truth and that you live authen-tically according to yours." We may call this approach individual-istic relativism.

We should not ignore the partial truths in these philosophies. Our perception of reality is definitely influenced by our position in society, our psychological mindset, our craving for power or po-sition within a system of power, and by our cultural boundaries. What we say and write does have implied meanings of which we may not have been aware at all as we spoke or composed our text. Yet our very ability to acknowledge the manifold limiting in-fluences on our perception of reality reveals our capacity to tran-scend these same limitations. None of the above critiques of knowledge would even be partially true if the above conditions and limits accounted for all that we claim to know.

If followed to its logical conclusions, cultural relativism eliminates what it wants to promote, namely the interest in other cultures and religions. Why should we bother to learn about many cultures and religions, if none of them leads to a better knowledge of reality, if each of them provides only practical advantages of functioning in a given society? Then why not rather limit ourselves to the culture which assures the best possible self-advancement? If all truth claims and all ethical norms are reducible to cultural norms or customs, we cannot be enriched by any cultural dialogue.

Moreover, our ability to translate a text from one language to another, even an ancient text of a language and culture that ceased to exist thousands of years ago, argues for the possibility of genuine communication. Although a translation is never perfectly accurate, it still shows that cultures separate from us and from each other in time and space have perceived reality in ways that we are able to understand. In fact, beyond a more or less objective understanding, we are even able to empathize with what they experienced. All this indicates the possibility of intercultural and interpersonal communication. Our awareness of being enriched by an exchange of views presupposes that by such an exchange we can gain a deeper and broader anchoring in reality.

Individualistic relativism leads to an even greater exclusivism and alienation. If each one of us has his/her own truth, then any dialogue becomes meaningless even within the same culture; we cannot be enriched by each other's views because one person's view is valid only for that person. Thus, interpersonal communication is a priori doomed to failure. The acute experience of isolation and estrangement among intellectuals may partly be rooted in the conviction that we can find no universal truth and meaning, but only a multiplicity of (perhaps sincerely held) personal opinions.

However, a wide-spread form of religious relativism closely allied with a certain form of mysticism concerns us here more directly. It has been often formulated in slightly different terms, but its essential thesis remains the same: in every religion we aim at an experience of the Divine or Transcendent Reality through different concepts, rituals and other practices. No matter how different these conceptualizations of the Divine and how different the religious practices are, they all conceptualize in different or even contradictory ways one and the same Divine Reality. The classic parable of this form of relativism is well known: a group of blind men are asked to touch different parts of an elephant and say what they think they touched. Obviously, they all will come to a different conclusion even though all of them touched the same animal. This approach, then, emphasizes the basic identity of the mystical experience and the relativity of any religious doctrine, since not only complementary but even contradictory doctrines may express the same Divine Reality.

This approach, which states that contradictory[2] statements may speak about the same unspeakable Transcendent Reality, implies that doctrinal assertions are ultimately irrelevant. Their truth claims must be relativized since what really matters is religious experience. At the same time, however, the philosophy of religious experience enunciates its own allegedly universally relevant and true doctrine, namely that religious doctrines cannot make truth claims. Hence, there is a latent inconsistency in this apparently plausible position.[3]

The above reasoning processes have already indicated for us the method we are going to use in this chapter. We have investigated the presuppositions of certain relativist philosophies regarding truth in general and religious truth in particular, and have exposed the inconsistencies in their approaches. As we attempt to

---

[2] Note that this philosophy does not simply assert that the different and opposing doctrines of various religions can be resolved in a higher synthesis, which would be an entirely different case.

[3] Cf. Ratzinger, *Truth and Tolerance*, 28-33. We need to investigate this philosophy more in detail when dealing with Hinduism and Zen Buddhism. But even now we should emphasize that, while religious experience is paramount in relating to Transcendent Reality, discursive knowledge (expressed in concepts and judgments) is inseparable from the experience itself and indispensable in evaluating the experience.

sketch out the method of a hopefully more adequate philosophy, we will engage in a similar inquiry into the implicit presuppositions of every branch of human knowledge. By investigating these presuppositions, we will show that one cannot deny them without tacitly presupposing their validity. As we further reflect on these assumptions, we will be led back to an ultimate explanation without which the assumptions would not be true.[4]

The Method of Philosophy and Its Search for the Absolute

As indicated above, philosophy deals not with a particular segment of empirical (i.e., observable) reality such as physics, biology or any other branch of the natural sciences does, but rather with those necessary presuppositions which scientific reasoning and everyday human experience take for granted. If these presuppositions were not true, all intellectual and practical human activity would be futile and meaningless, since it would not get us in touch with reality.[5] In what follows we will provide a few examples.

---

[4] Since in philosophy we are led back to the ultimate presuppositions of all knowledge, Akos Pauler, a great forgotten Hungarian philosopher, calls the method of philosophy reduction. Transcendental Thomists use a similar method called the transcendental method by which they analyze the necessary presuppositions of all human knowledge and action, the necessary presuppositions that precede and transcend any concrete act of the intellect and will.

[5] Of course, this is exactly what many postmodern philosophers assume to be the case. However, statements like 'we cannot go beyond language and its images to reality,' or 'we learn only about what we can do with things rather than what things are' are inconsistent. The denial of the possibility that our language (and the reasoning expressed in language) may reach reality claims some knowledge of both language and reality: how would you know that we cannot reach reality if you could not distinguish reality from your linguistic tools? Moreover, how would you know for what purpose you can use certain things unless you had some knowledge of what they are? Cf. J. Ratzinger, *Truth and Tolerance*, 186-191.

Universal Presuppositions

1. As we become aware of our own existence and of the world around us, a typical reaction is wonder and amazement: why do I, and in general, why do things exist rather than not exist? Yet not even the most rigorous scientific explanation of how the world evolved can answer this fundamental question. At the same time every scientific investigation would become a meaningless waste if scientists did not assume the reality, however tenuous and vague, of the object of their research.

Moreover, as we realize the amazing fact of our own existence, we perceive in the same experience that we might as well not exist. Our non-existence would not at all be unthinkable or impossible. Unless some unfortunate circumstances embitter us, we experience our non-necessary existence as a gift we have received rather than a reality we have brought about. That we exist as a gift and that we do not have to exist are two sides of a fundamental characteristic of our experience. In facing the world we perceive the same characteristic of non-necessity and gift also in other persons and in every object we observe. In philosophical language we call this gratuitous, non-necessary, gift-like character of every experienced being 'contingency.' We are vaguely aware of contingency in our daily lives, but only philosophy analyzes its implications. However, some dramatic experiences in our lives can do more than abstract philosophical reasoning. If we doubt the contingency of our own existence, a near-death experience or even a grave illness can awaken us to its reality. We experience the danger of physical death as threatening not only our bodies but our very selves. We feel threatened because we become aware of how precarious and ultimately non-necessary our existence is.

2. All scientists and thinking people assume that all phenomena they investigate have sufficient cause for appearing as they do. Otherwise, they would not search for an explanation. But scien-

tists do not study the very principle of causality[6]; they simply apply it in their own realm of competence by identifying the laws or patterns that explain certain physical, chemical or biochemical phenomena.

3. In doing research, scientists try out a number of hypotheses to explain certain observable phenomena, and they prefer the one which seems to them to come the closest to a true explanation. They may be skeptical of ever finding out "the final truth" about nature, but their motivation to continue their research presupposes a stubborn belief that they can describe more and more accurately what is going on. Even those who explicitly bracket any truth claim want to find out what hypothesis "works" in practical life. However, how could one figure out an economic way of using nuclear energy without knowing something about nuclear energy itself? Thus, the question of knowing reality, in other words, the question of true knowledge, remains implicit but unexamined in scientific research.

4. Scientists also accept the responsibility of giving a truthful report about their research. They agree in principle that it would be unethical to falsify the results of any experiment, although in practice every year several of them are caught cheating. Regardless of whether they act honestly or dishonestly, both groups of scientists accept the moral imperative to be truthful, but do not investigate the nature of moral obligation itself.

5. Scientists (and anyone who freely chooses a job) are usually convinced that their work serves a good purpose, even if they disagree on what constitutes a good purpose and what means are legitimate to achieve it. Thus most scientists would claim that stem cell research needs to be done for the good purpose of eliminating certain diseases. They also agree on the scientific facts involved (for instance, on the method of producing totipotent or pluripo-

---

6 Some physicists may object that Heisenberg's principle of indeterminacy in quantum physics contradicts this principle. However, the physicists themselves provide sufficient reason to suppose the unpredictable behavior of particles.

tent cells). Their disagreement centers on what is an ethically good or bad means to produce stem cells. The knowledge of ethical goodness is indispensable to their debate yet lies beyond the realm of scientific knowledge.

6. Many people (even outside the realm of Christianity's influence) agree that the highest ethical good is true love. Moreover, everyone admits that moral goodness (and true love in particular) is never perfect in this world. Anyone who has ever attempted to develop a "perfect friendship" or "perfect marriage" has experienced in a very personal way the limited and imperfect nature of true friendship and true marital love. We find in this life only limited goodness, only sparks or fragments of a more or less unselfish love. However, we usually do not reflect on what the reality of limited goodness presupposes.

7. Literary and art critics presuppose that in literature and art beauty is not simply a matter of taste. Even though much depends upon the "eye of the beholder," namely on one's subjective dispositions, there are pieces of literature and art that have been recognized as beautiful by most people of varying tastes. Literary and art critics analyze concrete pieces of art and literature; their study presupposes but does not investigate the ultimate reasons why something is more or less beautiful.

This brief and incomplete survey has indicated that in science, art, literature and daily human experience, there are universal assumptions that these disciplines and normal human interaction take for granted but do not investigate. The task of philosophy, then, is not the examination of a segment of empirical reality, nor is it just the description of the rules of meaningful discourse; philosophy explores what other branches of knowledge and general human experience presuppose but do not systematically examine. Thus, contrary to some uninformed claims, the philosophers' realm of investigation does not shrink with the advance of natural science, since their studies are situated on another level: they search out the foundations of all sciences and of all forms of human experience.

In what follows I will outline some examples of philosophical reasoning to show how we can conclude from the analysis of the above-mentioned presuppositions to their ultimate explanation, the existence of a Transcendent Reality without which none of these presuppositions would be true. Some of these reflections will be more elaborate than others; their convincing power will differently affect different individuals. Yet, I include all of them here in the same order as I have treated the presuppositions in order to show how every aspect of human experience calls for a Transcendent Reality.

From Presuppositions to an Ultimate Explanation

1-2. The presuppositions listed under # 1 and 2 need to be analyzed together. The awareness of our own contingency and the contingency of all things observed is based on the perception that none of these observed realities explain their existence themselves; they have been caused by something outside of themselves. If every cause in these chains of cause and effect were contingent, that is, if none had its explanation in itself, then nothing would be explained and we would simply postpone the explanation indefinitely. The only sufficient explanation for the existence of contingent beings that do not explain their own existence is a Necessary Being that is its own explanation.

A more difficult explanation could be summarized as follows: My awareness that I and the rest of the universe do not have to exist corresponds to reality only if I perceive my non-necessity and that of the universe in comparison to a real Necessary Being which or who cannot not exist. If the Necessary Being existed only in my mind rather than in reality, my awareness of contingence would be just a false, subjective experience with no foundation in reality.

3. When I become aware that there are more or less probable hypotheses in science, I strive to find that which is most prob-

able, in other words, that which comes closest to the truth. Thus, no research and no thinking can avoid an implicit reference to what is simply and unambiguously true. If all thinking implies a background awareness of that which is simply and unambiguously true, we must search for a sufficient explanation. How, then, can we explain that there are truths that are valid independently of our own thinking? What is the ultimate explanation for the validity of these truths that do not depend upon our own intellect?

There is also another way that leads from the implications of the natural sciences to Transcendent Reality. Every scientist presupposes that nature's processes follow intelligible laws; otherwise, he would not search for them. More precisely, these processes have been observed to correspond in remarkable ways to abstract mathematical formulae: nature "speaks the language of mathematics." What are we to make of this strange correspondence? How can we account for the fact that non-thinking matter is intelligible? If we assume that nothing can cause what it does not itself possess (an assumption we presuppose in every discipline and in everyday life), then non-thinking matter cannot cause thought patterns. It is inconceivable that a non-intelligent being could bring into existence a set of intelligent, highly sophisticated laws, which it would then dutifully obey. In that case, perhaps the human mind "causes" these principles of nature by projecting onto natural phenomena a set of laws that really come from man? If this were true, we would expect to be able to change these laws at our convenience. Yet what would happen if an architect simply ignored the laws of physics? The inevitable collapse of his building would be a forceful reminder that nature will not obey the arbitrary decisions of a human being; on the contrary, the laws of nature are only discovered by people, not created.

So in searching for an adequate cause, we find that neither nature itself nor the human mind offers a satisfactory explanation. We are compelled to postulate an intelligence higher than man's, a superior mind that does not, as we do, simply discover the laws of nature: it causes them.

4. If I acknowledge that there are certain values for which I ought to be willing to live and even die, I acknowledge the existence of a moral obligation in the depth of my own being, in my moral conscience. At the same time, I acknowledge this obligation to be above me, since it calls for an unconditional obedience which, however, I may freely disobey. But if I choose to disobey the command of my conscience, I feel guilty; in other words, I become aware that I ought to condemn myself for what I have done or failed to do. Thus a moral obligation emerges in my consciousness as "speaking" both from my inmost depth and with an authority that is superior to me and to any law of society. Provided that I perceive this obligation as absolute (that is, binding me unconditionally), I must conclude that its source can only be an Absolute (i.e. Transcendent) Person. For human beings cannot be unconditionally obligated by something less than themselves, such as an impersonal force, object or notion. Nor can we be absolutely obligated by other persons like us, since we perceive ourselves to be equal in dignity to them. Unconditional obedience to another human being would violate the sovereign dignity of my conscience, which remains the ultimate judge of whether or not I ought to obey or disobey a mere human command. The source of obligation cannot be simply my own person either, since I perceive my conscience's command as obligating me. Only an Absolute Person who is both infinitely above me and infinitely close to me (in the words of St. Augustine, closer to me than I am to myself) can obligate me absolutely, since only such an Absolute Person can command with the absolute authority that I perceive in the moral obligation, while simultaneously being so immanent within me as to issue the order from the deepest recesses of my own being, which is my conscience.[7]

5. When realizing that there are goods of lower and higher

---

[7]   Thus, conscience is not "the expression of the absolute value of the subjective self," as is ingrained in our culture, but rather the soul's "spiritual antenna," capable of perceiving a transcendent command. Cf. Ratzinger, *Truth and Tolerance*, 206-207.

degree, I am comparing these goods—implicitly but nonetheless unavoidably—to some standard. And since in this life I cannot conceive of any good the higher of which I could not imagine, this implicit standard in my mind exceeds all limitations. Indeed, the amazing fact in evaluating concrete and finite goods is that we do so in the vague but real awareness of Infinite Goodness beyond which nothing better can be thought. If we perceived this Infinite Goodness as not real but a mere abstract notion in our mind, this unreal 'Infinite Goodness' would appear as a lesser good than the real finite goods we experience in our life on earth. In other words, a mere imaginary standard would be a much lesser good than any concrete, finite good that really exists. To use a simple example, an imperfect wife is much better than a perfect wife who exists only in my imagination. Thus, if our experience that all the goods of this life are finite and imperfect is valid, Infinite and Perfect Goodness (to which we implicitly compare the goods of this life) must be real rather than imaginary.

6. The next step in our reflection is to perceive that, although the highest good that we can experience is unselfish personal love, in this world we can find it only to a limited degree: even the best friendship and best marriage fall short of perfect, infinite love. The experience of limited, imperfect love, however, implies a dim, but real background awareness of an Infinitely Perfect Love. If there were only relatively more or less perfect realizations of love, we would have no standard of evaluation. That even the most attractive experience of love here on earth can be seen as less than perfect implies that our standard of comparison is Infinitely Perfect Love. If this Infinitely Perfect Love were only a false figment of our imagination, our awareness of the finitude and imperfection of love on earth would also be false. However, most of us have at least a tentative intuition that a love which is both real and imperfect does exist between human beings. Thus, if this comparison between Perfect Love and imperfect love is to be true, both terms of the comparison must be real. If Perfect Love existed only

in our imagination, we would find imperfect but real love much more perfect than our imaginary dream of 'true love.'

7. In acknowledging that there are more or less beautiful things, we are comparing them—implicitly but nonetheless really—to what is infinitely beautiful, beyond which nothing more beautiful can be thought. In other words, in contemplating beautiful things that admit of more or less beauty, we have a dim but real background awareness of Perfect or Absolute Beauty.

I trust that after these short reflections the reader will have developed a tentative but growing insight that human experience includes in a multiplicity of ways the background knowledge (vague, obscure, and in need of explicit articulation) of Transcendent Reality. Our experience of contingency points to a Necessary Being, our caused existence is explicable only by the Self-Explaining Being, our search for scientific knowledge implies the validity of Truth, our awareness of unconditional moral obligation calls for the Absolute Personal Source of Moral Obligation, our experience of imperfect goodness and love for the existence of Perfect, Infinite Goodness and Love, our perception of varying degrees of beauty for the existence of Perfect Transcendent Beauty.[8] For lack of time and space we cannot show here in detail how the above-mentioned predicates belong to one and the same Transcendent Reality. However, we may develop an incipient insight into it: if to exist is good, the Necessary Being[9] that must

---

[8]   In the words of H. de Lubac: "Nothing can be thought without positing the Absolute in relating it to the Absolute; nothing can be willed without tending towards the Absolute, nor valued unless weighed in terms of the Absolute." de Lubac masterfully discloses the contradiction in the spirit of the one who denies God's existence: "the supreme contradiction is to lean upon God in the very act of denying him. That indeed is a judgment which denies and destroys itself, not only where its content is concerned, in itself, but by undermining its own structure and refusing the condition of its existence. No doubt the contradiction remains unseen because it does not intervene between two objective affirmations, but between objective and transcendental affirmations" (*The Discovery of God*, tr. A. Dru, Chicago: Regnery, 1967, 40).

[9]   The Necessary Being does not depend for its existence on any other being but on Itself; it must therefore contain in some transcendent way all perfections of being, thus, in this sense the Fullness of Being.

also be the fullness of Being is Perfect Goodness. Perfect Goodness, then, can very plausibly be perceived as Perfect Love, or rather
as the Perfect Transcendent Lover.

From the Unlimited Drive of the Person for Being, Truth and Goodness to the Existence of Absolute Being, Truth and Goodness

There is an alternate way to point to the existence of Infinite Transcendent Being, Truth and Goodness. The human mind is never
satisfied with what it knows; individually and collectively, human
beings constantly transcend their limits of knowledge. This impulse motivates personal intellectual progress and the unceasing
drive for more knowledge in society. In its fundamental dynamism,
the human mind strives towards unlimited knowledge, infinite
truth.

Similarly, the human will is not satisfied with limited goods
and limited existence. While setting different individual goals, we
all agree that we want in our own particular way the fullness of
joy, and this fullness of joy lies in the fullness of life. In every vo-
litional act, this dynamism towards fullness, and thus towards what
is infinite, manifests itself. We choose one good over another because that one appears at this moment the closest to the fullness
of joy for us. (We even choose what is morally wrong because we
convince ourselves that, here and now, this morally wrong action
is the best for us.)[10]

Further precision is needed here: the more we attempt to
fulfill our joy and life by indulging in the satisfactions of amassed
material goods, sensual pleasures, and worldly power, the more
unhappy and, indeed, unfulfilled we become. Only if we moder-
ate our desire for material things and strive for the fullness of Truth
and Love, does our capacity for joy grow.

---

[10] To those who choose suicide, death appears better than continued living.

Thus, our spiritual nature drives us to transcend all limited truths and goods and, instead, to strive toward infinite truth, goodness, and being.[11] From this dynamism of the human spirit we can conclude to one of two alternatives: either human existence is meaningless since it is doomed to frustration in its most basic drive, or it has been created for fulfillment in the fullness of Life, Truth, and Goodness. As C.S. Lewis remarks: if you spot a living fish on the dry ground, you conclude that water must be nearby. The human being is like the fish on the dry ground that yearns for the waters of unending life, truth, and goodness.[12] Therefore, unless we opt for the absurdity of the human condition, we cannot but conclude that the Fullness of Life, Truth, Beauty, and Love does indeed exist. However, for our purpose this last conclusion does not need to generate certainty; all we need is an incipient insight regarding the existence of such a Transcendent Personal Being Who is Love Itself. This tentative knowledge justifies the next part of this work, the study of world religions. If a Perfect Being Who is Love itself does exist and if he is indeed the source of our being, he must have manifested himself to humankind in some way and most probably in some or all of its religions.[13]

Human beings are psychosomatic unities, that is, simultaneously spiritual and material beings, and thus they live in space and time. Moreover, they are not isolated individuals but social beings who are born, grow, and become themselves in mutual interdependence and interaction. In other words, human beings live

---

[11] The irony of our spiritual nature is that we can freely stifle this transcendent dynamism by settling for intellectual or moral mediocrity. However, the resulting dullness and numbness of our life warn us that we have opposed our very nature, that we have suppressed the spiritual dynamism that is most valuable in a human person.

[12] Since we can stifle our desire for the waters of eternal life, the comparison is not perfect. The above reasoning is convincing only to those who are aware of the dynamics of their own spiritual nature.

[13] The use of the pronoun "He" in reference to this Absolute Love intends simply to characterize his personal nature rather than indicate his gender which would obviously contradict his transcendence. At this point we abstract from its analogical use within the mystery of the Trinity.

in history and are molded by historical events. Thus, if the Transcendent Lover exists, he would most likely adjust his self-manifestation to the historical nature of the human family; he would reveal himself not only in the depth of individual consciousness, but also in external, historical events that, affecting both the individual and the community, speak to the whole person, rather than to his soul alone.

Evidently, our investigation can target only what, at least in the broad sense, are historical manifestations of the Transcendent; we cannot examine a purely internal event of a religious nature that has not in any way been externalized. But we will also be open to specific, properly speaking, historical events of possible divine revelation; we will inquire into whether or not the Transcendent revealed himself by inspiring and shaping the history of communities and whether or not he himself in some way became audible, visible, and directly active in certain historical events.

A priori, many alternatives seem possible. For instance, we may find that each religion reveals the love of the Transcendent Lover with equal clarity and intensity, and that the differences resulting from the variety of cultures are only secondary. Another possible alternative would be that no religion reveals the Transcendent Lover, but rather all religions are distortions of the divine-human relationship, and the Transcendent One has provided another way for humankind to experience his love, for instance, in interpersonal human relationships. We can also conceive of a third alternative, according to which the historical manifestations of the Transcendent Lover center in one of the many religions, while his revelation in other religions is fragmentary or even partially distorted. We could continue this hypothetical list of alternatives almost indefinitely. If the Transcendent One is Love, however, we must a priori reject the alternative that he would arbitrarily exclude some people from any manifestation of his love.

Preliminary Observations

1. Transcendent Love's direct revelation in the depths of the soul is related to, but does not coincide with, its external, historical manifestations. An inner revelation, received by way of intuition, may have many degrees of perfection that do not necessarily coincide with the perfection of the different forms of the Transcendent One's historical manifestations. Thus, on account of God's universally active Spirit, a Hindu mystic may have a deeper awareness of the Divine than a practicing Christian.

2. We will search in the major religions of the world for signs in the communal history and personal experience of their members that could reveal the presence and activity of the Transcendent and Necessary Being, the Absolute Source of Moral Obligation, the Infinitely True, Beautiful, and Good, the One Who is Love Itself. Where the Transcendent One truly manifests himself, all the above perfections will be experienced to varying degrees and in various combinations. However, since the human being's loftiest desire aspires to pure love, we will search above all else for the self-manifestations of Perfect Love.

3. The insight that Perfect Love is the central mystery of the Transcendent One cannot be proved by philosophical reasoning alone. Still, we can show that Perfect Love presupposes all the above perfections. By reflecting on the experience of the "most loving persons" in history, we may describe pure love as the unselfish engagement in seeking to bring about the good of another by valuing his/her being and fostering his/her goodness and beauty through the offering of one's actions and even one's life. Love, then, in this sense presupposes, affirms, and fosters being as true, good, and beautiful, especially the being of a person.

4. At this point, the reader may want to call attention to a serious difficulty for our method: "How can you say that your method of investigating and comparing world religions is objective when you evaluate them in the light of a principle which is

self-evident only to believing Christians? If you declare that the full revelation of the Absolute must be the revelation of Absolute Love, you have already stacked the cards in your favor, for you have presupposed that the most basic principle of Christianity is true."

(a) I would respond by asking the objectors what they mean by "objective." If by "objective" they mean the approach of an uninvolved observer who investigates and describes religious phenomena from an indifferent viewpoint, then I would concede that my approach is far from being "objective." However, such an objective approach which observes a religion from the outside will end up seriously misunderstanding and misrepresenting the observed religion. A religion can be understood only if—to use a felicitous expression of Paul Ricoeur—we develop a hypothetical faith in it. In other words, we should try to see and understand ourselves, the world, and the Absolute through the eyes, the mind, and the heart of those who believe in that religion. Hypothetical faith in a religion should include maximum empathy, our being on the same wavelength as the adherents of that religion. Empathy for the believer will be our best guarantee for reducing the misunderstandings of the religion to a minimum. The result, I hope, will be a presentation with which competent adherents of that religion would find themselves in agreement.

(b) If by "objective" the objectors mean not to prejudge the value of a religion before examining it, in this sense, I hope, my approach will be objective. When saying that the highest religion or religions will be the one or the ones in which Absolute Love reveals itself most fully, I rely on universal human experience rather than on the explicit data of Christian religion. Human beings, even outside the boundaries of Christian faith, agree that pure love is the most important perfection in our universe. To the Christian, that many non-Christians describe pure love in terms that are very close to the Christian experience of agape is explained by God's gift of grace not only to Christians, but to all human beings.

5. As said before, I assume in my readers a basic familiarity with Christian doctrine, ritual, and moral teaching. Thus, no separate chapter on Christianity will be added, but other world religions will be compared to it throughout the book. Within each chapter the major structures of a religion will be related to the corresponding ones in Christianity. After treating most of the world religions, I will summarize what appears common in each of them, or at least in most; then the unique features of the Christian religion in its relationship to other religions will appear even more clearly. In the last part of the book I hope to show that the claim of Christianity to possess the historically full revelation of God's love in Jesus Christ is phenomenologically plausible and historically justifiable. At the same time, Jesus Christ will appear as the key to uncover the Christic structure of a universal, general revelation, the partial and often ambiguous signs of which need to be evaluated critically and integrated into Christian theology. Thus, through the encounter with other religions, Christian revelation will more effectively discover and actualize its own fullness. After describing the need and tasks for this dialogue with other religions, I will explain the relationship between dialogue and the Christian task of universal evangelization. The book will be completed by a "Reader's Guide" to encourage further readings and to check the readers' comprehension of what they have studied. An Appendix on the Logos doctrine of St. Justin will provide a sample of how the early Fathers evaluated and assimilated pagan religious philosophies.

PART II
A Survey of World Religions

Chapter I

PRIMITIVE RELIGIONS

1. The Experience of the Sacred

Historians have two major sources regarding primitive religions, the archaeological findings of statues, paintings and tombs that attest to primitive human beings' beliefs in gods and in an afterlife, and the beliefs of primitive people in our own age. The archaeological findings do not provide evidence for belief in transcendent creator gods. But one cannot deny the existence of such beliefs among primitive people based on this lack of evidence, since the very transcendence of these gods, just as in the case of the God of the Hebrews, may have prevented any kind of material representation. At the same time, our knowledge of primitive tribes living in the early twentieth century as man had lived in the Paleolithic age provides a much richer storehouse of religious beliefs, including beliefs in the existence of transcendent creator gods. If we assume that, at the beginning of civilization, all humankind held beliefs similar to those of the primitive tribes in our age, we can reconstruct the religions of primitive humankind with a sufficient degree of probability.

Primitive people did not discover the existence of god(s) by philosophical reasoning as we have arrived at postulating the existence of a personal God in the previous chapter; rather, they discovered the Divine by immediate experience. Living in close contact with nature, they became spontaneously aware that there is behind the phenomena of nature a mightier and more fascinating reality that may appropriately be called "the Sacred." They felt the solidity and permanence of the Sacred in huge rocks, its majesty in cloud-covered, ragged mountains, its life-giving, renewing power in springs and streams, its threat to reduce everything to chaos in the raging waves of the ocean. Primitive tribes, however, were not pantheists. They knew that nature is not god, but all phenomena of nature appeared to them as a hierophany, a manifestation of the Sacred; to use the words of R. Otto, they experienced the Sacred as *"mysterium tremendum et fascinans"*: a frightening and yet immensely attractive mystery.

The Sky God and Lesser Gods:
Conflict between Transcendence and Immanence

One cannot prove whether or not all humankind worshiped only one god in the beginning of its history.[1] Some very primitive tribes, however, such as the South American Indians living in the region of Tierra del Fuego, did practice monotheism. M. Eliade, perhaps the most important commentator on the amassed data of primitive religions, has this to say:

> What is quite beyond doubt is that there is an almost universal belief in a celestial divine being who created the universe and guarantees the fecundity of the earth (by pouring rain down upon it). These beings are endowed with infinite foreknowledge and wisdom; moral laws and often tribal ritual as well were established by them during a brief visit to the earth; they watch to see

---

[1] Here, of course, we deal with history after the Fall. We know from biblical revelation that before the Fall the first man and woman had believed in one God and had a personal relationship with him.

that their laws are obeyed, and lightning strikes all who infringe on them.[2]

Note both that the sky god is not identical with the sky, but rather lives in the sky, and that his eternity, power, majesty and infinity are not deduced by logical reasoning but are directly revealed in the eternity, power, majesty and infinity of the sky.

In spite of being the Supreme Creator, the heavenly god has been gradually forgotten or pushed to the periphery of primitive religious consciousness. When discovered by modern historians, they were not the central object of worship and sacrifices:

> The Hereros, a Bantu people from South-West Africa, call their supreme god Ndyambi. Withdrawn into the sky, he has abandoned mankind to the lower divinities. For that reason he is not adored. "Why should we sacrifice to him?" said a native. "We do not need to fear him, for he does not do us any harm, as do the spirits of our dead." The Hereros, however, do offer prayer to him when they have some unexpected piece of good luck.[3]

Other sky gods are prayed to only in calamities, when the lesser gods fail to help.

Thus, in the religious consciousness of primitive peoples the transcendence of the heavenly god is distorted into aloofness and distance. They increasingly think of him as irrelevant and unhelpful in fulfilling their daily needs; as the Bantus say: "God, having

---

[2] M. Eliade, *Patterns in Comparative Religions* (reprinted in Lincoln, NB: Univ. of Nebraska Press, 1996), 38. Note that Eliade relies to a large extent on the data W. Schmidt and his disciples, Catholic missionaries, gathered and published in the first half of the twentieth century in their monumental work: *Ursprung der Gottesidee*, vols. 1-12 (Münster: 1926-55).

[3] Eliade, *Patterns*, 47-48.

made man, pays no further attention to him." The following song
expresses the resignation of the Fang tribe in Equatorial Africa:

> Nzame (God) is on high, man below.
> God is God, man is man.
> Each is at home, each in his own house.[4]

The same conviction prevails everywhere among primitive
peoples, in Australia, Africa, South America, and in the islands
of the Pacific Ocean.

As societies developed, they turned more and more to lesser
gods believed to satisfy people's vital needs better. This took place
in different ways: at times, the children of the sky god took over
the day-to-day government of human life; in other cultures the
sky god himself turned into a more available lesser god, such as a
god of thunder and rain who, married to the goddess, mother
earth, would cause the fertility of the soil; in other cases, the heavenly god just faded away and other gods took over.

The shift to lesser gods occurs most dramatically when primitive tribes turn from pastoral life to agriculture: the settled, agricultural life leads to the discovery of sexuality and fertility as a
divine force, and thus gives rise to belief in fertility gods. They
become the center of religious life, since the survival and multiplication of people were believed to depend on them. However,
the fertility gods and goddesses, such as Baal and Ashtarte in the
Canaanite religion, were no longer truly divine: no longer the
guardians of high morality, their support could often be manipulated by a ritual of some kind.[5]

And so a tragic conflict appeared right at the beginning of
the history of religions: divine transcendence (God being infinitely
above all created reality) is in irreconcilable conflict with divine

---

[4]   *Ibid.*, p. 49.
[5]   Sacred prostitution is a good example of the moral decadence the cult of fertility gods
       has brought about.

immanence (the closeness, the availability of God). Primitive humankind cannot imagine for itself a god who would be both truly transcendent and truly immanent, infinitely higher than us and yet infinitely close to us. Divine transcendence is distorted into distant and aloof sky-gods; divine immanence into semi-divine heroes who are no longer the supreme guardians of morality but may be forced into serving human needs. This movement from transcendent sky god to fertility gods reveals not only a grave deficiency in the general religious sensitivity of humankind, but also the deep-seated desire to find a god who is both truly divine and truly responsive to human needs. We might say that the dynamics of primitive religions cry out for a god made flesh, a god who is truly Emmanuel, 'God with us.'

The Bible and the Primitive Idea of God

At this point, it is appropriate for us to compare the biblical experience and notion of God to the primitive.

The God of the Bible remains both immanent and transcendent. Uniquely in the Old Testament, transcendence and immanence, instead of becoming distorted and mutually exclusive, are not only in harmony, but inseparably united. Indeed, it is God's transcendence, the almighty power of his infinite love, that inspires and enables him to remain close to his people. In spite of Israel's repeated infidelities, Yahweh remains ever faithful. The periodic punishments of his people serve the purpose of his plan of mercy: he draws closer and closer to his people, teaching and forming them so that, at the end, a faithful remnant (Mary and the disciples) may be ready to receive him when, by becoming man, he accepts through his people full solidarity with all humankind. Note that the Incarnation does not create a half human, half divine hero; Jesus is no Hercules, no Indra of the Hindu mythology, but a true human being and almighty God in one person.

2. Myth

Myth in primitive religions means something very different from our ordinary usage. From among the many available attempts at understanding myth, my essay is based on Eliade's description.[6] Rather than being a "fictitious narrative," myth in the mind of primitive peoples narrates what alone is truly real: it is the story of the beginnings. The actual life, activity, and history of primitive peoples gain validity and meaning by reproducing myth in ritual.

The myths of the primitive sky gods are rare and simple. For instance, the supreme god of the Maori, Io, creates the world—not unlike Yahweh—by simply uttering commands: "Let darkness become a light-possessing darkness... let there be one light above, let there be one light below."[7]

Most myths in primitive religions, however, seem to emerge at the stage when the sky gods fade into oblivion or begin to be transformed into more active but less transcendent gods, such as a male sky god who becomes the sexual partner of mother earth, a goddess who is imagined as the original womb of all emerging life.

The primitive understanding of myth includes four important points: (a) the myth describes a sacred event like the beginning of the gods, of the cosmos, and of man. (b) The myth takes place at the beginning, before empirical history, in a time perceived as primordial or "sacred." (c) The protagonists of the myth are superhuman beings (gods, demi-gods, demons) whose activities (struggles, murders, and sex life) constitute the beginning of the cosmos and of man. Often, the world and/or the human race emerge as the result of the murder-sacrifice of a god.[8] (d) For

---

[6] Cf. M. Eliade, *Myths, Dreams and Mysteries* (New York: Harper & Row, 1967).

[7] M. Eliade, *Essential Sacred Writings from Around the World* (HarperSanFrancisco, 1992), 86.

[8] See, for instance the myth of Purusha in Hindu mythology. It is not entirely clear whether freely or against his will, but Purusha is sacrificed by the gods, and the cosmos is the result of this sacrifice (See Eliade, *Essential Sacred Writings*, 226-228).

primitive people the "really real" events are the mythical events; all that happens in their own history is nothing more than a repetition or imitation of the primordial, mythical happening.[9]

Another form of origin myth is that of Paradise and the Fall. Primitive man "remembers" a beginning when heaven and earth were not yet separated, when man easily conversed with the gods, was free from toil, did not have to die, and understood the language of the animals.[10] After the Fall (which is the result of a fault or simply a bad choice) only the shamans can fly up to heaven for a short period of ecstasy.

Myth and Christianity

Christianity is at times referred to as a myth in the history of religions. If by "myth" the author means a set of symbolic narratives with religious meaning, narratives that are viewed as either historical or fictional, the term may be misleading, but is not false. However, if the word "myth" is used in the more restricted sense as described above, we can admit only a very vague similar-

---

[9] A good example is the Babylonian myth of creation (cosmogony): at the beginning there was a combat between Marduk (a chief-god) and Tiamat (a monster-god representing the forces of chaos and darkness). Finally Marduk killed Tiamat and created the cosmos from Tiamat's dismembered body and created man from the blood of the slain demon Kingu. Another such example is the god Dionysos (Bacchus) who was killed and dismembered, but later on he rose again from the dead. The devotees of Dionysos participated in this sacred event when celebrating his feast. They believed that they were given new vitality, "new life," by this participation. A slightly different form of the same creation myth is that of celestial-chthonic hierogamy: it derives vegetative, animal and human life from the archetytpal intercourse between a storm-god or rain-god and mother earth.

[10] A most illuminating myth is from Indonesia, narrated by the natives of Poso: In the beginning the sky was very near the earth and the Creator used to let down his gifts by a rope. One day he lowered a stone, but the first man and woman refused to take it. The Creator complied and pulled back the rope and, next, instead of a stone, he sent down a banana. Our ancestors, of course, eagerly consumed it. Then came a voice from heaven: "Had you chosen the stone, your life would have been changeless and immortal. Since you chose the banana, you shall die and your children will step into your place." The story has an amazingly deep religious meaning: our ancestors did not trust in the providence of the Creator: that lack of trust in God's goodness is the origin of human mortality. See Eliade, *Essential Sacred Writings*, 140.

ity between the mythical world view and Christianity, namely that both Christianity and the primitive myths express the belief that the universe, humankind, and all human activities depend on a higher, transcendent order. Creation out of the sacrifice of a god has a vague similarity with the Christian belief in the new creation resulting from the free self-offering of the Son of God. But a more careful analysis of the two world views reveals some fundamental differences:

(1) When describing the primordial history in Genesis 1-11, the biblical authors indeed display a mythical language and way of thinking (e.g., the tree of knowledge of good and evil, the garden of Eden, the talking serpent, etc.). At the same time, however, the Genesis narratives present a polemic, or "anti-myth," in which Israel explains her own beliefs about the beginnings by contrasting them with the myths of the surrounding peoples, in particular the Enuma Elish of their Babylonian conquerors. Thus, the biblical authors insist that the one God created everything (not out of some pre-existing matter)[11] by "his word" (not through a cosmic struggle in which he had to overcome other gods). Moreover, human sexuality is not the imitation of divine sexuality: the God of Israel, although he is spoken about as a "he," transcends gender and has no sex partner.

(2) In the rest of biblical revelation, which begins with the history of Abraham (Gn 12) and ends with the vision of the heavenly Jerusalem (Rv 21-22), the Bible reverses the mythical world view. In the latter, the real event is the primordial mythical event and the rest of history has value only insofar as it repeats the prehistorical myth; time is cyclical, and no real progress or novelty may occur in history. Christianity's central belief, however, affirms God's entrance into human history; he chooses a people for himself and educates them in order to prepare a remnant for the fullness of time, when God himself will come in the flesh and renew

---

[11]   The belief of "*creatio ex nihilo*" (creation out of nothing) is the result of a developing understanding. See its clear formulation in 2 Maccabees 7:28.

all humankind. Thus, in the Christian view, time is not cyclical, but linear: God has gradually entered history and we still expect his coming in glory for the consummation of his Kingdom. Christianity, then, gives new meaning to time and history: there is progress, a growing fulfillment in human history, rather than an endless reiteration of the original cycle.

3. Rites

The rites of primitive religions may be defined as the dramatic or recitative re-enactments of the mythical event.

For example, in Babylon, on the last and first days of every year, the people re-enacted dramatically, with two groups of actors, the cosmic battle between Marduk and Tiamat. They believed that in this rite they became contemporaneous to the sacred event of creation, when Marduk overcame the forces of chaos. Thus, through the ritual re-actualization of creation, the world, which threatened to fall back into chaos at the end of the year, was enabled to continue as an orderly universe for another year.

In the primitive imagination, creation was conceived of as emergence from the waters. Water was the symbol of formless chaos, potentiality without any distinct shape, and the source and beginning of all things. Thus immersion into water (baptism) in primitive ritual meant a relapse into chaos, the disintegration or "death" of one's former being. The re-emergence from water signified a rebirth: one's former being along with his sins had been dissolved in water and a new creature emerged to a new life.

Sacrificial rituals are a special form of rite. As we have seen, in religions where one still recognizes a transcendent sky god, sacrifices are rare. They consist mainly of the offering of food (vegetables, animals) or sometimes one's own blood; the motivations of the sacrificers are thanksgiving, expiation, and petition.[12]

---

[12] See W. Schmidt, *Urpsrung der Gottesidee*, vol. 6, pp. 445-457.

In agricultural societies, the sacrifice is often believed to re-peat the murder-sacrifice of a divine being through symbolic ac-tion (for instance, through the offering of an animal, human be-ing, vegetable, or drink), and thereby to assure the re-creation and continuation of the world and the well-being of society.

Primitive Rites and Magic

Especially in the case of the re-enactment of a murder-sacrifice, the rite often degenerates into a form of magic; in other words, it becomes an attempt to control and manipulate the Di-vine Power or Person. The sacrificer believes that by the perfor-mance of the rite he can force the Sacred Power to do his will. Obviously, this is the reverse of any authentic religious relation-ship, in which the creature freely submits himself to the will of the Creator.

Yet primitive rites are not necessarily magic; they are rather ambiguous in themselves and can be put to both religious and magical use. An example of sacrifice as expression of gift of self is the Vedic sacrifice of soma juice in India, which is believed to be a re-enactment of the murder-sacrifice of the Divine Being Purusha. The book *Hindu Spirituality* describes the goal of this sacrifice in a deeply religious way as the thankful offering of one's own life to the Absolute:

> Once man realizes his place in the scheme of existence he is obliged to sacrifice in thankful recognition of all that life has offered him. By pouring oblation into the fire, the sacrificer gains access to the World of Light and having thus emptied himself of impurities is refilled with the nectar of life which pours down from heaven and so enjoys good health and, with all his faculties fortified, a full span of life.[13]

---

[13] *Hindu Spirituality*, vol. 1, ed. K. Sivaraman (New York: Crossroads, 1989), p. 30.

Primitive Rites and Israel

The rituals of Israel are the re-enactments not of the creation account of Genesis, but of the acts of Yahweh in history, acts which created and liberated Israel. Thus, the liberation from slavery in Egypt was celebrated at Passover, the giving of the Law at Sinai at Pentecost (Shavuot); indeed, the whole elaborate system of sacrifices was connected with the Covenant into which Yahweh entered with Israel (thanksgiving for the Covenant, expiation for sins committed against the Covenant, celebrating the communion established by the Covenant). Yet the more ancient cosmic reference of the rites is retained: for instance, the feast of Passover is combined with the Feast of the Unleavened Bread, an agricultural feast, and Shavuot is also a harvest festival.

Note that for Israel the remembering of Yahweh's powerful deeds in history means far more than a mere psychological recalling of past events. When celebrating, Israel believes that she participates in the past saving acts of God, in much the same way that primitive tribes, when performing a rite, believe they participate in the sacred time of creation. At the same time, the commemoration of the great saving events of the past is also an anticipation of an even greater, definitive saving act. For instance, at the time of Jesus, the Jews were expecting the appearance and mighty acts of the Messiah at the time of the Passover.

Primitive Rites and Christianity

Christianity neither destroys the cosmic symbolism of the most primitive rituals nor negates the meaning of Jewish rituals; rather, it claims to fulfill their promise by its own rites. It preserves the cosmic symbolism and the reference to God's interventions in the history of Israel, but sees them as preparations for the final saving event, the death and resurrection of Jesus Christ. The Christian sacraments extend to us Christ's saving work (and his personal sacrificial presence in the Eucharist) and anticipate its consummation at the end of history. For instance, baptism in primitive religions signified dying to one's former self and becoming a new creation. In Jewish history the baptism of proselytes commemorated and re-enacted the crossing of the Red Sea and Jordan, which made Israel into a nation. All this is taken up into the rite of Christian baptism as its preparation. But the dying and rising to new life in baptism is believed to be first and foremost a share in the death and resurrection of Jesus Christ.

While the inherent ambiguity of primitive rites may turn into magic almost imperceptibly, the Christian rite is, by its very nature, opposed to magic: in his sacrifice, Christ does not try "to force God's hand," but acts as the perfect worshiper of his Father.[14]

Conclusion

The desires and the world-view of religious men and women can most clearly be analyzed in primitive religions. It is for this reason that, before any other religion, we first explored the structure of the basic phenomena of tribal or primitive religions in some detail; in particular, we have discussed the meaning of the primary religious symbol, the sky, as well as the meaning of myth and ritual. We have also noticed that Christianity claims both to correct and to fulfill these desires in a way that surpasses our expectations.

---

[14] The Christian rite, of course, may be abused as magic, but this abuse goes against its very nature, while the rites of primitive religions are inherently ambiguous: a rain dance, for instance, may be authentically performed as a request of prayer to the Great Spirit or as an automatic means to bring about rain.

Chapter II

HINDUISM

Hinduism, along with Buddhism, fascinates our contemporary Western culture; it attracts in particular those people who, disillusioned with the quest for material wealth, but unaware of the mystical tradition of Christianity, hunger for a deep religious experience. The more pleasure people taste and the more gadgets they own and control, the more frustrated they may become, since none of these makes us happy. Then the spiritual peace and bliss that the Sacred Texts and gurus of the East offer may become a powerful attraction.

An additional incentive for some people is the Hindu gurus' promise to actualize our hidden divine energies and, thus, to lift us above the limitations of a conventional human life.

Towards the middle of the second millennium B.C., Aryan tribes migrated to India from the north. The different forms of Hindu religion may have derived from the blending of the religions of the native Harappans (who lived in northern India near the Indus River and had developed a highly sophisticated agricultural society), of the native Dravidians (who lived in southern India), and of the immigrating Aryans.[15] During its long history, Hinduism has undergone considerable transformations and has developed simultaneously in different directions. It has some common features, but no fixed creed or organized structure similar to

---

[15] T.P. Burke, *The Major Religions. An Introduction with Texts* (Cambridge: Blackwell, 1996), pp. 15-16.

Christian churches. In this course, we can only give a survey of the main stages of its development, list its most important sacred writings, and characterize some of its major trends.

1. History

Vedic Religion (1500–800 or 600 B.C.)

This epoch[16] is characterized by the worship of many lesser gods, even though it preserved evidence of an earlier stage in which Dyaus-Pitar, the Sky-Father,[17] was worshiped. In the Vedic hymns there are still references to him as "the Sky that knows All" (Atharva Veda, 1.32.4), and occasionally they invoke "the Sky Father" (Ibid., 6.4.3.). But the highest god in the age of the Vedas is Varuna, who, though still a heavenly god, is much less distant than Dyaus-Pitar: he is an all-knowing, powerful sovereign ruler over the cosmic, moral, and liturgical order (rta).[18] Several hymns, similar in tone and content to the biblical Psalms, invoke him, exalt his holiness, and ask for his pardon. Yet, in the Vedic period even Varuna is retreating from the center of religious consciousness; Indra, the god of storm, battle, biological vitality, and fertility, becomes the most popular god of this period.[19]

The sacred writings of this period, first handed down orally for a long time before they were put into writing, are the four Vedas[20] (Rg Veda, Sama Veda, Yajur Veda, Atharva Veda). They consist of a collection of hymns addressed to different gods, and

---

[16] Scholars provide different approximations for the duration of the Vedic period.

[17] Cf. "*Deus pater*" in Latin.

[18] Cf. M. Eliade, *A History of Religious Ideas* (Chicago, IL: Univ. of Chicago Press, 1978), vol. I, pp. 200-203; Burke, *Major Religions*, pp. 17-19. His name Varuna is related to the Greek sky-god's name, Ouranos.

[19] Indra, high on soma juice killed the primordial dragon Vrta and out of his dead body created the earth. See *Rg Veda* I.32.

[20] *Veda* literally means knowledge.

they contain sacrificial formulas and magic spells. Attached to each collection of hymns are prosaic treatises called the Brahmanas, which explain the rituals of the sacrifices. At the end of the Vedic period, so called "forest treatises" (Aranyakas) were added to the Brahmanas; these meditations present an obvious challenge to the Brahmanas' exaggerated ritualism. Written by hermits living in the forest, they contain philosophical speculation, just like the latest Vedic hymns. The Aranyakas continue in the Upanishads,[21] both of which herald a new stage in the development of Hindu religion.

Upanishadic Period (800 or 600–300 B.C.)

While the Vedic religion centered on the sacrifices to the gods that represented the sacred character of life in this world, the Upanishads deny not only the reality of this world, but even the reality of the distinction between individual selves. What we superficially perceive as our own egos, our mental operations of sensing, thinking, and willing, as well as the accompanying consciousness on the basis of which we establish our separate identities, are only appearances. Those who overcome ignorance realize that nothing else but Brahman exists.[22] The real self in me, in other human beings, and, in fact, in every apparently different thing, is Atman, *the* Self, which is identical with Brahman. It is infinite Being, Consciousness, and Bliss, and no human speech or thought can express It. It is "neti, neti," neither this nor that.

What hinders us from discovering Brahman in ourselves is our self-centeredness. As soon as we make the existential discovery of the one true reality, our false conceptions of distinctions between beings disappear; then calm and peace set in:

---

[21] *Upanishad* means literally "sit near to (a teacher)."

[22] Brahman originally meant the sacred or magic power present in everything.

> Therefore, one who knows this, becoming pacified, controlled, at peace, patient, full of faith, should see the Self in the Self alone. He looks upon everyone as it. Everyone comes to be his Self; he becomes the Self of everyone. He passes over all evil; evil does not pass over him. He subdues all evil; evil does not subdue him. He is free from evil, free from age, free from hunger, free from thirst, a Brahman, whoever possesses this knowledge. (Brihadaranyaka 4.4.28, tr. by Hopkins)[23]

As long as one does not develop a complete detachment from all desires, including the desire for existence as a distinct "I", one does not achieve moksha, the deliverance from the necessity of being reborn again and again into the world of false appearances. He will be constantly reincarnated, either into a higher or lower caste, or even as an animal or plant. This wheel of birth-death-rebirth (samsara) is regulated by the law of karma: one is reborn according to the cumulative effects of one's good or bad deeds.

In the later Upanishads, Brahman is described in terms more personal than before. The texts switch from designating Brahman as "It" to addressing him as "Lord." No longer just the object of meditation, He is also addressed in prayers of praise and admiration. The world, however, is still perceived as a mere appearance, Maya,[24] but in some texts this colorful multiplicity manifests something of Brahman.

Contemplation, and through it the knowledge of Brahman, is to be obtained through yoga,[25] which, in the later Upanishads, means a combination of physical and spiritual exercises that aim first at establishing control over our sensory and biological func-

---

[23] The quote is taken from Burke, *Major Religions*, 22.

[24] The word *Maya* comes from the same root as magic, connoting a magic trick. The world is the result of Brahman's *lila*, a playful display of divine energy.

[25] Yoga etymologically is the same word as the English yoke. In general it means the pathway to spiritual liberation. Cf. Burke, *Major Religions*, 23-24.

tions, such as breathing and even heartbeat, and thus attaining the actualization of our divine energies, and eventually lead to a pure awareness of the identity of our deepest Self (Atman) with Brahman.

Classical Hinduism (300 B.C. to 500 A.D.)

In classical Hinduism (influenced strongly by the Dravidian South) the trend towards a more personal understanding of the Absolute further intensified. Those Hindus who studied the Upanishads believed that one could worship the Absolute Divine Reality under the form of any of the personal gods (devas). The most popular personal gods became Vishnu and Shiva. Brahma[26] creates the world, but Vishnu takes over after creation and rules it with great benevolence toward humankind. Shiva has a frightening, destructive aspect, and is also called "the Destroyer," but he is also the source of life; his dance both destroys and brings life to the world.[27] Brahma is not worshiped, whereas Vishnu and Shiva are. Vishnu has several avatar(a)s (descents or earthly forms of the gods). The avatars serve the purpose of rescuing humankind in times of physical or moral danger. Most avatars have animal forms, for instance, the Fish (Matsya) and the Boar (Varaha), but the most famous ones are human forms, Rama and Krishna. Krishna especially is the object of bhakti (loving devotion).

The stories of the avatars are told in the Puranas and in the great epics of Hindu literature, the Ramayana and the Bhagavad Gita (Song of the Lord), which is itself only part of a larger epic poem, the Mahabharata.

---

[26] Brahma is the masculine form of Brahman, a personal creator God rather than the originally impersonal Absolute.

[27] While Shiva may be worshiped as a concretization of Brahman itself, he has retained his aspect of fertility god, often represented by the "*lingam*," a stylized phallic symbol, while his wife has many characters and names like Parvati, the goddess of beauty or Kali, a frightening, evil spirit with fangs.

The Bhagavad Gita (composed probably in the 1st century B.C.) has remained the most popular Hindu religious text even up to our days. It constitutes a new high peak in the history of Hindu religious thought. The Absolute, Ineffable, but Impersonal Brahman of the Upanishads appears here as a personal God who descends and becomes visible as Krishna, the Lord; in fact, he disguises himself as the charioteer of a warrior, Arjuna. He dispels Arjuna's anxieties about the incoming fratricidal war, and encourages him to fulfill his caste duties by fighting as a warrior. Though it addresses the god Krishna as a person, even the Bhagavad Gita maintains a certain pantheism: what really exists behind the phenomenal world is the one, unchangeable, immortal Self:

> He who considers this One[28] the killer
> and he who considers this One the killed,
> both of them do not know.
> This One does not kill, nor is It killed.[29]

Krishna explains to Arjuna various ways of "liberation" from samsara, the cycle of continued re-birth and death:

(a) The best way is bhakti, loving devotion to Krishna, fixing one's mind on him, doing everything for his sake. He who lives in this way enters Krishna and finds in him a true home.

(b) Those who meditate on the impersonal, "unmanifest, undefined, and imperishable" (Brahman) and restrain their senses, are equal-minded toward all and rejoice in the good of all; they also attain Krishna, even though this route is more difficult.

---

[28] "This One" refers to Atman embodied in humans. In a battle only the bodies, mere appearances, are killed.

[29] *Bhagavad Gita with the Commentary of Shankaracharya.* Tr. Gambhirananda (Calcutta: Advaita Ashrama, 1998), 2,19: 122.

(c) One who has a hard time focusing in meditation or loving devotion should use yoga, the discipline of exercise.

(d) If someone cannot do yoga, let him do his duty unselfishly, by abstaining from its fruits. In other words, let him do his duty just because it is his duty, not for attaining any tangible gain from its performance.

Medieval Period

While the average Hindu continued to worship one of the personal gods, religious philosophy moved beyond the stage of spontaneous insights, and systematic treatises appeared on the scene.[30] Three major philosophers need to be mentioned. Their central problem was the relationship between God (the Self, Brahman), the individual selves, and the material world.

Sankara (788-820?) is the most important representative of the advaita (non-dualist) school of philosophy. By interpreting the Upanishads, he concludes that for those in the state of ignorance (which is the state of ordinary perception) the world and individual selves appear as different objects. However, for the one who acquires knowledge through the practice of ethical virtues, devotion, and contemplation, only Brahman exists. His "I" and everyone else's "I" (Atman) are identical with Brahman:

> The existence of Brahman is known on the ground of its being the Self of everyone. For everyone is conscious of the existence of (his) Self, and never thinks "I am not." If the existence of the Self were not known, everyone would think "I am not." And this Self (of whose existence all are conscious) is Brahman.[31]

---

[30] These treatises are commentaries on the Brahmasutra (also called Vedanta Sutra), an enigmatic summary of the Upanishads which consists of brief and obscure aphorisms.

[31] *A Sourcebook in Indian Philosophy*, ed. S. Radhakrishnan & C.A. Moore (Princeton: Princeton Univ. Press, reprinted in 1989), 511. See also 506-543.

To Sankara, creation and the destruction of creation are as natural as the inhaling and exhaling activity of a living creature, yet, strangely, creation does not fulfill a need on the part of Brahman; it is lila, a divine play, recreation, or sport.

Ramanuja (11th century A.D.) represents a qualified nondualist (advaita) position. He was concerned about safeguarding the religious relationship between Brahman and human beings. According to him, a non-qualified advaita position destroys the possibility of bhakti (loving devotion) and adoration of God: if my immediate self is Brahman, logically, I would end up worshiping myself. Therefore, Ramanuja affirms a real and abiding difference between individual selves and the highest Self, who is within these individual selves as the individual self is in his body. Yet the dependence of individual selves on Brahman does not negate their moral responsibility; the Lord (Brahman) rewards their good deeds and punishes their sins according to the rule of karma.

The individual selves are in real bondage because their bodies are subject to pain and pleasure. The "knowledge" that such bondage is unreal cannot be true. We need the Lord's grace to be released of the bondage that we have deserved through our actions (in this life or in a previous life): "The cessation of such bondage is to be obtained only through the grace of the highest Self pleased by the devout meditation of the worshiper."[32]

Even after release (moksa) from samsara (the cycle of birth-death-rebirth), the individual self does not disappear; he finds his bliss in the worship of the Lord.

Yet an unsolvable ambiguity remains. The individual self is of an essentially different nature than the highest Self, and yet the former is described as part of the latter, and even more ambiguously, the individual self is a "distinguishing attribute" of the highest Self.[33] Thus, pantheism is still implied by Ramanuja's philosophical system.

---

[32] *Ibid.*, 552. See also 543-555.
[33] *Ibid.*, 555.

Madhva (1238-1317 A.D.) teaches dvaita (dualism) between the individual selves and Brahman, the Supreme Being whom he worships in the form of Vishnu. Even though creation is eternal (as in the previous philosophies), there is a fundamental difference between "God and the individual self, between God and matter, between individual selves, between selves and matter and between individual material substances."[34]

Madhva describes God in highly personal terms: "The glorious Lord confers knowledge (on the devoted self) for his righteousness, and absolves him from sin and leads him to eternal bliss; (such is the boundless mercy of the Lord)."[35] While Vishnu is the embodiment of the infinite Spirit, lesser gods serve as intermediaries in the soul's ascent to him. Madhva's followers considered their master also as an embodiment of Vayu (Breath, Spirit), whose role was to mediate the spiritual ascent.

According to Madhva, however, not every soul is able to obtain release from samsara for eternal bliss in God, but only those who are nobly inclined. There are two other groups of souls, those who have a mixed inclination and those of ignoble inclination. This fundamental disposition of the soul cannot be changed without destroying the soul itself. God respects the innate tendency of each type and his grace saves only the nobly inclined.[36]

The Creator-creature dualism of Madhva has never become the mainstream of Hindu philosophy; yet, in spite of its polytheistic language, the repudiation of the body, and the determinism of human destiny, Madhva's insights show a remarkable affinity with the Judeo-Christian tradition.

---

[34] *Ibid.*, 508.

[35] *Ibid.*, 567.

[36] See *Hindu Spirituality*, vol. I, 306. Madhva's three categories of souls reminds the reader of certain trends of gnosticism which also use a tripartite division of the human race and restrict salvation only to the first group and to some of the second while excluding all who belong to the third group.

Modern Period

In the modern period, different forms of the classic and medieval period of Hindu religion continue to flourish. In addition, two new features have arisen.

The first may be called an inclusive approach to religions in general. Hinduism itself comprising many different and even contradictory trends, encountered other religions such as Buddhism, Christianity and Islam (just to mention the largest ones). As a result of such manifold contacts, many of its adherents developed the conviction that every religion is a different path to the same goal. Ramakrishna (19th century), one of the greatest representatives of this inclusive approach, said:

> All doctrines are only so many paths; but a path is by no means God himself. Indeed, one can reach God if one follows any of the paths with wholehearted devotion.

Ramakrishna himself tried to live according to the tenets of the major religions. He lived for a while as a devotee of Vishnu, then a worshiper of Shiva; he also lived as a Muslim and as a Christian. He claims to have found the same God through all these different paths.

He also perceives the same Savior figure in many different forms:

> The Savior is the messenger of God. He is like the viceroy of a mighty monarch. As when there is some disturbance in a far-off province, the king sends his viceroy to quell it, so wherever there is a decline of religion in any part of the world, God sends his Savior there.[37]

---

[37] This text is quoted by H. Smith, *The World's Religions* (San Francisco, CA: HarperSan Francisco, 1991), 74.

Another form of modern Hinduism adopted the missionary spirit of Christian denominations and began to preach certain forms of Hindu religion to Westerners.[38]

This short and incomplete survey has shown the great variety within Hinduism; in fact, one should speak of Hindu religions
rather than Hinduism. Yet, there are some common characteristics that, in the mind of all Hindus, distinguish orthodox Hindu
thought and religions (astika) from heterodox deviations (nastika)
such as Jainism, Buddhism, and Sikhism:

(a) Even though they interpret the Vedas differently, all forms
of orthodox Hinduism accept the Vedas as containing the
Eternal Truth or Eternal Law: Sanatana Dharma.

(b) They all insist on the primacy of the spiritual self, whether
they recognize only one Absolute Self or, in addition to that,
many individual selves as well.

(c) They all believe in samsara, the transmigration of souls according to the law of karma.

(d) The destiny of the soul is immortality in union with the Absolute, either by discovering its identity with Brahman or by
living in contemplation and adoration of Brahman.

(e) All those who deny the existence of the spirit as distinct from
corporeality cannot call themselves Hindus.

2. Hinduism and Christianity

Every comparison and dialogue between Hinduism and
Christianity runs the risk of oversimplification because of the great
diversity within Hinduism. Nevertheless, some general observa-
tions may prove helpful.

1. Christianity appreciates the emphasis on the primacy of
Spiritual Reality, yet affirms that also our bodies, transformed by

---

[38] Cf., for instance, the Hare Krishna Society.

the Holy Spirit, as well as a new universe, will share—each creature in its own way—in God's eternal life.

2. Aside from Madhva's philosophy, which has never become mainline in Hindu thought, Hinduism looks at the world as Maya, the result of a divine "play" (lila) that exists either merely as an appearance for the unenlightened mind or as the external form or body of Brahman.

Christianity agrees that creation reveals the playfulness of God's wisdom rather than fulfilling a genuine need in God (Proverbs 8:1-31). However, in the creation of spiritual beings, angels, and humankind, we believe that God also reveals his freely given love. Nor do Christians view creation as Maya, mere appearance; although in comparison to creation God is the "really real," the absolute fullness of being, consciousness, and bliss (in Sanskrit God is "sat, cit, ananda"), Christians view creation also as real and valuable—distinct from God, yet dependent on him.

Indeed, creation manifests God's beauty, goodness, and perfection, but Christians cannot see created selves as a "distinguishing attribute of God" or his external form or body; we see an infinite qualitative difference between Creator and creature.

Yet we may find a common language for Hindus and Christians to describe how the world manifests God's perfections. In the Christian tradition, when ascribing a created perfection to God, we use the threefold way of affirmation, negation, and supereminence. For instance, we say that God is existent, good, true, and beautiful (via affirmationis). But we must immediately add that God is not existent, good, true and, beautiful, namely, not in the limited manner creatures are understood to be existent, good, true, and beautiful (via negationis). Finally, we conclude that God is existent, good, true, and beautiful in an infinitely more perfect way than we can conceive of (via supereminentiae). This dialectic safeguards God's transcendent perfection while still providing a true way of speaking about God: there is an analogy between Creator and creature. The perfections of a creature are similar, yet, at the same time, more dissimilar than similar in comparison to the transcendent perfection of God.[39]

3. The doctrine of unqualified or qualified advaita (the non-dualism of individual selves and the Highest Self) may, in certain texts, be the inaccurate transposition of mystical language into metaphysical conceptuality. Christian mystics also speak about a quasi-dissolution of the human self into the "ocean" of God's infinite love. But in the experience of Christian mystics, fusion or union never abolishes the infinite difference between God and man; the fusion does not occur on the level of being or nature, but on the level of personal love, the gift of God's infinite condescension by which he raises us to himself. The doctrine of advaita, however, may express, in other texts, the conscious or subconscious desire of sinful humankind to achieve equality with God, which is a re-enactment of original sin.

4. Christian theology sees in the identification of the ineffable and transcendent Brahman with one of the Vedic gods, like Vishnu or with one of the avatar(a)s like Krishna or Rama, the innate desire of humankind, often deepened and purified by grace, for an incarnate god who shares our lives and saves us from our misery.

However, we do not see these gods or avatars as savior figures equivalent to Jesus Christ. Krishna and Rama may have some foundation in distant history, but as described in the Ramayana and the Bhagavad Gita, they are mythological figures, neither fully divine nor fully human. Nor do Hindus believe that through Krishna and Rama God takes upon himself our sins and sufferings in order to save us through his death and resurrection. Rama and Krishna resemble more the docetic or gnostic Christ, who only appears to be human, disdains suffering, and redeems us by his knowledge. Christ compares to Vishnu and Krishna as a (God-

---

[39] The doctrine of the Upanishads that God is both *asti asti* (it is) and *neti neti* (it is neither this, nor that) could converge with the Christian dialectic of the triple way if the divinity's personal nature were acknowledged by the Hindu discussion partner.

inspired) dream to its (God-given) fulfillment that exceeds the boldest desires of the dreamer.

5. The law of karma is close to the Christian doctrine according to which every free human act has an immanent effect on the soul. A good act performed with God's grace increases our similarity to God, while an evil act distorts it.

The Hindu, however, believes that his karma, the immanent effect of his good and evil acts, determines his next stage in the cycle of samsara. Only if he is free of every attachment to the self does the soul obtain moksha and achieve his true Brahman nature, according to the advaita school.

The doctrine of reincarnation (samsara) is unacceptable to Christianity. Philosophically, reincarnation is impossible, since the human being is the unity of soul and body rather than a soul imprisoned in a body; our body belongs to our personal identity. Thus, the rebirth of the same person into another body is inconceivable, since in another body he would not be the same person. He would not even be the same soul, since the soul itself is changed by the body.

But Christianity rejects reincarnation mainly on theological grounds. According to the Gospel, we receive one life here on earth as a preparation for eternity, rather than an indefinite number of life cycles. We have to "work out" our salvation before we die, in this life. For Christians, then, time on earth is invaluable, because in it they build up, through their free decisions enabled by God's grace, their eternal participation in God's Trinitarian life of love.

Catholic Christianity, however, knows about the existence of Purgatory: those souls who die in the state of sanctifying grace (as God's children, with the love of God in their hearts) but are still burdened by residual sinfulness (such as some selfishness, vanity, or greed) need to be fully purified before they see God face to face. Only those with a pure heart, who have completely restored their likeness to God, will see God face to face.

6. Christians appreciate the importance of contemplation and

especially of loving devotion (bhakti) in the various trends of Hinduism. However, they reject any self-divinizing tendency: our union with God and our awareness of God is always a gift of God's undeserved grace.

7. Yoga, the combining of physical and breathing exercises with spiritual techniques for the purpose of realizing the identity of one's Atman with Brahman, needs to be evaluated carefully. Evidently, the Christian does not accept its self-divinizing goal. Yet, its physical exercises performed in a calm, contemplative spirit can be of great help for the Christian's spiritual life. The yogic exercises calm the body and help us "achieve" peace with our body so that our bodily drives and instincts no longer paralyze our prayer life. In fact the yogic exercises can positively help us in our intellectual and spiritual pursuits. Our physical and psychic energies, including the sex drive, may be harnessed and sublimated by the yogic exercises in order to promote mental concentration, prayer, and meditation.

However, we should keep in mind that the yogic exercises cannot cause our union with God; they simply help eliminate the obstacles of nervous tension, distraction, and physical inertia, which hinder the cooperation of our body with God's grace and with our free will.

8. In the last part of the course we will return to the tendency of modern Hinduism to claim a basic equivalency of major religions as different roads to the same God. Our study of the different types of gods has already revealed the simplistic character of a relativist approach to religion.

9. Although prohibited by the Indian constitution, the caste system remains influential in Hindu culture even today.[40] Human

---

[40] The historical origin of the caste system is disputed. Some scholars claim that the conquest of the dark-skinned native population by the fair-skinned Aryans and the resulting inequality of rights and duties had to be justified religiously and perpetuated socially. Most orthodox Hindus disagree with this sociological explanation. The four major classes of Vedic times from which the many castes and subcastes have later developed are: the priestly

beings are born into a higher or lower caste or into the crowd of the casteless "untouchables" because of merits or demerits (karma) inherited from their previous lives. The untouchables were prohibited from participating in official worship and sacrifices.

The caste system is evidently incompatible with the equality and oneness of all human beings in Christ: "There is neither Jew nor Greek, there is neither slave nor free, there is neither male nor female; for all are one in Christ Jesus" (Gal 3:28).

---

caste (Brahmins or Brahmans), the warriors, princes, administrators (Ksatryas) the merchants, farmers (Vaisyas) and servants, unskilled laborers (Sudras). The untouchables or outcastes are at the bottom of society. Hindus could marry and dine only within their own caste.

Chapter III

BUDDHISM

Buddhism derives historically from Hinduism. Its origin is connected with the teaching and word of an historic person, Siddhattha Gotama (in the Pali language), or Siddhartha Gautama (in Sanskrit), who is called by his disciples Buddha (The Enlightened One). He is also called Sakyamuni, the sage of the Sakya tribe.

1. Buddhist Writings

The traditions concerning the life and teaching of Buddha were committed to writing several centuries after his death. The most complete collection has been preserved in the Pali language and is called the Tipitaka (Three Baskets). Some traditions of probably later origin have also been preserved in Sanskrit.

2. Siddhartha Gautama

We know very little about the personality and life of Siddhartha. Yet even though we possess no documents contemporary to his life and teaching, we can establish some facts concerning his life and teaching with varying degrees of historical probability. Born as a son of a royal family in northern India, he lived probably between 563 and 483 B.C., in a time period of religious confusion and transition. The ritualism of the masses and the forest hermits' extreme asceticism and pantheistic contemplation (as attested in the Upanishads) characterize the epoch.

Siddhartha lived a happy, carefree life with his wife and son, until one day he discovered the shocking fact of human suffering. He could no longer live amidst wealth and luxury. He left his wife and son and set out to find deliverance from suffering. After many unsuccessful attempts, such as extreme fasting, mortification, and philosophical speculation, he decided to sit in meditation until he would find the way of liberation from suffering. After forty days he finally obtained "enlightenment" and discovered the way to deliverance. It is at this point in life that he became the Buddha. He wanted to share his discovery with suffering humankind, so he went from city to city, preaching his doctrine, recruiting followers, and meditating. His first disciples were organized into monastic communities.

These may have been his last words before he died:

> Be lamps to yourselves.... Betake yourselves to no external refuge. Hold fast to the truth as a lamp. Hold fast as a refuge to the truth. Look not for refuge to anyone beside yourselves.... Decay is inherent in all component things! Work out your salvation with diligence. (Maha-Parinibbina Sutta, II, 33; VI, 10, quoted by J.A. Hardon, *Religions of the World* [NY: Image Books, 1968], I, 102.)

3. The Original Doctrine of Buddha

Due to much uncertainty and conflicting claims regarding the chronology of written sources, we can reconstruct the original doctrine of the historical Buddha only to a certain degree of probability. The Buddha does not speculate about God or gods, about the eternity or non-eternity of the world, not even about the nature of Nirvana, the state of final deliverance. In one of his parables, he compares the state of unenlightened human beings to the man who hurts from an arrow lodged in his chest; such a man will not engage in metaphysical speculation about the eternity or non-eternity of the world, but will want to get the arrow out and stop the pain. So the Buddha's interest focuses on one practical question: how can we achieve liberation from the misery of suffering? The doctrine of the "four noble truths" sums up his solution:

1. The first truth is the knowledge of suffering (dukkha). It is not enough to have a theoretical knowledge about it. You have to have an experience, an existential knowledge which affects your life. Then you will discover that

> ... birth is painful, old age is painful, death is painful, sorrow, lamentation, dejection, and despair are painful. Contact with unpleasant things is painful, not getting what one wishes is painful. In short, the fivefold clinging to existence is painful (grasping for bodily form or shape, pleasant feeling, attractions of the will, internal fancies, mental consciousness). (Dhammapada XXII, quoted by Hardon, *Religions of the World*, I, 103.)

In other words, the first truth consists in the insight that human existence as lived by those who have not yet achieved the state of "enlightenment" is nothing but suffering.

2. The second truth reveals the cause of suffering: frustrated craving. As long as man desires pleasure, prosperity and even his own existence, he is constantly frustrated and, as a result, he suffers.

3. The third truth deals with the purpose of the Buddhist's quest: the extinction of suffering. This is possible only by discovering that the "I," the personal, distinct self of a human being, is unreal. The person is only "a convenient designation, a mere name" which stands for five groups or "aggregates": matter, sensations, perception, mental formations (emotional inclinations), and consciousness. But there is no one who possesses these aggregates.

Craving arises from the delusion that I am someone who wants to possess pleasure, prosperity, and existence. If I discover that I am not, and that I cannot say this or that is mine, then the craving ceases, and peace and calm set in, which is Nirvana, "the state beyond pleasure and pain." It must be made clear, therefore, that in spite of some Western interpretations, original Buddhism advocates not only the ethical quality of unselfishness, but a metaphysical selflessness, i.e., it teaches that the human self (person or I) is unreal; to think otherwise is to live in an illusion.

4. The Fourth Truth points out the way, the "Holy Eightfold Path to Nirvana."[41] Here we can only summarize the eight steps, or rather the eight interconnected aspects of the one Path:

(1) "Right Understanding," namely the understanding of the first three Noble Truths.

(2) "Right Thought" or "Right Intention" presupposes that "all that we are is the result of what we think." In other words, if we abstain from hateful, greedy, and lustful thoughts and cultivate loving thoughts, our thoughts and intentions will gradually change our actions and ourselves.

"Right Speech," "Right Conduct," and "Right Livelihood" are all concerned with moral conduct (sila). The most important moral principle of action in Buddhism, just as in Hinduism, is nonviolence: ahimsa.

(3) "Right Speech" means not to cause harm by lying, gossiping, or idle talk. Speak graciously and with benevolence.

(4) "Right Conduct" avoids causing any harm by abstaining from killing, from stealing, from intoxicants, and from unchaste acts. The latter means that monks should live a celibate life, and married people should use restraint in sexual pleasures. Strict Buddhists are also vegetarians; they abstain also from harming animals.

---

[41] The eightfold articulation of the Path comes probably from a later stage of Buddhist doctrine.

(5) "Right Livelihood" means that Buddhists should not accept occupations which interfere with their spiritual progress, such as being butchers, brewers, arms dealers, or prostitutes. The last three steps of the Path describe the unfolding of a contemplative attitude (samadhi or samatha).

(6) "Right Effort" requires a steady and whole-hearted application of the will to get rid of all destructive mindsets, such as vengefulness, resentment, lust, and greed. The Buddha explains it in the following way:

> Those who follow the Way might well follow the example of an ox that marches through the deep mire carrying a heavy load. He is tired, but his steady gaze, looking forward, will never relax until he comes out of the mire, and it is only then that he takes a respite. O monks, remember that passion and sin are more than the filthy mire, and that you can escape misery only by earnestly and steadily thinking of the Way.[42]

(7) "Right Mindfulness" means a peaceful, steady self-presence, a deep honesty with oneself. We should not run away from facing ourselves, we should not deny feelings and motives which we would like—out of shame—to sweep under the rug of our consciousness. By becoming aware of our true feelings and our bodily sensations, we are no longer enslaved by them. We can be delivered from the obsession of psychic and physical pain in this way.[43]

(8) "Right Concentration" includes several stages. After the conquest of "desire, hatred, sloth, fear, and doubt" the ascent through various stages begins. At the end the world, with all its joys and sufferings, vanishes from consciousness and the Buddhist

---

[42] The saying is quoted by H. Smith, *The World's Religions* (San Francisco, CA: HarperSanFrancisco, 1991), 109.

[43] In describing the Eightfold Path I am indebted especially to Burke, *The Major Religions*, 64-65 and H. Smith, *The World's Religions*, 103-112.

reaches a state of perfect equanimity. One is released from samsara and attains Nirvana when a state beyond consciousness and unconsciousness is reached.[44]

The original phase of Buddhism does not deny the existence of the Hindu gods, or of Brahman, but it does not advocate prayer, sacrifice, or any kind of communication between the gods and humans. As far as salvation is concerned (which means to be released from the wheel of existence and to obtain the state of Nirvana), human beings are left to their own resources. They alone have to work out their salvation; not even the monastic community to which they belong can offer much help. The notions of creation and "grace," or the saving love of a personal god, are totally absent from what is probably the original doctrine of Buddha.

Yet, even original Buddhism seems to know about Absolute Reality. Nirvana[45] is negatively the extinction of all desire and the realization of the state of non-self: anatta (Pali) or anatman (Sanskrit). Yet, it is not pure nothingness. It is the "realm of the immortal." It is true that early Buddhism emphasizes this aspect of liberation from the cycle of samsara, but an early Pali text attributes the following speech to Buddha:

> There is, O disciples, an unborn, an unoriginated, uncreated, unformed. Were there not, O disciples, this unborn, unoriginated, uncreated, unformed, there would be no possible exit from the world of the born, originated, created, formed.[46]

Another text speaks about the Absolute in even slightly personal terms:

---

[44] See H. Dumoulin, *Zen Buddhism: A History*, vol. I. *India and China* (New York: Macmillan, 1988), 15-19. Dumoulin underlines the probable influence of Yogic meditation on the Buddhist stages of "Right Concentration."

[45] *Nirvana* in Sanskrit, *Nibbana* in Pali. The literal meaning according to Dumoulin "denotes a motionless rest where no wind blows, where the fire is quenched, the light has been extinguished, the stars have gone out, and the saint has died" (*Zen Buddhism*), p. 111.

[46] Udana VIII, 3, quoted by Dumoulin, p. 20.

The great ocean is deep, immeasurable, unfathomable.
So also… if the existence of the Perfect One be mea-
sured by the predicates of corporeal form: he is deep,
immeasurable, unfathomable as the great ocean.[47]

Similarly, the saint, arhanta (Pali) or arhat (Sanskrit), who
reaches Parinibbana (complete Nirvana at the moment of death)
is like an extinguished flame that—in contemporary Hindu belief—exists in a subtle, invisible form. Yet "there is no word to
speak of Him."[48]

This early notion of Nirvana as the extinction of flame is il-
lustrated by the following dialogue:

"Sire, disciples are to conduct themselves for as long as
life lasts with the Buddha as guide, with the Buddha
as designation."
"Very good, revered Nagasena. But is there a Buddha?"
"Yes, sire, there is a Buddha."
"But is it possible, revered Nagasena, to point to the
Buddha as being either here or there?"
"Sire, the Lord has attained Nirvana in the Nirvana el-
ement that has no groups of existence still remaining.[49]
It is not possible to point to the Lord as being either
here or there."
"Make a simile."
"What do you think about this, sire? When some flame
in a great burning mass of fire goes out, is it possible
to point to the flame as being either here or there?"
"No, revered sir. That flame has ceased to be, it has dis-
appeared."

---

[47] Samyutta Nikaya, IV quoted ibid.
[48] Suttanipata, quoted ibid.
[49] Groups of phenomena composing an existent entity.

> "Even so, sire, the Lord has attained Nirvana in the
> Nirvana element that has no groups of existence still
> remaining. The Lord has gone home. It is not possible
> to point to him as being here or there."[50]

In the course of its long history Buddhism developed many schools and branches. Of what survives today, Theravada and Mahayana (with its many ramifications such as Pure Land, Zen, and Tibetan Buddhism) are the dominant forms. Theravada ("the Way of the Elders") has its center today in Sri Lanka and can be found in most countries of Southeast Asia, such as Burma, Thailand, Laos, Cambodia, and Indonesia. Its emerging opponents, the Mahayana Buddhists, condescendingly named the Theravada along with other Buddhist schools the Hinayana, the "lesser vehicle," that is, a less effective means to Enlightenment.

The Theravadins rely chiefly on the "third Basket" of the Pali canon, called Abhidamma, and they claim it represents the original teachings of Sakyamuni. They venerate the human Buddha as a great sage but do not deify him. They describe Nirvana chiefly in negative terms as the extinction of the (apparent) self. Their ideal is the monk who belongs to the Sangha (the monastic community), goes begging for his once-a-day meal, lives a celibate life, and develops the four Noble Virtues of loving-kindness, compassion, equanimity, and joy in the well-being of others. But the Theravadins concentrate on release from samsara and reaching Nirvana all by themselves; they cannot rely on any supernatural help for this purpose. Once they reach Nirvana, they have no scruples of entering it, since they cannot help anyone else except by their example.

---

[50] Quoted in *The Teachings of the Compassionate Buddha*, ed. by E.A. Burtt (New York: The New American Library, 1963), 117-118.

5. Mahayana Buddhism

Mahayana Buddhists rely mainly on the Sanskrit canon of Buddhist writings. The earliest Mahayana scriptures date back probably to the first century B.C., although traces of Mahayana teachings can be discovered even in the oldest Buddhist scriptures. Today Mahayana prevails over the Theravada in China, Japan, Korea, Vietnam, Tibet, and Nepal.

Mahayana Buddhists also insist that their teaching is the authentic interpretation of Siddhartha Gautama. When Siddhartha reached enlightenment, they claim, he did not enter Nirvana, but, moved by pity, returned to the crowds and began to preach and help everyone else to reach Nirvana as well.

The Theravada ideal can be perfectly realized only by the monk, whereas Mahayana presents its teachings to everybody, including those who choose to remain in the world.

While it further develops an essential feature of original Buddhism, the practice of karuna (compassion), Mahayana also reabsorbs some of the central elements of Hinduism.[51]

The characteristics which distinguish Mahayana from Theravada may be summarized under the four following headings:

The Re-emergence of Absolute Reality

Absolute Reality is conceived of very much like the Hindu Brahman, except it has a different name: Buddha nature. Buddha nature is the true reality of every sentient being, but only those can experience it who at the end of the Path reached enlightenment and obtained wisdom (prajna) in contemplation. But no one

---

[51] Buddhism became widely influential in India in the third century B.C. during the reign of Asoka, the ruler of the Mauryan Empire of North India. But gradually the number of its adherents decreased to a small minority in India while Hinduism reasserted itself and strongly influenced even the Mahayana school of Buddhism.

can describe this universal Buddha nature without offending against its transcendence. Some trends in Mahayana even call it Universal Emptiness.

The historical Siddhartha Gautama was only one of the earthly emanations or manifestations of the universal Buddha nature. However, there are innumerable other Buddhas, all manifestations of that one Buddha nature. In fact, every sentient being is a potential Buddha and all are called to actualize their Buddha nature.

The distinct reality of the individual human person is not recognized in Mahayana. Through Enlightenment we discover the unreality of our egos and of the limits of our own body as we realize that we and all other Buddhas are identical with the cosmic body of the one Self-Existent Buddha (Dharmakaya). This realization enables us to enter Nirvana.

Karuna

Contrary to the individualistic attitude of Theravada Buddhism, Mahayana Buddhists believe that we can help everyone else by imparting our own merits to others. Thus compassion (karuna) is the most important virtue for the Mahayana Buddhist, just as equanimity (upekkha) is for the Theravadin.

The Bodhisattvas

The salvation of others is so important that the ideal for the Mahayana is no longer the arhat or aranta, the saint who attained Nirvana, but the bodhisattva (a being fixed on enlightenment) who refuses to enter Nirvana because he prefers to exercise a ministry of mercy so that others can reach Nirvana.

The ideal of the bodhisattva stems from the Indian spirit, for which images, desires, wishes, and vows are as much realities as are humans and their deeds. With their enlightened insight, they embody the Great Compassion (mahakaruna).[52] Originally they were highly revered heavenly beings, savior figures for the masses second in importance only to the Buddhas.

A later development added great historical figures to the heavenly beings, such as the Buddhist philosopher Nagarjuna. Eventually all holy, enlightened individuals were honored as bodhisattvas. In fact, at the beginning and throughout their monastic life, Zen disciples commit themselves by vows to follow the way of the bodhisattva.

Yet, the heavenly bodhisattvas keep even now a special place in the religious consciousness of many Buddhists. They dwell in heaven, but in answer to prayers, they come down in innumerable "incarnations":

> The Bodhisattvas, finding their joy in smoothing away the sorrows of others, descend into hell as swans swoop into a clump of lotus flowers. The deliverance of creatures is for them an ocean of joy drowning everything else.... Have one passion only: the good of others.... All who are unhappy, are unhappy from having sought their own happiness. All who are happy, are happy from having sought the happiness of others.[53]

The Saving Buddhas

Since Siddhartha Gautama and everyone else who fully realized his Buddha nature belongs to the realm of Absolute Reality, religious imagination turns to these Buddhas as savior figures who have infinite compassion for humankind, which wallows in the mire of unceasing reincarnations. Many Mahayana Buddhists in general, but especially those belonging to the Pure Land branch

---

[52] Dumoulin, *Zen Buddhism*, p. 31. In describing Mahayana, I am chiefly indebted to this classic of Buddhist history, pp. 27-39.

[53] Bodhikaryavatara, ch. VII.

of Mahayana, ask for the help of the Buddhas in their misery. Meditation remains essential in all forms of Buddhism, but for these people supplications, ritual, and the unceasing invocation of Buddha's name become part of their life.

In the later philosophical school of Yogacara the problem of the countless personal Buddhas and the one Buddha nature is resolved in the doctrine of the three bodies of the Buddha. The first body is the Apparitional Body of the individual Buddhas. The second is the Enjoyment Body, the personalized, perfected form of the Buddha who can be personally addressed by the devotees under this aspect. The third is the Cosmic Body of the Buddha (Dharmakaya), which is all individual Buddhas seen as the one consummate Absolute Reality:

> The cultic need for veneration was able to clothe the blessed body of the Buddha in an unspeakable splendor of light and beauty, endow it with infinite wisdom, power, and compassion, and depict his pure Land as the home of all human yearnings. The metaphysics of this Buddhology is cosmotheistic, and its corresponding anthropology, mystical. The deepest concern of the human individual must be the attainment of the enlightened view, for only the enlightened can grasp the perfect reality that is the Buddha. At the same time, enlightenment signifies the realization of one's deepest self—the Buddha nature inherent in all sentient beings.[54]

6. Buddhism and Christianity

What we said about the Hindu idea of Brahman and the world in comparison to Christian beliefs applies also to the rela-

---

[54] Dumoulin, *Zen Buddhism*, 33.

tionship between the universal Buddha nature and the Christian understanding of God. Here I will focus on the teachings of the Four Noble Truths from a Christian perspective, the figure of the bodhisattva, the saving Buddha, and the notion of compassion in Mahayana Buddhism.

1. In the eyes of the Buddha, unenlightened human existence is nothing but suffering because all desires are doomed to ultimate frustration. This indeed follows logically from his ignorance of any Loving Personal Absolute.

On the other hand, Christianity believes that existence is real and good and that we have been created to share in God's own joy, because our beginning, our life, and our end originate from, and are guided by, an Infinite Love. Consequently, every moment and event of our existence is providential; even repented sins and sufferings, endured or accepted in love, are conducive to ultimate fulfillment.

Yet, we can agree with the Buddhist that the person without even an implicit faith who considers human life a cosmic accident, a fleeting moment emerging from nothing and sinking into nothing, is indeed entitled to feel miserable.

2. Again, if there were no Loving, Personal Absolute, the Buddhist would be right in claiming that frustrated desires are the cause of suffering. If, however, there is a Loving, Personal Absolute, then every human being, even those with only an implicit faith in him, has some sort of intuition that our deepest longings are not absurd, but in some way or another are destined to be fulfilled.

From a Christian perspective, the cause of suffering is sin in its multiple forms: original sin committed at the dawn of human history and affecting all human beings, as well as personal sins creating socio-economic structures and psychological conditions which make human lives miserable.

In a dialogue with Buddhists, however, we can find some common ground, since sin is always the cause or result of a false desire. When we sin, we desire something against the order of reality, and ultimately in every sin we desire to be our own gods; such desires indeed distort our existence and our relationships, and so they become the cause of suffering.

3. If there were no Loving Personal Absolute, it would be logical to follow the advice of the Buddha: extinguish all desires. But since we believe that we are created by an Absolute Love to share in the personal communion of the Triune God, we cannot accept as our goal the extinction of all desires. Rather, we should purify our desires by redirecting the sinful desires that crave for unreality and by becoming aware of our deepest needs, a need for Infinite Truth, Goodness, and Beauty, a need for Infinite Life and Love. The ideal of the Christian is not to extinguish the fire of human passion but rather to purify and intensify its flame. Rather than developing a stoic resignation, we should develop a realistic sense of appreciating everything according to its real value.[55]

Moreover, Christ did not come to reveal the unreality of the human self but to show concretely by his death and resurrection how infinitely God values every human self.[56] Therefore, in the Christian view, human existence is valuable. It has to be purified and transformed by sharing in the death and resurrection of Christ; but God will fulfill our inmost desires beyond our boldest expec-

---

[55] Recall the famous saying of St. Bernard: "*Sapiens est cui res sapiunt prout sunt*: The wise person is the one to whom things 'taste' as they are." In other words, the wise person values instinctively everything according to its true value, neither less nor more.

[56] We can show the reality of our "I" even philosophically. None of us is a mere "stream of consciousness," a constantly changing bundle of thoughts, feelings and volitions. In and beyond the continuous stream of human consciousness there is an "I" who remembers the changing ideas, emotions and volitions of the past and anticipates those of the future. Without a (constantly changing yet permanent) "I" we would not have the awareness of our own personal identity. Moreover even if we could bracket all that our consciousness contains, all emotions, thoughts and volitions, there would always remain the bracketer, the person himself/herself.

Moreover, how can change exist without something or someone changing? If something or someone is changing, there are beings that change rather than mere change without beings. If something is changing, then something is, namely, that which is undergoing change: the dialectic of changing and continuing identity cannot be avoided unless we deny the reality of change itself.

tations. Christ came that we "may have life and have it to the fullest" (Jn 10:10).

Yet, there is room for dialogue even here. The Buddhist might admit that the desire for Nirvana, for a state of peace and unspeakable tranquility, should be cultivated and only the lower desires extinguished.

As said before, a Christian can never accept that our personal selves are illusions, falsely perceived manifestations of one universal Buddha nature; we know that each personal self is the object of an Infinite Divine Love that creates, develops, and guides the self into full conformity with the divine image for eternal life. Every human individual is so precious in God's eyes that the incarnate Son has shed his blood for each one of us.

In a dialogue, however, we should recover the partial truth of the Buddhist doctrine by understanding the "I" not metaphysically but ethically. Within an ethical language game, it is true and ought to be emphasized more than Christian ethics usually does that our egos are illusory and the source of all self-deception. The balloons of our false self-image, our overblown egos, need to be recognized, pierced, and deflated if we are ever to come back to reality and avoid unnecessary suffering.[57]

Christians also believe that, in this world, we cannot eliminate all suffering. But we can turn all our sufferings to our good and to the good of others, insofar as we accept them out of love as a share in the cross of Christ. Then suffering may serve both as atonement for our sins and others' and as a means of deepening our love for God and our fellow human beings. In fact, we cannot truly love in this world without suffering.

4. The ethical demands of the Eightfold Noble Path are, with some notable exceptions, similar to those of Christian morality. We also want to be present to ourselves in honesty and truth and

---

[57] This, of course, is only another way of showing that the source of suffering is sin, the false cravings that create an overblown ego.

to abstain not only from evil deeds but also from evil desires. Yet, the goal of moral purification for the Christian is not peace, equanimity, and detachment, but unselfish love (which calls for involvement and struggle and yet provides peace even in the midst of tension and conflict).

5. The figure of the bodhisattva who wants to take upon himself all the sufferings of the world is the closest among the figures of non-Christian religions to that of the Suffering Servant (Is 52:13-53:12). A great difference, however, lies in the fact that the Servant atones for the sins of humankind against a personal God, while the bodhisattva liberates all sentient beings from bad karma, the immanent effect of evil actions.

6. The figure of the saving Buddha to whom Buddhists pray for liberation resembles the figure of Christ the Savior. Yet, the saving Buddhas are believed to be saviors of all sentient beings not only of the human race.

7. Buddhist compassion and Christian charity seem, at first glance, identical. Buddhist compassion, however, extends in the same way to every living being. Theoretically, a tiger or the microbes in a human organism are as much objects of compassion as a human being. This all-embracing universality of karuna diminishes its personal quality. People cannot be valued truly if they are loved with the same love as the bacteria that feed on their bodies. Christians also respect and love (or at least ought to love) every creature; there is among all creatures a universal brotherhood in God. But for the Christian, one human person is more precious than the whole material universe, since every human person is created in God's image and redeemed by the cross of the incarnate Son of God.

Another difference between Buddhist compassion and Christian love is derived from their contrasting views concerning the human person. For the Buddhist, the reality of the human person is either an illusion (original Buddhism) or identical with the one universal Buddha nature (Mahayana). So compassion is directed to help one discover this truth. However, if the human person *as an individual* is only an illusion, how can he/she be loved for his/her own sake as Christianity commands it? If the Buddhist wants to be totally present to another human being, he will experience that true love discovers the very core of the other person, the irreducible uniqueness of the other, and he will want to affirm and appreciate that unique person. Moreover, a true lover reaches the beloved in spite of and through the constant changes that the beloved undergoes; he remains faithful and aims at the eternal flourishing of the beloved.

However, the doctrinal system of Buddhism is one thing and the concrete experience of a Buddhist another. In spite of their doctrine, Buddhist experience frequently attests to a genuine love which is akin to the Christian experience.

7. Zen Buddhism

Zen Buddhism originated from an adaptation of Mahayana Buddhism to Chinese Taoism and was later transplanted from China to Japan. Presently, Zen is the most attractive form of Buddhism for the West.[58]

The adherents of Zen, like the other branches of Buddhism, derive their school from Siddhartha Gautama. One day, they explain, the Buddha held up a flower, and looked at it for a long time without saying a word. One young man in the audience began to smile and the Buddha looked at him approvingly. This young monk became enlightened without hearing a word, but just by looking at the flower, and thus he became—they say—the founder of the Zen school of Buddhism.

---

[58] Zen is the Japanese equivalent for the Chinese word *ch'an* which comes from the Sanskrit word *dhyana* meaning meditation. According to a legendary tradition, Bodhidharma carried over the Zen tradition to China in the 6th century A.D. and, according to Japanese sources, it spread to Japan in the same century.

This story presents all the essential elements of Zen Buddhism: no word is spoken, no teaching imparted, and enlightenment results not from the studying of Buddhist scriptures, the sutras, but from a silent gesture of the Buddha.

Every day Zen Buddhists spend long hours in silent meditation, sitting in the lotus position (zazen), the goal of which is enlightenment (satori), an experience that is beyond any conceptual knowledge. In the words of Professor Habito:

> What zazen is meant to realize is not a thought or idea or image about something, no matter how lofty or profound, but the direct experience of the pure fact of being, right here and now, with every breath: a pure fact of being wherein the opposition between the subject and the object is overcome or dissolved.[59]

The Rinzai school of Zen Buddhism practices "koan" (a Japanese word corresponding to the Chinese word "kung-an"[60]). A koan is a weird action, a paradoxical story, question, or statement whose purpose is to break down the usual ways of logical thinking and make the meditator aware that we are to reach reality directly, without concepts and words.[61]

In spite of their claim that experienced reality cannot be conceptualized, Zen Buddhists speak at length about their unspeakable experience, and many of them explain it by relying on a metaphysics and epistemology that is common in Mahayana Buddhism.

---

[59] Ruben L.F. Habito, *Healing Breath. Zen Spirituality for a Wounded Earth* (Dallas, TX: Maria Kannon Zen Center publications, 2001), 63.

[60] Its original meaning is public record or public notice.

[61] Here is a simple koan: "A monk said to Chao-chou, 'I have just entered this monastery. Please instruct me.' Chao-chou said, 'Have you had your breakfast?' The monk replied, 'Yes, I have.' Chao-chou said, 'Wash your bowls.'" Enlightenment, then, does not come from theoretical knowledge but from being fully present to what I am doing and even more, to be one with what I am doing and thereby one with all that is (See Habito, *Healing Breath*, 77).

Most of them[62] assume that enlightenment occurs when all dual-
ity between the mind and the world of phenomena disappears and
the meditators become pure consciousness, in which they experience themselves one with the totality of reality. The result is ec-
static joy, an exuberance of energy, a total "connectedness with
oneself and with all that is."

A Christian Perspective on Zen Buddhism

There is no reason for anyone to doubt that such experiences
can occur, since the testimonies which describe them speak with a
directness and authenticity that could hardly be faked. What is experienced in satori, however, is open to a variety of interpretations;
in fact, there might exist in what is called satori very different kinds
of experiences that Zen Buddhist experts do not differentiate.

In some cases satori could be the experience of feeling one
with nature, the universe, earth, plants, animals, and human beings on an instinctive, intuitive level. Such a union does not need
God's grace but only an awakened self that is in touch with its
subconscious drives and energies. Perhaps the myth of Antaeus
can shed light on such an experience. Antaeus remains invincible
as long as he is in touch with his mother Earth. Once he loses
contact with her, he becomes weak. For modern Westerners who
have lost touch with themselves and with nature, feeling one with
all of "be-ing" on a level that liberates their subconscious energies
becomes a most attractive experience.

However, no human being can live in a neutral state regarding God's call to supernatural life. Either he has accepted the call
of grace (or is in the process of accepting it), or he has rejected it
(or is in the process of rejecting it).

In the latter case, the one who experiences satori may interpret this experience of oneness as becoming divine and all-pow-

---

[62] D.T. Suzuki, a well known Zen Buddhist writer, is one of the few exceptions.

erful: he may think that his consciousness is everything and everything real is nothing else but his own consciousness; the "All" and "Absolute" is actualized in him. In other words, his satori is a climax of self-divinization; it is original sin reenacted.

However, if someone in the state of grace experiences satori, this may result for him in an implicit experience of God himself, mediated through the actualization of his unity with the rest of creation. Indications that this second kind of experience have taken place are signs of gratitude, humility, moral purity, and self-giving love in the enlightened person.

Yet, in both cases, if the enlightened person was raised in a Mahayana philosophical system, he may (mistakenly) express his satori as becoming aware of an ontological non-duality between his consciousness and the rest of reality. Evidently, such a pantheistic interpretation is incompatible with Christianity.

The Philosophical Foundations of Zen Buddhism

Since Zen Buddhism is so popular in our culture, we need to investigate its philosophical and theological presuppositions in the Mahayana tradition.

a) Reflections on the Epistemology of Experience

1. While maintaining the ontological distinction between the knowing subject and the world, a (broadly) Thomistic epistemology views the process of knowing as beginning with an undifferentiated experience of the object and culminating in a differentiated, more enlightened experience or insight in which the knowing subject and the object of knowing become one in the "*esse intentionale*," in the order of intentional being. Such an insight is the result of more or less elaborate logical operations (forming concepts, making judgments, constructing an argument, etc.) regarding the object of knowing. In each epistemological judgment,

by expressing the link between a subject and a predicate through the copula "is," the knowing subject participates in the being ("the is-ness") of the object known. Thus, knowledge in the Thomistic tradition does not terminate in concepts but in judgments. Concepts do not affirm anything to be real, judgments do. The purpose of forming concepts is only to create tools to approach the knowable content of objects. But we can affirm the object's existence and its "suchness" only in judgments. The end-point of an epistemological process, then, is a mediated immediacy, an insight that results from a set of judgments about the object in question. Through the insight the knower participates in the being of the world known. An insight may in turn become the starting point of a deeper and clearer experience of the same reality, an experience in which not only one's intellect but also the will and emotions participate, an experience that results in a real union of one's being with the being of the experienced reality.[63]

2. When experiencing something new, we must be aware that our previously formed concepts and judgments influence our interpretation of the undifferentiated first experience. Although our prior notions do affect our new experience, yet, upon reflection, the new experience should result in refining or changing our previous concepts and judgments.

---

[63] The process described above applies to sub-personal objects. Persons as persons, however, can only be known through faith. For example, if I look at an alpine meadow, it is an undifferentiated experience which, nonetheless, comprises more than the sum total of sensory impressions. Then I may explore the individual plants of the meadow in detail and the beautiful harmony that results from the configuration of every detail. Afterwards, I may take a second look at the whole in which the already obtained discursive knowledge of the parts and of the whole will result in a richer and more articulate insight into the meadow. This insight may result in an experience in which I "love" the meadow more than at the beginning of the process of knowing and I experience a kind of direct union with it. In personal relationships the first undifferentiated experience of the encountered person may also result in the acquisition of conceptual knowledge *about him*. However, if I want to know the person himself, I must believe what he says about himself. Believing another person means that I rely on this person as trustworthy: thus it is only in a real union with him do I know him. Loving another person implies an even deeper union of my being with that of the beloved; yet, union in true love affirms and embraces the real difference between the two friends.

3. Should we decide to eliminate all concepts and judgments from our experience, this conscious rejection of making any judgment about our experience will necessarily result in a judgment, namely, that our experience is alien to concepts and judgments. Thus, by trying to separate discursive knowledge (concepts and judgments) and experience, we involve ourselves in making a new judgment and thereby demonstrate the epistemological absurdity of complete separation between experience and discursive knowledge in the process of knowing.

4. We should, however, recognize that the type of knowledge in which experience prevails (both the undifferentiated and especially the differentiated experience) gets us in touch with reality in a much more comprehensive way than the knowledge that is predominantly discursive: in experience, reality affects our whole being; in discursive knowledge, only our intellect. Yet discursive knowledge eliminates doubts, clears up ambiguities, and provides precisions that will reinforce and deepen the experience itself.

In the case of experiencing values, in other words, the real, the good, the true, and the beautiful, our final goal is not merely a conforming of our intellect to the object of knowledge (a union of the knower with the object in the intentional order) but a *connaturalitas*, a transformation of our whole being under the impact of these value-experiences.

b) Application to Zen

After outlining the process of knowing in Thomistic epistemology, it appears most likely that the Zen Buddhists' vehement rejection of conceptual knowledge targets another theory of knowledge, that which terminates in concepts rather than in union with the object of knowledge.

On the other hand, if Thomistic epistemology is true, the Zen Buddhists' flat rejection of any discursive knowledge is self-contradictory. They cannot avoid speaking about their experience in terms of discursive knowledge, as is amply documented by the enormous amount of Zen literature. At the same time, we admit with the Zen Buddhist that experience ("mindfulness," "looking deeply" in Zen literature) is indeed both the beginning and the end of the process of knowing reality. This mindfulness, however, cannot be opposed to discursive knowledge, but rather must be its beginning and its end, since the goal of discursive knowledge is to transcend itself in a certain kind of union with the object of knowledge. Moreover, mindfulness—at the risk of losing itself— has to acknowledge its need for interpreting and evaluating one's experience in terms of concepts and judgments. In fact, everyone writing or lecturing about Zen is doing that in different ways and to varying degrees.

1. Concretely, then, if "looking deeply" means an experience of becoming one with the object of our experience in a *sui generis* mode that Thomists call the order of the *esse intentionale*, this union of object and subject does not call for a pantheistic view of reality. From this epistemological realization we cannot jump to the metaphysical conclusion that subject and object, mind and matter, are one and the same ontological reality.

In fact, such a conclusion would contradict the Zen experience itself, which is characterized by becoming alive to, alert to, and enriched by direct contact with reality. If it were only a becoming aware of one universal consciousness, how could it embrace the world in all its dazzling variety and otherness? The experience of oneness with the object of experience is better explained by the above-mentioned Thomistic understanding of insight than by a pantheistic universal consciousness. If only consciousness exists, and that without a conscious subject, neither the variety of objects and their enriching effect on the knowing subject nor the experience of consciousness are explicable. In other words, the consciousness of manifold and different realities presupposes a unifying center that is the subject of consciousness; the experience of being enriched by the manifold and different objects of knowledge presupposes an ontological difference between the knower and the world.[64]

2. Could the experience of the "emptiness" of things affirmed by Zen not be explained better by moral and existential notions than by metaphysical ones, which imply that the phenomenal world has no underlying reality? To put it simply, an alert presence to the objects of our experience, and, even more, a radically unselfish love call for the radical deflating of our egos, for emptying ourselves of all preoccupations, concerns, worries, and petty ambitions. We must be one "big, receptive empty space" in order to embrace the world, especially the world of persons. But ontologically, this emptying of the self results in the perfection of the self, which can grow only in loving, self-emptying relationships.

3. The Zen Buddhist teaching that by being one with "the dependent co-arising of all phenomena" you reach Nirvana could be more precisely formulated in this way: it is in and through the experience of the changing world, which could exist and could not exist, that we become aware of its necessary ground, namely the Being which cannot not exist.

Is this necessary Ground of Being that has caused all contingent beings to exist personal or impersonal? Certainly, it cannot be personal in the sense of a limited, finite, individual subject. But Christian revelation speaks about this Necessary Being as a supremely loving and freely loving communion of Infinite Persons. Moreover, the Son came so that he might give himself completely to each one of us in the Holy Spirit. Christian religious experience, then, is more than wakefulness (looking deeply), and compassion; it is the awareness that an infinitely powerful love wants to embrace and transform each one of us.

---

[64] For more details on a modern Thomistic epistemology see Bernard Lonergan, *Insight, A Study of Human Understanding* (New York: Harper and Row, 1978).

Chapter IV

THE RELIGIOUS PHILOSOPHY
OF TAOISM AND CONFUCIANISM

The primitive Chinese religion's notion of the heavenly God has never entirely vanished from the Chinese religious consciousness. In fact, it developed further during the Chou dynasty (1111-249 B.C.). The Emperor ruled by Heaven's Mandate, and thus represented the Will of Heaven for his subjects. If, however, the emperor failed to observe virtue (te), he would lose his right to govern. In addition to the Lord on High or Heaven, the Chinese also believed in many spiritual beings, demons, and spirits of ancestors, to whom they offered sacrifices.

Here we will investigate the most important trends of Chinese religious philosophy rather than of the popular religions of many gods, demons, and ancestors.

Besides Zen Buddhism, which spread from China to Japan as well, Taoism and Confucianism are typically Chinese world views. Taoism is more mystical; it is oriented towards wordless contemplation, withdrawal from pressure-filled activity, and living in harmony with nature. Confucianism concerns itself with the practical wisdom of building a humane and just society. Yet, as we will see, these two seemingly antithetical philosophical trends share many points of convergence.

1. Taoism

Traditionally, Lao Tzu (6th century B.C., possibly a contemporary of Confucius) is considered to be the author of a famous small book, Tao-Te-Ching (The Classic of the Way and Its Virtue) that provides inspiration for this philosophy. Chuang Tzu (399-295 B.C.) further developed the Taoist heritage.[65]

In what follows, I will summarize the notions and images of the Tao-Te-Ching.

a) Tao

Tao existed before heaven and earth, undifferentiated and complete; it depends on nothing and does not change (25).[66] It is the one ultimate, eternal principle: invisible, inaudible, intangible, the "mother" of all things, the beginning of heaven and earth. Tao itself cannot be named, but all that have names derive from Tao. Image, form, and essence are all in Tao, but Tao itself is dim, dark, and elusive (1, 21). At times Tao seems to be identified with Non-Being (28).

Tao is impersonal; one cannot pray to Tao. It does not create out of nothing by a personal act of the will, but by dividing itself into the many visible things by way of begetting (42).

All tangible and visible things carry either yin (the female, passive principle) or yang (the active, masculine principle); harmony in the world derives from the combination of these two forces (42).

Tao seems similar to the logos of Stoic philosophy in the West, the ultimate rational principle of all things.

---

[65] Cf. Wing-Tsit Chan, *A Sourcebook in Chinese Philosophy* (Princeton, NJ: Princeton Univ. Press, 1973), 3-5; 136-138.

[66] The numbers refer to the short chapters or rather poems in the Tao-Te-Ching.

b) Taoist Morality

Taoist morality does not discard the traditional Chinese view that virtuous life means following the way of Heaven (the term "Heaven" meaning an impersonal form of the heavenly God) (59). Heaven saves and guards those people who have mercy (or deep love).

In the Tao-Te-Ching, however, Heaven is not the Ultimate Principle, but rather originates from Tao; therefore virtuous life consists ultimately in following Tao. At the same time it can also be described as following nature, since all of nature reflects Tao (16, 21, 23).[67]

The one who follows Tao is identified with Tao (23). Whoever opposes Tao will soon perish (28, 55). The wise man is the virtuous man who is aware of the needs of others and is good to both those who are good and to those who are not good because virtue is goodness (49). He also repays hatred with virtue (63).

While the sage's softness and readiness to bend like a reed (22) rather than to be broken like an oak tree by the wind seems at places nothing more than a clever strategy for survival, humility means something much deeper in Taoist thought. It holds the secret to achieving supreme moral strength. Thus, the wise man dares not to be 'number one'; he refuses to put himself on a pedestal in order to shine and to be admired. But precisely this attitude of humility reveals his inner strength, courage, leadership, and nobility (22, 67). Simply put, he does not compete, so the world cannot compete with him (66).

The wise man "acts without action" (wu wei: 63). He screams all day long but does not become hoarse (55).

If he is a ruler, he rules without using force; in fact, he rules

---

[67] I used here the translations of Wing-Tsit Chan, *A Sourcebook in Chinese Philosophy*, 139-176 and Gia Fu Feng & Jane English, *Lao Tsu, Tao Te Ching* (New York: Random House, 1972).

without any action. The ruler's virtue and lack of cravings transform his subjects into virtuous people (57-58).

The wise man is like a little child (55); even though he is
shy and humble, people look to him and listen to him (49). His
bones are soft, his muscle is weak, yet he has a firm grip. Insects,
wild birds, and beasts will not attack him (55).

He has not experienced sexual intercourse, yet he is whole
and his manhood is strong (55).

The wise man appreciates silence: "He who knows does not
speak" (56) and certainly does not argue. He "learns to become
unlearned" (64). To have extensive (conceptual) knowledge is a
sign of lack of wisdom (81).

Chuang Tzu further developed the mystical vision of Tao-
Te-Ching. His goal is complete spiritual freedom, which he attains by accepting Nature in all its transformations; it does not
matter for him whether he is a man dreaming about being a
butterfly or a butterfly dreaming about being a man. He accepts
death by claiming that death is only a transformation into another
life form.[68]

Taoism and Christianity

Taoist morality comes close to Christian moral teaching on
several counts. There is a clear resemblance between obedience
to Tao and to the Natural Moral Law. Beyond the requirements
of the Natural Law, the Taoist's understanding of humility and
universal goodness may be inspired by God's grace. Christianity,
like Taoism, sees humility as essential to our spiritual quest. The
sage's attitude toward hatred and toward those who are not good
comes very close to the Christian love of the enemy.

However, the underlying visions of reality in Christianity and

---

[68] The treatise attributed to Chuang Tzu is called Nan-hua chen-ching. See more on it in
A Source Book, 179-210.

in Taoism are substantially different. In Taoist philosophy there is no personal God whom we are called to imitate, to whom we can pray, and in whose grace and love we can share. The Taoist sage is good to those who are not good because that is virtuous behavior, not because he intends to imitate the attitude of a personal God who forgives our sins and overcomes hatred by his love.

Moreover, te, the Chinese term for virtue, means also the latent power of things, the mysterious energies that may make the sage immortal. Thus, the ambiguous meaning of te reveals for us the ambiguity of the Taoist sage's moral quest. The practice of te may mean a high degree of moral perfection in absolute obedience to Tao. But in religious Taoism it often degenerates into the sage's self-sufficient quest for immortality, either spiritual or physical, through enhancing his life force. He uses breathing exercises, meditation, fasting, and even alchemy to achieve immortality by his own efforts. In this case, then, Taoist ethics aims at the exact opposite of the Christian ideal; instead of accepting deification through God's grace as a gift, he intends to be a god on his own—original sin reenacted.

2. Confucianism

Throughout the more than four thousand years of Chinese civilization, Confucius (K'ung Fu-tzu) exerted the greatest influence on Chinese philosophical thought and behavior.[69] According to later traditions he lived from 551 B.C. to 479 B.C. It is not easy to find the real Confucius behind the many layers of legends. In legendary accounts he was transformed into a diplomat and successful statesman, and during the Han dynasty (206 B.C. to 220 A.D.) into an infallible Divine Sage.

We can reconstruct the outline of his life only with some degree of probability.

---

[69] Confucius is the latinized form of the name K'ung Fu-tzu: Grand Master K'ung.

Born in the state of Lu (modern day Shantung) from a noble but poor family, he lost his father at an early age. He was a "self-made man who became perhaps the most learned man of his time."[70] He held the job of a police magistrate, perhaps even becoming a minister of justice. Either fired by his prince, or voluntarily relinquishing his job, Confucius became an itinerant teacher wandering from state to state with some of his disciples. He offered his services to several princes but none of them wanted to appoint him to any important job. He spent his last years in his home state. In his lifetime he resolutely disclaimed the title of Divine Sage or even a "good man." He claimed only one unique quality: "The unwearying effort to learn (not abstract knowledge, but self-improvement) and unflagging patience in teaching others" (Analects VII, 33).

Confucius' influence is unparalleled, not only in China, but also in Korea and Japan. It soon overcame the rival school of Mo-Tzu and was adopted into the official ideology of the Chinese Empire during the Han dynasty.[71] While originally Confucianism was nothing more than a moral philosophy, Neo-Confucianism (a conflation of Taoist and Buddhist views with Confucian morality) came to prominence in the past eight hundred years, and provided a metaphysical doctrine to explain all of reality.

The Chinese communist state attempted to eradicate Confucian thought from the nation's consciousness. Yet recently, recognizing the bankruptcy of their Marxist ideology, and the need for credible moral standards, even China's communist leaders began to encourage the resurgence of Confucian morality.

---

[70] *A Source Book in Chinese Philosophy*, tr. & compiled by Wing-Tsit Chan (Princeton, NJ: Princeton Univ. Press, 1973), 17.

[71] Mo-Tzu's philosophy (479-438 B.C.) rivaled in influence that of Confucius for several centuries. Heaven in Mo-Tzu's thought is much more active in human affairs than according to Confucius. Heaven directs all the affairs of man and the world; nothing is left to fate. Morality depends on Heaven's Will. The criterion of moral right is what benefits man; whereas for Confucius what is morally right should be cultivated for its own sake while he admits that doing what is right causes happiness. Mo-Tzu stresses universal love rather than love centered on family relations, and he opposes any kind of war.

Confucian Morality

Most commentators on Confucius and his teaching belittle the role religion plays in his thought. It is true that Confucius discouraged speculation about the "Beyond" and that he wanted to keep the spirits at a distance. Nevertheless, "Heaven" (T'ien) in the sense of a Transcendent, Absolute Reality who has some personal characteristics, plays an essential role in his life and teaching.

Confucius evaluates his whole life in relationship to Heaven's Will. Learning about morality for him meant learning about the Will of Heaven. And he reached maturity by interiorizing Heaven's Will so that the spontaneous desires of his heart were in harmony with it:

> Confucius said: "At fifteen I set my heart on learning. At thirty I was firmly established. At forty, I had no more doubts. At fifty, I knew the will of Heaven. At sixty, I was ready to listen to it. At seventy, I could follow my heart's desire without transgressing what was right" (II, 4).[72]

He is aware that Heaven begot the moral power of virtue in him, a power that renders him fearless (VII, 22). He claims that no human being knows him, but only Heaven (XIV, 37). He is in awe of Heaven's edicts (XVI, 8). The most important task in life is to know Heaven's Way. Once you know it, you might as well die (IV, 8). Heaven can be prayed to, but if one is in the wrong with Heaven, there is no one else to pray to. The implication seems to be that whoever opposes Heaven, opposes also the world of heavenly spirits (III, 13).[73]

---

[72] The following numbers refer to chapters and verses in the Analects, the collection of the sayings of Confucius and his disciples. See *A Source Book*, 22.

[73] Note that later Chinese philosophers understood Heaven's decrees more and more impersonally as moral order or moral destiny. Cf. *A Source Book*, 23.

If one intends to follow the Way of Heaven, he should develop his te, the inner moral force or virtue that Heaven has begotten in him (VII, 22). As this paraphrase indicates, virtue for Confucius is not a straitjacket stifling the spontaneity of a human being, but is rather the unfolding of his innate human potential. We should constantly strive to become more virtuous. For Confucius this is the only worthy goal for all learning.

Confucius does not discuss whether or not we are born good; Mencius, one of his followers in the fourth century, will claim that we are. Confucius, on the other hand, while stressing the power of unlimited perfectibility in us, admits that he never met a human being who has reached the pinnacle of moral perfection, which he describes as jen, translated either by "humanity" or "Goodness." Only the Divine Sages or Emperors of past epochs could be described as having realized jen.[74]

That the supreme moral value is "humanity," or acting according to our human nature, reveals the profound humanism of Confucius. Ethical perfection is to become fully and perfectly human. However, the elusive character of jen discloses its transcendence. Jen is at our side, and Confucius has not seen a man who did not have the power to realize it in himself; yet he has seen no one (including himself) who has actually embodied it.

Confucius considers jen such a transcendent perfection that he rarely speaks about it. One may be a gentleman and yet not have obtained jen (XIV, 7). He does not know whether even those who have no craving for domination, no vanity, no resentment, no covetousness would qualify for jen (XIV, 2). He can only say that unselfishness (to recognize others' merits rather than his own) and shu (actions derived from like-heartedness) lie in the direction of jen (VI, 28). Shu means that one has the heart of the other

---

[74] Jen originally meant either a free man as opposed to ming (subject) or (with a small change in writing) a man possessing the qualities of his tribe. Later it came to mean human being in general and the perfection that is appropriate for a human. Cf. A. Waley, *The Analects of Confucius* (New York: Vintage Books, 1989), 27-29.

in himself so that his own feelings can serve as a guide for doing what the other person needs.

He who has obtained jen has no reason to grieve; he can never be unhappy (IX, 28). But situations may arise in which he has to give his life for achieving jen (XV, 8, VIII, 13).

The more easily obtainable ideal for Confucius is that of the chün-tzu, translated either as "gentleman" or "superior man."[75] The gentleman is characterized by an all-pervading nobility of spirit. His opposite is the common man or the small man. The gentleman strives to do what is right, while the small man does what is beneficial to him. He calls attention to the good qualities in others, not to their defects; the small man does the exact opposite (XII, 16). He does not grieve that people do not recognize his merits, but he grieves at his own incapacities (XIV, 32). He does not fear or grieve when looking into himself, since he finds no taint there (XII, 4). He is dignified but never haughty, while the opposite is true of the small man (XII, 16). The gentleman is so reliable that if you should entrust to him either an orphan or the welfare of a state, he would prove trustworthy and competent in both cases.

The moral force of the gentleman is such that even people above him will be influenced by it (XIV, 24).

He appreciates education, the arts, and especially music. He studies not for impressing people but for the sake of self-improvement (XIV, 25).

Confucius is not an unconditional pacifist, but he wants to minimize the use of force and claims no expertise in warfare (XII, 7; XII, 19; XV, 1).

The social structure of society is based on the five relations:

---

[75] The history of the etymology of chün-tzu is very close to that of "gentleman." Originally the expression meant "son of a ruler" or "son of the nobility." Later the social connotation was forgotten so that chün-tzu for Confucius simply means a man of noble character. Since "superior man" can be easily misunderstood, I will use here the translation "gentleman." Cf. Waley, *Analects*, 34-38.

relationship between father and son, between elder brother and younger brother, between husband and wife, between older and younger persons, and between prince and minister.

Among these relationships the one between father and son is archetypical and strongly influences the other relationships. Society is healthy if everyone behaves according to the propriety of his social position (XII, 11).

In order to have a stable government, soldiers, food, and the trust of the common people are needed. Of these three the most important is the trust. A government can survive without soldiers and even food, but not without the trust of the common people (XII, 7).

Confucianist and Christian Morality

As a high-ranking Chinese convert explained, his Confucianism was for him a providential preparation for Christian morality.[76] Hardly any moral advice of Confucius needs to be discarded when one embraces Christian morality. In fact, almost all of it should be followed. I know of no other non-Christian moral teaching that approximates in so many areas what Christianity recognizes as the Natural Moral Law. We may also detect the effects of God's grace in Confucius's personal interiorization of the moral law, in his insistence on the unconditional obedience to doing what is right, and on the readiness to seek Goodness (Humanity) even at the expense of one's own physical life.

At first reading, Confucius seems to teach that one has to follow the Way of Heaven by one's own power. Yet there are some intimations of a transcendent force at work in those who sincerely seek Goodness. Confucius mentions that Heaven begot the moral

---

[76] See Jean Ching Hsiung Wu, *Du Confucianisme au Catholicisme* (Rome: P. Universita Gregoriana, 1948), 24. He was the ambassador of the Republic of China to the Holy See before the Communist takeover.

force in him and that this force is available to all human beings; most of them, however, do not avail themselves of it.

There are, of course, obvious differences between Christian morality and that of Confucius. He is part of a patriarchal society and does not show enough appreciation for women. He knows and teaches neither that we should love our enemy nor that we are called to share in God's own love for our fellow human beings. Nevertheless, according to Ching Hsiung Wu, he is "a Catholic in spirit":

> Is it not clear that for Confucius Heaven is all powerful, all wise and all good? Unfortunately, the Confucianists did not grasp this essential point in the thought of their master. They preached only filial piety toward parents and completely ignored filial piety toward God. In the hands of the Confucianists the nascent theism of Confucius degenerated into an impoverished pantheism. In the history of China there is no greater man than Confucius because no other man has had such a filial attitude toward God.[77]

---

[77] *Ibid.*, 25-26.

Chapter V

ISLAM

1. Muhammad, the Seal of the Prophets

The chief source for our reconstruction of the life, deeds, sayings, and personality of Muhammad is the Hadith (literally, statement), a large body of literature that began to be put into writing two hundred years after the death of the Prophet. Even Islamic scholars question the authenticity of certain Hadith collections, while they accept others that, although formulated late in time, reflect what these scholars perceive as the authentic spirit of Islam.[78]

Muhammad was born from the Arab clan Quraish around 570 A.D. in Mecca. He came from a family that practiced monotheism, the legacy of Abraham. According to Islamic sources, his family derived itself from Ishmael, the son of Abraham. His father died before Muhammad was born, his mother, when the child was six, so Muhammad was raised first by his grandfather, then by his uncle. As a young man, he was employed by a wealthy widow named Khadijah. He acted for her as the overseer of her caravan of camels on journeys to Syria. He gained her full trust,

---

[78] My chief source for his life is the article "Muhammad" from the *Concise Encyclopedia of Islam* (ed. C. Glasse, San Francisco: HarperSanFrancisco, 1991) and J. Renard, *Responses to 101 Questions on Islam* (New York: Paulist Press, 1998).

and at the age of forty Khadijah became Muhammad's wife.[79] Muhammad was deeply religious from a young age and spent considerable time in prayer and meditation in the hills of the countryside. One night around the year 610 (now commemorated on the 27th of the month Ramadan) he had a troubling visitation: the angel Gabriel commanded him to recite God's message ("qur'an" means recitation). Muhammad was deeply shaken and sought counsel and reassurance from Khadijah, who became the first believer in the authenticity of her husband's prophetic mission. The second visitation came about a year later, after which the messages, and sometimes visions, became more frequent. Muhammad believed that his mission, received from Allah through the mediation of the angel Gabriel, was to proclaim Allah to be the only God and, thus, to restore the primordial religion of Adam and Abraham. In this one authentic religion humankind must submit itself to its Creator in total obedience.

In Mecca the majority of people were polytheists, who believed in many lesser gods and goddesses along with Allah, the chief god. Muhammad came from the ranks of the hanifs, who believed only in the one God Allah, but Christians and Jews also lived in the area of Mecca. Muhammad could not read or write, so, barring direct revelations from God, his only way to learn of Jewish and Christian traditions had to come through oral traditions from local Jews and Christians.

In Mecca, Muhammad's initial proclamation did not meet with great success. The city made its living from the pilgrims who came to worship its 360 idols of the many different gods and goddesses, and the merchants were afraid that, if Muhammad's religion should spread among the people, they would lose all their

---

[79] Until her death, she was Muhammad's only wife and the Prophet preserved the greatest respect for her throughout his life. Later, Muhammad married ten more times and had nine wives at one and the same time. In addition, he had also two concubines. In the Arab society of his days, polygamy and concubinage were an accepted practice. According to the *Concise Encyclopedia of Islam* Muhammad said that "dearest to him were 'prayer, perfumes and women,' all that in this world is fragrant of paradise" (281).

income. The hostility against the Prophet grew so strong that he and his adherents migrated to Yathrib about 300 miles to the north, a city that later became known as Medina, "the city of the Prophet." In Yathrib the Prophet was received favorably and soon became the city's sole religious and political leader. The year of Muhammad's flight or migration (Hijra), 622 A.D., became the first year of the Islamic calendar. Its importance for Muslims derives from its being the year of the foundation of the first Islamic society. In Medina Muhammad prohibited the worship of all gods but Allah, established set times for daily public prayer, and set Friday as the day of the main weekly religious service.

Meanwhile the violent skirmishes between the people of Mecca and the Muslims of Medina escalated until Muhammad finally decided to return to Mecca with a large army in 630. The city surrendered to him and Muhammad had all the idols of the gods and goddesses smashed. He transformed Mecca into an Islamic city according to the pattern followed in Medina. Nevertheless, he preserved the Ka'bah ("cube"), a large cubic stone structure that contains the Black Stone, and made it into the center of pilgrimage for all Muslims. All the images of pagan gods and goddesses were painted over, but according to Islamic tradition the Prophet did not allow the image of the Virgin Mary with her Child to be eliminated. In 632, the year he died, Muhammad led the first pilgrimage to the Ka'bah.

2. Survey of Islamic History

After the death of Muhammad Islam split into two major groups. One was led by the son-in-law of Muhammad, named Ali, who claimed appointment by the Prophet himself. The larger and politically and militarily more successful party chose Abu Bakr, a father-in-law of the Prophet. These successors were called Caliphs, both political and spiritual leaders. The faction of Ali became known as the Shi'ite Muslims,[80] while the majority follow-ing Abu Bakr and his able successor Umar became identified as the People of the Sunna (sunna: custom, tradition) or Sunni Muslims. Today about 85% of all Muslims are Sunnis.

Already during his last years, the Prophet became the most powerful political and religious leader in Arabia. In a century af-ter his death, his zealous followers conquered millions of people from India to Africa to Spain. Only the army of Charles Martel was able to halt the Islamic advance, at Tours and Poitiers in 732, and thus prevent for the time being the further conquest of Eu-rope. In conquered countries, polytheists were given only two choices: convert to Islam or be executed. Christians and Jews, however ("People of the Book" along with Zoroastrians, Sabians [their identity is unclear] and Hindus), were allowed to remain in their religion, but they had to pay taxes to the Islamic authorities.

The expansion of Islam spearheaded by the Arab armies led to a flourishing Arab culture. Many of the mosques erected in the Islamic world became masterpieces of religious architecture; phi-losophy, mathematics, the natural sciences, and medicine flourished and made great advances. For instance, the thought of Aristotle became known to Christian Europe through the media-tion of Islamic scholars such as Avicenna (Ibn Sina) who wrote extensively on logic, metaphysics, psychology, astronomy, and medicine. He was the author of a highly respected book, *The Canon of Medicine*. Western civilization owes also the decimal system of arithmetic and the development of algebra (itself an Arab word) to the Arab-Islamic world.

However, in the eleventh century Turkish armies conquered Baghdad, the religious-political capital of the Arab Empire. As a result, the Seljuk Turk Sultan claimed political leadership over all

---

[80] Ali's successors came to be called imams. They had great spiritual authority, and some Shi'ites even attributed to them divine powers. According to the largest faction of this branch, the twelfth imam went into hiding and will appear only before the end of the world. Most Iranians and 60% of all Iraqis are Shi'ites.

Muslims, and the Baghdad Caliphate was reduced to a secondary position of spiritual leadership until it completely disappeared. The Ottoman Turks conquered Constantinople in 1453 and gradually extended their Empire over the Balkans and most of Hungary. Their armies were halted only near Vienna. At its height the Ottoman Empire stretched from near Vienna to the Caucasus to Yemen in Eurasia, from Alexandria to Algeria in Africa. Its demise was slow; the last Turkish troops left the Balkans only at the end of the 19th century. The final collapse came only after World War I, when a secular Turkish Republic, established by Kemal Ataturk in 1922, replaced the Islamic Empire.

3. The Qur'an

The Qur'an, published by Muhammad's followers a few decades after his death, is believed to contain the unadulterated word of God as it came to Muhammad verbatim from Allah through the mediation of the angel Gabriel. Muslims consider the Qur'an the miracle of Muhammad for its supreme beauty and for its fidelity to God's revelation. The Qur'an was needed because God's previous revelations as contained in the Hebrew Bible (called Torah in the Qur'an) and in the New Testament (called Gospel) were corrupted in the process of transmission. In order to avoid the same fate, Muslims carefully preserve every word of the Qur'an in its original Arab form and every Muslim has to memorize at least some parts of it in the Arabic language. The Qur'an consists of suras which do not form a sequential history as the books of the Bible do; yet they contain much historical material that is often vaguely and at times closely similar to the biblical stories of both Testaments.

One of the greatest Islamic scholars of our time describes the Qur'an in these terms:

The text of the Qur'an is... not based on long periods of compilation and interpretation by human agents. Rather, the Qur'an is the actual Word of God as revealed to His messenger and is like Christ for Christians, who is himself the Word of God brought into the world through the Virgin Mary. She, therefore, plays a role analogous to that of the soul of the Prophet; both are pure, immaculate, and virginal before the Divine Word.

To understand the spiritual significance of the Qur'an, it is essential to remember that the Qur'an was a sonoral revelation. The first words of the Sacred Text revealed by Gabriel surrounded the Prophet like an ocean of sound as the archangel himself filled the whole of the sky. The sound of the Qur'an penetrates the Muslim's body and soul before it appeals to his mind. The sacred quality of the psalmody of the Qur'an can cause spiritual rapture even in a person who knows no Arabic. In a mysterious way, this sacred quality is transmitted across the barrier of human language and is felt by those hundreds of millions of non-Arab Muslims, whether they be Persian, Turkish, African, Indian, or Malay, whose hearts palpitate in the love of God and whose eyes are moistened by the tears of joy upon simply hearing the Qur'an chanted.[81]

4. The Prophet Muhammad

Muhammad is highly respected by Muslims as a peace-loving, kind, and wise leader, the model of all virtues. He is not wor-

---

[81] S.H. Nasr, "The Qur'an as the Foundation of Islamic Spirituality," *Islamic Spirituality. Foundations*, ed. S.H. Nasr (New York: Crossroad, 1987), 4.

shiped, but revered as a prophet, a messenger of God.[82] He is, however, the last of the prophets, the "seal of the prophets," whose mission was to re-establish definitively the original Muslim religion that existed before the sin of Adam, and was restored again and again to its original purity by a series of prophets, such as Noah, Ishmael, Moses, and Jesus.

5. The Message

God is one, has no partners or associates, does not beget, and is not begotten. "Allah is a proper and true Name of God, through which man calls upon him personally."[83] He is the all-powerful creator, supreme majesty, and supreme beauty. Yet, his most frequent name, almost a synonym for Allah, is al-Rahman, "the Merciful One." This quality of God seems to have been unknown to the Arabs before Muhammad's preaching.[84] The first surah of the Qur'an sums up concisely what our relationship to Allah should be:

> In the name of Allah, Most gracious, Most Merciful.
> Praise be to Allah
> the Cherisher and Sustainer of the Worlds;
> Most Gracious, Most Merciful;
> Master of the Day of Judgment.
> Thee do we worship,

---

[82] Muslims distinguish two kinds of prophets: 1. "Rasul" means literally "messenger," or envoy. They bring a new revelation or new religion. The above mentioned prophets belong to this higher category. Of course, for Muslims even a new religion is nothing more than the restoration of the corrupted original Muslim religion, which simply means the right, original relationship between God and man, that of obedient surrender. 2. "Nabi" literally means "prophet" and his mission takes place within an existing religion. Hadith literature put their number at one hundred and twenty-four thousand. Thus, humankind cannot claim that they were not warned of God's universal judgment.

[83] *Concise Encyclopedia of Islam*, 35.

[84] *Ibid.*, 37.

And Thine aid we seek.
Show us the straight way,
The way of those on whom
Thou hast bestowed Thy Grace,
Those whose (portion)
Is not wrath,
And who go not astray.[85]

Man is created upon the form of God the all-merciful; his vocation was to be God's vice-regent on earth. Should he cut himself off from the Mercy and Light of God by his free will, he will enter not paradise but hell after the Great Judgment. In many Islamic traditions it is maintained that some less serious sinners may be purified by fire after death. However, neither hell nor paradise last for all eternity, since only God is eternal. Heaven and hell last "for perpetuity, that is, for an indefinite duration." Those in hell will eventually lose consciousness. In paradise there will be different degrees of happiness, and, according to some traditions, only the "blessed" and not the "saved" will see God face to face.

Islamic tradition also knows about a certain form of "*apokatastasis*": God necessarily creates, but his creations return to him after a certain length of time and there will be a period when God alone exists (*apokatastasis*). After this intermediate stage, he will begin to create another world. With the cessation of creation, including all beings distinct from God, paradise and hell will cease as well.[86]

The rank and file Islamic believers, however, do not indulge in such speculations. They believe in eternal life with a resurrected

---

[85] Note that Surah, a chapter of the Qur'an literally means step or degree. Since the Qur'an is directly God's Word in Arabic, it cannot be translated according to Islamic belief into other languages. Every 'translation' is considered only a paraphrase. In this chapter I quote a version that is widely used by Muslims in the United States: *The Meaning of the Holy Qur'an*, revised translation and commentary by Abdullah Yusuf Ali (Brentwood, MD: Amana Corporation, 1993).

[86] See *Concise Encyclopedia of Islam*, 43-44.

body in paradise, in which all our purified desires will be satisfied and we will enjoy the presence of Allah:

"Enter ye therein
In Peace and Security;
This is a Day of Eternal Life!"
There will be for them
Therein all that they wish—
And more besides
In Our Presence.[87]

6. The Five Pillars of Islam

Islamic religion has five "pillars" on which it "rests" and from which it draws its strength. The word "Islam" means surrender or submission and the "Muslim" is the person who has surrendered to the one God.

1. Shahadah is the profession of faith; it is short and simple, yet its full acceptance includes all that is essential for salvation. Muslims maintain that it obtains its full, "sacramental" force only if it is recited in Arabic: "Asshadu al-la ilaha illa-Llah, wa ashhadu anna Muhammadan-rasulu-Llah", "I perceive (and bear witness) that there is no god except Allah and I perceive (and bear witness) that Muhammad is the Messenger of God."

The first shahadah corrects the sin of Adam (eating of the forbidden fruit) that took objects for divine reality. The second acknowledges the revealing function of the last Messenger,

---

[87] *The Meaning of the Holy Qur'an*, 50:34-35. Seyyed Hossein Nasr, the great Islamic scholar, teaches a more sublime interpretation of Qur'anic Paradise: "Now the description of paradise seems at first sight to be simply the sublimation of earthly pleasures, including sexuality. In reality the reverse is true. Every legitimate experience of a pleasing nature here on earth is only a shadow and reflection of paradisal reality. The most intense physical experience for the human being, which is sexual union, is a reflection of the union of the soul with God and reflects on its own level something of that supreme joy and expansion" (*The Heart of Islam*, San Francisco: HarperSanFrancisco, 2002), 247.

Muhammad, but also that of the previous messengers, in fact, that of the whole creation.[88] If one repeats this confession of faith often, with all his heart, he will expunge from his being the tendency to set up idols in place of the true Absolute.

2. Shalah is ritual prayer recited five times a day in Arabic, at dawn, at noon, in the afternoon, at sunset, and at night. It should be done in the state of ritual purity, normally after an ablution, it is oriented in the direction of Mecca, and it consists of silent and aloud prayers, bows, and prostrations. Not only the mind and heart, but the whole person prays, including his/her body. The Muslim prays these canonical prayers in the name of all humankind, in fact, of all creation.

Charles de Foucauld, a young, agnostic French officer in Africa, discovered the reality of God as he watched his Muslim soldiers pray with a deep awareness of God's awesome presence. Later, he returned to his Catholic faith, and, as priest and hermit, began to serve the poorest Muslims, the Tuaregs, in Africa.

3. Zakah is alms-giving to the poor directly or to the Islamic state that supports the poor from these taxes. There exists a definite scale of obligatory almsgiving on most kinds of property and income.

4. Sawm (fast) is obligatory during the ninth month of the Islamic calendar from dawn to sunset: no eating, drinking, or sexual enjoyment is allowed during the hours of daylight. The purpose of the fast is manifold: it establishes a spiritual discipline, makes prayer easier, intensifies the solidarity with those who have nothing to eat, and can be offered as a sacrifice for expiating sins.

5. Hajj (pilgrimage). Every Muslim who is capable financially and physically must make this greater pilgrimage to Mecca and to some places adjacent to it once in his life. He will visit the Grand Mosque at Mecca and walk around the Ka'bah seven times. The

---

[88] *Concise Encyclopedia of Islam*, 359-360 & Renard, *Responses to 101 Questions on Islam*, 33-39.

Ka'bah is not an idol but a concrete symbol that helps Muslims to become aware of God's presence. According to Muslim belief the Ka'bah was built by Adam and restored by Abraham. Thus, the pilgrims who visit and touch the Ka'bah get in touch with the pure state of religion that had existed before the sin of Adam. They are renewed inwardly and become aware of the unity of the world-wide Muslim community, which consists of many races and cultures.

The jihad (holy war) is not compulsory for all Muslims, and there is a great variety of interpretations about what constitutes a holy war. The general Muslim interpretation of jihad is restricted to a war in defense of Muslim religion and society. Yet extremist groups consider Western society as a whole a mortal enemy of Islamic morality and Islamic law (shari'ah) and therefore they see terrorist activities as legitimate self-defense against the West and against apostate, excommunicated (takfir) Muslims. The primary meaning of jihad for many Muslims, however, is spiritual: it is fighting our own sinful tendencies, or even more generally, it is striving for an upright life in obedience to God.

7. Sufism

Sufism is the esoteric (inner) or mystical dimension of Islam, while the keeping of the shari'ah, the external laws and guidelines issued from the Qur'an and the Hadith, is its exoteric (external) aspect.[89] All are called to practice the shari'ah, but not all are called to tariqah, the spiritual path of the Sufis. The latter do not simply keep the Five Pillars of Islam, but seek an intimate, loving union with God.

Islamic sources insist that Sufism has been present in Islam from the beginning, the first Sufi being Muhammad himself and

---

[89] The suf means white wool, the preferred garment of the Prophet and of the Sufis.

the most important source of inspiration for the Sufis coming from
the Qur'an and the Hadith. Take, for instance, the following
Qur'anic statements:

> God is near to man, "nearer to him than his jugular
> vein" (50, 16). "He is the best and most beautiful rec-
> ompense" (73, 20). He illuminates the hearts of those
> who invoke him morning and night with humility, ven-
> eration and love; He shelters His friends from fear and
> sadness.[90]

According to a hadith, Muhammad described the stages of
spiritual development in the following way: the first stage is al-
islam, voluntary submission and obedience to the external laws;
the second stage is al-iman, faith. At that point grace enters the
heart and the Muslim begins to see and love the laws of God. The
third stage is al-ihsan, perfect virtue: the Sufi becomes completely
free from worldly concerns and dedicates his body, soul, and spirit
to God's will. As one Sufi said: "The Sufi is he who possesses nothing and is possessed by nothing."[91]

The goal, then, of the Sufi is a complete emptying of himself, a material and spiritual poverty. One has to get rid of the false
ego, the inflated self-importance, in order to open up to God's
presence.[92]

Ibn 'Ata' Allah said:

> The source of every disobedience, indifference, and pas-
> sion is self-satisfaction. The source of every obedience,

---

[90] J.L. Michon, "The Spiritual Practices of Sufism," *Islamic Spirituality*, 267. Note that Surah
73:20 is quoted here in the translation of this article.

[91] *Ibid.*, 267.

[92] The poor are called faquir in Arabic, darwish in Persian. These two words obtained a
pejorative connotation in several languages because of the magic practices, extreme
mortifications, and trance dancing (which induce an artificial ecstasy) that some groups
of the Sufis practiced. But these are considered deviations by mainline Islamic groups.
See *Concise Encyclopedia of Islam*, 377-380.

vigilance, and virtue is dissatisfaction with one's self. It is better for you to keep company with an ignorant man dissatisfied with himself than to keep company with a learned man satisfied with himself. For what knowledge is there in a self-satisfied scholar? And what ignorance is there in an unlearned man dissatisfied with himself?

In addition to humility, love of neighbor is also essential for the Sufi. They like to quote Muhammad: "You will not enter paradise until you love one another."

Another division of the mystical path consists of (1) the way of purification characterized by fear, (2) the way of love and sacrifice, and (3) the way of knowledge. This last stage is not a mere intellectual knowledge but "identity between the knower and the object of knowledge," which is the end goal of the spiritual journey. In spite of such pantheistic statements, Sufi scholars insist that their mystical doctrine is not pantheism. The "unity of Being" (wahdat al-wujud) means that the mystic sees God everywhere, not that God is reduced to everything; He remains supremely transcendent.[93]

8. Islam and Christianity

As a great prophet, Jesus (Isa ibn Maryam) has a special place in Islam. He is born virginally from Mary after the message of an angel (3:45-47). He preaches already from the cradle, performs miracles, and prophesies the coming of Ahmad-Muhammad (61:6). He is called a "Spirit from God and the Word of God" (4:171). The Jews crucify his likeness; they did not kill him because Allah took him to himself. He confesses before Allah that

---

[93] *Ibid.*, 378-379.

he has not worshiped any other God but Allah and did not consider himself God. His role was similar to those of the great prophets before him, to return people to the original Adamic religion that is Islam.

Islam rejects the doctrine of the Trinity as contradicting the absolute unity of God. God does not beget and is not begotten.[94] It is very likely that the Qur'an thinks that Christians attribute physical begetting to their God. According to some Hadiths, Jesus will come back at the end of time and destroy the Antichrist.[95]

Christians should not ignore that Islam meant a great step forward in the cultural, moral, and religious developments of the Arabs, Turks, and some other nations that lived in the state of polytheism and idolatry. God's infinite majesty, glory, and beauty acknowledged and proclaimed five times every day in humble prayer of adoration, praise, and thanksgiving have impressed some fallen away Christians to the point of finding their way back to Christianity.

At the same time, Islamic domination beginning in the 7th century, although not requiring the conversion of Christians, in fact reduced to a negligible minority a well-established Christianity in Asia Minor and in Africa. By its very nature, mainline Islam has always aimed at the establishment of an Islamic society, governed by Islamic law, the shari'ah. Just as Muhammad himself, his successors, the Arab and, later, the Ottoman caliphs, attributed to themselves both supreme spiritual and political power. Since the end of the Ottoman Empire in 1922, no one could credibly claim such a title for the Muslim world, yet striving for an Islamic state remains a strong trend among Muslims even today, especially in those societies in which Muslims constitute the ma-

---

[94] "How can He (Allah) have a son
    When He has no consort?" (6:101.)
[95] See S.H. Nasr, *The Heart of Islam*, 246.

jority.[96] Obviously, the ideal of fusing religious and political powers creates problems for the Christian minorities in Islamic countries and makes a theoretical dialogue between Christian and Islamic theologians difficult.

At the same time, there are countless Muslims who want to live in peace with Christians and whose deep piety and goodness are an inspiration for us.[97] Listen to these words of Seyyed Hossein Nasr:

> [Muslims] must even extend their hand in friendship to those Christian and primarily Protestant evangelists who express ignorant, hurtful, and even malicious and egregious views about Islam. Muslims must in this case turn the other cheek and prove in their actions that for them also Christ is sent by God and his words revered.[98]

The deeply religious, peaceful Muslims may be a providential warning and a powerful witness in God's hands for contemporary Christians who have forgotten about the majesty of God. Only a genuine rediscovery of God's infinite greatness, power, and holiness can bring us to appreciate his infinite humility in becoming one of us in Jesus of Nazareth.

---

[96] We must admit, though, that in Medieval Muslim Spain Christians and Jews enjoyed relative freedom while, after the *Reconquista*, Muslims and Jews either had to convert or emigrate. Those who stayed and did not convert, faced the Inquisition. Yet, Saudi Arabia, a modern Islamic state, punishes not only Christian evangelization, but theoretically, even public Christian worship.

[97] The twofold aspect of Islam (violence in fighting for Islam and peaceful piety) revealed itself dramatically in the story of the Cistercian Trappist monks at Tibhirine, Algeria. These monks, with Fr. Christian de Chergé as their Prior lived in Algeria for the explicit purpose of praying with and for the Muslims. When the Islamic terrorists threatened with execution every foreigner who did not leave the country, their Muslim neighbors were begging the monks, their friends, to stay with them. They did stay and they were executed. The people in the area mourned them as their own brothers. See Marie-Christine Ray, *Christian de Chergé prieur de Tibhirine* (Paris: Bayard Éditions, 1998).

[98] *The Heart of Islam*, 305.

Chapter VI

JUDAISM

The scope of this study is not the religion of the Old Testament but rather the development which defined the religion of the great majority of Jews in conscious opposition to Christianity. So we have to begin with outlining Jesus' relationship to his own people.

1. The Attitude of the Jews towards Christ

The majority of the Pharisees rejected him for healing on the Sabbath, for forgiving sinners, and for admitting the forgiven sinners into table fellowship. Their outlook on salvation was opposed to that of Jesus: the Pharisee wanted to merit the coming of the Kingdom by virtuous deeds, while Jesus taught that the Kingdom cannot be merited, since it is the free gift of a forgiving God (cf. Mt 20:1-10).

Yet some of the Pharisees and scribes accepted Jesus (Jn 3:1-2; Mk 12:28-34). Both Jesus and the Pharisees believed in the resurrection of the dead and in the existence of angels; in this they opposed the Sadducees (Lk 20:27-40, Ac 23:6-10).

The Sadducees were materialists and believed only in this life on earth. They jealously guarded their privileges and their control over the Temple and its income, which the Romans allowed them to keep. They turned against Jesus because they feared that Jesus' cleansing of the Temple would deprive them of this last power base. According to John, they were afraid that the

Messianic enthusiasm around Jesus would result in a Roman intervention and the loss of the last vestiges of national independence (Jn 12:45-53).

The Zealots seemed to sympathize with Jesus. Simon the Zealot, one of the apostles, may have been a former Zealot (Lk 6:15), and perhaps also Judas Iscariot. They, however, became disappointed in Jesus because he twice declined to lead a potential Messianic uprising, first in the desert after the multiplication of the loaves, then in Jerusalem at his last solemn entry into the Holy City (Jn 6:15; Mk 11:1-10).

The Essenes shared some beliefs with Jesus, such as the indissolubility of marriage and the value of celibacy. But their hatred for sinners and their hope that the Kingdom would come through their perfect observance of the Law separated them from Jesus.

The crowds during Jesus' public ministry were enthusiastic about his miracles and especially about the multiplication of the loaves (which was perceived as a Messianic sign of repeating the miracle of the manna in the desert), but the majority did not heed his call to conversion. When Jesus entered Jerusalem before his last Passover, the crowds received him enthusiastically as the new David until it became obvious that Jesus was either unable or unwilling to accept the role of the glorious, military Messiah. Disappointed and frustrated, they could easily be manipulated by the leaders to demand Jesus' crucifixion.

2. History of Judaism after the Resurrection of Jesus and the Spreading of the Church

After the Resurrection, the small band of Jewish disciples grew into a sizable community in Jerusalem and in Galilee. They participated for a while in Temple worship but they also had their own Eucharistic celebrations in private homes (cf. Ac 2:42-47).

The history of the primitive Christian church in Galilee may be much more important for the shaping of Gospel traditions than it is generally assumed. Excavations in Capernaum unearthed the ruins of a domestic church, a private home (of Peter's family?) turned into a church in the 1st century A.D.[99]

The majority of the Jews, however, turned against Christianity. The relationship became especially embittered when the nascent Church began to admit a large number of pagans without imposing the ritual laws of Moses on Gentile Christians. As a result, in the second half of the first century Christians were gradually banned from the synagogues and, after the destruction of the Temple by the Romans in 70 A.D., the separation was finalized.

The destruction of the Temple in 70 A.D. and the failure of the messianic Bar Kochba rebellion in 135 to rebuild it have profoundly influenced the reorganization of Judaism as a religion in conscious opposition to Christianity.

As the Sadducees' authority, based on the performance of the Temple liturgy, disappeared with the destruction of the Temple, the Pharisees became the undisputed leaders of reorganized Judaism. Their academy in Iamnia (Yavneh) became the first important center of rabbinic scholarship. The problems they faced were enormous. Two failed uprisings resulted in the end of the Temple worship, the soul and center of Jewish piety for almost a millennium. Hopes in the near coming of a victorious Messiah were crushed and, after John the Baptist, no more prophets arose in Israel.

Toward the end of the 1st century the Pharisees defined the canon of the Jewish Bible more narrowly than the Alexandrian canon had done centuries before them.[100] Instead of Temple wor-

---

[99] Cf. Jerome Murphy-O'Connor, *The Holy Land. An Oxford Archaeological Guide from Earliest Times to 1700,* 4th revised ed. (Oxford-New York: Oxford University Press, 1998), 218-220.

[100] The Pharisees applied four criteria of canonicity: (1) The books had to be in harmony with the Torah (Pentateuch); (2) they had to have been written before the time of Ezra, (3) in Palestine and (4) in Hebrew. On this basis they eliminated from the Alexandrian canon (which the Catholic Church has retained) Judith, Wisdom, 1st and 2nd Maccabees, Tobit, Baruch, Sirach and parts of Daniel and Esther.

ship and sacrifices, the Pharisees and scribes proposed daily life as continuous Temple worship, the sanctification of the Divine Name. Consequently, they extended the rules of ritual purity that used to apply only to the Temple activities of the priests to the whole realm of everyday life. All of Israel should live "as a holy nation, a people set apart."

Instead of the priest, prophet, or messianic king, the rabbi, well versed in the knowledge of the Torah, became the Jewish leader, the center of the Jewish community (living either in the Holy Land or in exile). In the words of J. Neusner, the rabbi became the "the incarnate Torah." Their actions and their way of applying the Torah served as authoritative guidance for the actions of future generations. Thus, in addition to the Bible, the Talmud (oral commentaries on the Law of Moses, wise sayings, and stories developed around historical events) was written down between 300 and 500 A.D.[101] The five books of Moses and the Talmud form the Torah, the Law of God. The rabbis insisted on the strict observance of all the 613 commandments deduced from the Torah. Yet the best rabbis understood the Torah in a way that is not far from Christ's interpretation of the Law. For instance, Rabbi Simlai explained that all the 613 commandments were rightly reduced by Isaiah to two: "Thus says the Lord, keep justice and do righteousness" (Is 56:1).[102] R. Akiba declared: "This is the most fundamental principle enunciated in the Torah: 'Love thy neighbor as thyself'" (Lv 19:18).[103] According to Yohanan ben Zakkai the preservation of the Temple was not an end in itself. He taught that there was another means of reconciliation between

---

[101] It exists in two forms, the Palestinian and Babylonian Talmud. The Talmud consists of the Mishna that had been completed in the third century and of the later Gemara. Both parts contain Halakhah (legislative texts) and Haggadah (stories, exhortations). First viewed as a mere interpretation of the Bible, the Talmud later assumed the character of divine revelation in the Jewish mind.

[102] *Makkot* 24a.

[103] *The Talmud. Selected Writings.* Introd. Ben Zion Bokser & Baruch M. Bokser (New York: Paulist Press, 1989), 28.

God and Israel, so that the Temple and its cult were not indispensable. What was the will of God? It was doing deeds of loving kindness: "I desire mercy, not sacrifice" (Hos 6:6) meant to Yohanan, "We have a means of atonement as effective as the Temple and it is doing deeds of loving kindness."[104]

Once it became known in the Empire that Christians did not belong to the Jewish religion, which was officially tolerated by Rome, they were exposed to religious persecution. The Jews looked at Christianity as a most dangerous heresy and so they often cooperated with the pagan authorities in the persecution of Christians.

With the conversion of Europe to Christianity, especially in the Middle Ages, the situation became thoroughly reversed: the Jews were discriminated against by Christians.

For instance, the Fourth Lateran Council in 1215 prescribed that they should wear a distinctive dress, and not appear in public during Easter. They were not allowed to hold public office, and in some cases had to pay tithes to the Church.[105]

As a compensation, they became skillful merchants and rich bankers. (They were allowed to charge interest for lending money, while Christians were not allowed to do so in the Middle Ages.) Their separate existence, their refusal to become Christians, the popular misconception that they are *en groupe* responsible for the death of the Son of God, and their wealth led from time to time to persecutions, pogroms, and expulsion from one country after another (England, Spain).

Yet, the ghetto helped them to preserve their culture, their religious identity, and their religious and social autonomy.

Moses Maimonides, the greatest medieval Jewish philosopher, showed that Jewish beliefs and practices are not irrational

---

[104] J. Neusner, "Varieties of Judaism in the Formative Age," *Jewish Spirituality*, ed. A. Green, *World Spirituality*, vol. 13 (New York: Crossroad, 1986), p. 195.

[105] See Fourth Lateran Council, # 68-69, in *Decrees of the Ecumenical Councils*, ed. Norman P. Tanner, vol. I (Washington: Georgetown Univ. Press, 1990), 266-267.

and summarized the basic tenets of Jewish faith in 13 creedal statements that have remained normative up to the modern age.

Although Israel wanted to safeguard jealously the transcendence of God, many Jews had the intuition that their God could
not remain indifferent to the sufferings, sins, and obedience of his
people; in fact, they became convinced that Yahweh must be pas-
sionately involved in their history. Thus, certain trends in Judaism asserted that God suffers with his people. Zohar, a master-
piece written in Aramaic that belongs to the mystical tradition of
Kabbalah, goes even further. It explains that by obeying the commandments Jews reunite the feminine aspect of the divinity
(Shekhinah) with the masculine one (Tif'eret) that has been split
into two halves by the sin of Adam.

The mizwot (commandments) are an invitation to realign
the human and divine wills, a mystical means to restore the harmony between the Blessed Holy One and his Shekhinah. The
human being thus comes to the aid of God. He can raise
Shekhinah from the dust of exile (1:191b) and actualize divine
being. Of one who performs the mizwot, God says, "It is as if he
has made Me.... Since they [the Blessed Holy One and his
Shekhinah] are aroused above you to join together... you have
indeed made them" (3:113a).[106]

As a result of the Enlightenment and the French Revolu-
tion, the ghettoes were abolished and the Jews were allowed to
join the mainstream of European society. Their integration into
modern society, on the one hand, enriched the cultural life of
Europe; on the other, it led to the loss of faith in many Jews and/
or to a "watered-down" form of Jewish religion that became mainly
a way of life (keeping the Torah) rather than faith in the God of
Abraham, Isaac, and Jacob, the God who chose his people for a
unique purpose and will send the Messiah to establish his reign.
Many Jews also gave up belief in the resurrection of the dead and

---

[106] D.C. Matt, "The Mystic and the Mizwot," *Jewish Spirituality*, 387.

immortality of the soul and concentrated on earthly goals. The "enlightened" Jews began to emphasize a Messianic Age rather than a personal Messiah. But the notion of this Messianic Age often appeared to mean little more than belief in the progress of mankind, which would gradually eliminate all social evils, violence, war, and poverty.

The persecution of the Nazis led to the slaughter of about six million Jews during World War II and hastened the creation of the state of Israel. Jews realized that they would not be safe unless they have their own country and independent state. With the backing of the United Nations, the Jews who immigrated to Palestine beginning at the end of the 19th century proclaimed the state of Israel in 1948. In the ensuing war with its Arab neighbors and Palestinian Arabs, Israel expelled a large number of Arabs from that part of Palestine which was to become their state. In the 1967 war, initiated by the Arabs, Israel occupied the ancient part of Jerusalem, the West Bank (former Samaria and Galilee), the Gaza strip, and the Sinai desert. When Israel concluded a peace treaty with Egypt, Sinai was returned to Egypt, but the other territories remained under Israeli occupation. This explains the present day situation of conflict and growing tension.

The Holocaust (Shoah) caused a major religious trauma for many Jews. A few could discover in it a sign of continuing divine election; they saw it as God's imposition on his people of the destiny of the Isaian "Suffering Servant." But for many who had beforehand reduced faith in the Messianic Age to an exaltation of human progress and morality, the two World Wars and Shoah were a scandal: How can the human race ever arrive at peace and prosperity, if science and technology only improved the effectiveness of killing and torture in the 20th century? And above all else, how could God permit the monstrosity of the Shoah? Many lost their faith, while others concluded that God could not prevent evil but suffered along with his people.

Yet, even in our century there were many Jews, including

simple people and learned theologians, who preserved a deep faith in the God of Abraham, Isaac, and Jacob and bore powerful witness to Him before the world. Two names ought to be mentioned here, the German philosopher-theologian Martin Buber and the charismatic Polish-American rabbi and author Abraham Joshua Heschel. Both have drawn from the spirituality of Hasidism, an 18th century spiritual movement among Eastern-European Jews, and from existentialism. Both saw the vocation of the Jew to sanctify the Divine Name by his everyday actions.[107]

While the Church did not condone the persecution of the Jews in the Middle Ages, it sanctioned certain forms of discrimination as explained above. However, concerning the death of Jesus, already the *Catechism of the Council of Trent* in 1566 emphasized that "the guilt in us seems more enormous than in the Jews, since according to the testimony of the same Apostle, 'If they had known it, they would never have crucified the Lord of glory' (1 Cor 2:8); while we, on the contrary, professing to know him, yet denying him by our actions, seem in some sort to lay violent hands on him."[108]

Vatican II made it clear that "what happened in Jesus' Passion cannot be blamed on all the Jews then living, without distinction, nor on the Jews of today. Although the Church is the new people of God, the Jews should not be presented as repudiated or cursed by God, as if such views followed from the Holy Scriptures." The Council also quotes St. Paul, according to whom, in spite of their temporary unbelief, "the Jews still remain most dear to God on account of their fathers, for (God) does not re-

---

[107] There are some differences between the two men: Buber rejected rabbinic Judaism with its insistence on minute observance of the Law while Heschel remained within the rabbinic tradition but tried to give a spiritual meaning to the observance of the commandments. Buber saw every human being as a divine spark and saw the role of the Jews in re-uniting all these divine sparks to God.

[108] *Catechism of the Council of Trent for Parish Priests* (New York: J.F. Wagner, 1923), 50-61; 362-365.

pent of the gifts he made nor of the calls he issues" (Rm 11:28–29).[109]

3. The Relationship between Judaism and Christianity

What unites us?

At the beginning of the Christian movement, Christians were not called Christians (christianoi: followers of Christ), but they considered themselves faithful Israelites who attended the Temple liturgy in Jerusalem and synagogue services in the countryside. They believed in Jesus as the fulfillment of the Messianic hope of Israel, the person in whom all of God's promises to his people and humankind were fulfilled.

When in the 2nd century Marcion proposed a Christianity without the books of the Old Testament, the Church rejected his truncated Bible as well as his belief that the God of Jesus Christ is a God different from that of the Old Testament. The Christian Church has kept this Jewish heritage in spite of the Marcionite attack.

1. The first part of the Eucharist, the Liturgy of the Word, is patterned after the synagogue service, except for the addition of the New Testament readings.

2. The bulk of the Liturgy of the Hours, the official public prayer of the Catholic Church, is the Book of Psalms: priests, religious communities, and some lay people pray the whole Psalter within a cycle of four weeks. This is more than a formal link between the two peoples. The Church offers her praise and thanksgiving, her lamentations and anguished cries for help, by actualizing as her own the praise, thanksgiving, and supplications of Israel.

---

[109] "Declaration on the Relationship of the Church to Non-Christian Religions," #4.

3. The two most frequently used words in every Christian prayer come from Jewish worship: "Amen" (I accept it in faith) and "Alleluia!" (Praise God).

4. The Christian Eucharist, based on the Last Supper of Jesus, grew out of the Jewish Passover Meal. Moreover, the structure of Eucharistic Prayers, according to most recent studies, developed from the todah, a sacrifice of praise and thanksgiving in Jewish liturgy.

5. In the Catholic Eucharistic liturgy reformed after Vatican II, the prayers we use in offering the bread and wine before consecration have been taken from Jewish prayers of blessing before eating the bread and drinking the wine: "Blessed art thou, O Lord our God, king of the universe who bringest forth bread from the earth." "Blessed art thou, O Lord our God, King of the universe, who createst the fruit of the vine."

6. Jesus of Nazareth, as well as his mother and his first disciples are, without a single exception, Jewish.

Shared Beliefs and Beliefs Close to Jewish Beliefs

1. We believe in the God of Abraham, Isaac, and Jacob, creator of heaven and earth. Every morning in the official prayer of the Church we say with Zechariah, "Blessed be the Lord the God of Israel." Every evening we conclude our Vespers with the canticle of Mary, in which we testify to God's fidelity to his people: "He has come to the help of his servant Israel" (Lk 1:68; 1:54). A Christian believes that God will be faithful to him in his own personal life because he believes that God has been faithful to Israel throughout her history.

2. We believe that God chose Israel as his own adopted son for a special mission for all humankind. He liberated them from Egypt by mighty deeds and wonders and introduced them into the Promised Land, and in spite of their sins, he remained faithful to Israel and always kept a remnant faithful to him.

3. We believe that God gave Moses the Torah, the Law by which Israel became a nation consecrated to the worship and service of God in a unique way.

4. Following St. Paul and the perennial teaching of the Catholic Church (most recently formulated by Vatican II), we believe that "the Jews still remain most dear to God because of their fathers, because (God) does not repent of the gifts he made nor of the calls he issues."[110] God has a special plan for Israel and his providence will preserve them until the end of history.

5. With St. Paul we believe that we, Gentile Christians, were grafted as "wild olive shoots" into the noble olive tree, the Israel of the Fathers, and that we share in the rich sap of the root. We do not support the root, the root supports us (Rm 11:17-18).

6. The Hebrew Bible is also part of our Bible. We read, proclaim, and listen to it as God's own Word that addresses us every day.

7. Just as Pharisaic Jews traditionally believed in the resurrection of the dead and in everlasting life for the just in the Kingdom of God, so do we believe.

8. Even though we believe that the Messiah has already come for the first time as the Suffering Servant of Isaiah (52:13-53:12), we still await his glorious coming at the end of history.

What divides us?

The same Jesus of Nazareth, the same Hebrew Bible, the same common heritage is, for the time being, also a separating wall between us.

1. We believe that the promises given to Israel and recorded in the Hebrew Bible began to be fulfilled in Jesus of Nazareth.

2. The greatest stumbling block for a believing Jew seems to

---

[110] Romans 11:28-29, quoted by the "Decree on Non-Christian Religions" of Vatican II, #4.

be the Christian claim that in the itinerant prophet, Yeshuah of Nazareth, the God of Israel himself came to rescue his people and that the believing remnant of historic Israel became the seed for a universal gathering, the Church. The Hebrew Bible strictly prohibits the worship of any man. How do Christians dare to worship a man and still claim to be strict monotheists and the heirs of Israel?

Tasks for Dialogue between Christians and Jews

Christians should apologize for the discriminatory measures of the Middle Ages, for periodic persecutions of their Jewish brothers and sisters, and for not doing enough to rescue the Jews during the Nazi persecutions of World War II.[111]

Both sides should strive to clear up misunderstandings about each other's practices and beliefs. We should also try to understand more deeply each other's faith and even learn from each other. All these tasks are possible without giving up our distinct identities.

Here I refer only to some of the problematic issues that need to be cleared up in dialogue.

1. The Gospels, if read according to the intention of their authors, do not justify anti-Semitism, not even anti-Judaism. How could they be anti-Jewish if they were all written by Jews? Were the Pharisees anti-Jewish because they opposed the Sadducees, or the Essenes because they opposed both groups? In fact, the Gospels can be understood only if we read them in conjunction with the Hebrew Bible. At the same time, we must admit that Christians often abused the Gospels to justify discrimination and persecution against the Jews.

---

[111] This was recently done by Pope John Paul II and by a document issued by the Doctrinal Congregation of the Holy See and by a statement of the French bishops. At the same time we must not forget the heroic acts of many bishops, priests and lay Christians as well as the silent but most effective rescue work of Pius XII.

2. Christians should not single out observant Jews as if they were guilty of "pharisaism." Self-righteous bragging about good works before God could be worse in a Christian than in a Jew. A faithful Jew who finds his joy in sanctifying the Divine Name by obedience to the commandments, and a faithful Christian who strives to sanctify God's Name by obedience to the Law of Christ are closer to each other than normally perceived.

3. We should explain to our Jewish friends that Christian belief in the Incarnation does not require us to worship a mere man. We believe that the God of Israel entered into such close solidarity with his people (and through that people with all humankind) that he has taken on a full human nature as his own so that he may carry our burdens and thereby restore us to communion with himself. God is the ultimate subject in Jesus and, when worshiping Jesus, we worship God in his human nature.

The Christian doctrine of the Incarnation respects God's transcendence, while the post-biblical Jewish beliefs that God in his divine nature suffers with his people, that he cannot prevent suffering, or that our obedience actualizes while our disobedience splits God himself, are a direct attack on God's transcendence.[112] These non-biblical Jewish beliefs show that Israel wants to believe in a God for whom Israel does really matter, who is totally involved in the life of his people. But, ironically, her refusal to accept the mystery of the Incarnation results in speculations that destroy her most cherished treasure, the biblical notion of God, by reducing it to the figure of a more powerful brother (and sister).[113] Belief in such mystical speculations does not disqualify someone from being regarded as a Jew, but belief in the Incarnation does, even though in the latter God's transcendence is safe-

---

[112] According to Christian faith God truly dies on the cross but in his human nature, his divinity cannot be destroyed. If divinity is destroyed, what can save us?

[113] However, we must admit that not all Jews accept these post-biblical speculations which offend against God's transcendence.

guarded while his utter solidarity with his people is affirmed. Is such a position consistent?

4. Christians should stop practically being Marcionites.[114] We need to rediscover and appreciate the Jewish roots of Christianity if we do not want to misunderstand our own Christian faith. Without the Old Testament, our New Testament becomes unintelligible and distorted. If we seriously investigate its Old Testament preparation, the Incarnation appears in a new light. God has stooped down first of all to his own people, Israel; he has become man by becoming the new, perfect Israel. This is well shown in the Gospel of Matthew: Jesus is brought back from Egypt as Israel was, he undergoes the same temptations that historical Israel underwent, except that Jesus did not succumb to them. The fact that Jesus fulfilled the prophecies which apply to Israel appears already in one of the earliest kerygmas (1 Cor 15:4).[115] Thus, the Incarnation means first of all that God the Son has become (the embodiment of) eschatological Israel. Or, from another perspective, it is in Jesus that Israel has fully become the first-born son of Yahweh. God, then, became man by becoming the perfect Israel. From this biblical perspective the Incarnation is first an exaltation of Israel, and only in this sequence is it then the exaltation of all humankind as well.

5. Christians and Jews can await together the coming of the Messiah, a coming which, according to Jewish belief, will be his first, according to Christian belief, his second, glorious coming.

---

[114] As explained above, Marcion rejected the entire Old Testament and kept from the New Testament only the Letters of Paul and the Gospel of Luke (without the infancy narrative). He opposed the God of the Old Testament, a God of vengeful justice, and preferred the merciful God of Jesus Christ.

[115] The statement of 1 Cor 15:4 that Jesus "was raised on the third day according to the Scriptures" makes sense only as a reference to Hosea 6:2 where the prophet speaks in the name of the remnant of Israel: "On the third day he will raise us up to live in his presence." Jesus is that new Israel God has raised up. The representative embodiment of a whole people in one person is foreign to modern thinking but standard practice in ancient Jewish literature.

At the same time, Christians must take seriously the Jewish "no" to the Messianic claim of Jesus. As a rabbi put it so candidly at a dialogue session, "Jesus does not fit the job description of the Messiah." Indeed all the prophecies agree that the Messiah will bring peace to Israel and to the nations. And where is that peace? It seems that violence has only increased throughout the two thousand years after Jesus' birth. How can Jesus be the Prince of Peace if his followers have not stopped fighting and, for 1600 years, reduced their Jewish brothers and sisters to tolerated secondary citizenship and periodically even persecuting and lynching them? Enlightened Jews, of course, do not attribute the Shoah to Christians, and they acknowledge that the official Catholic Church always opposed violence to the Jews and that Pope Pius and many other bishops and priests saved hundred of thousands of Jews during WW II. But this does not change the fact that Jesus did not bring political peace. How should Christians evaluate the Jewish challenge to us, "no peace—no Messiah"?

The risen Lord greets his disciples by "shalom – peace" (Lk 24:36, Jn 20:19-21). In John he repeats this greeting twice. The words of Jesus are more than a customary Jewish greeting. He not only wishes peace but bestows the Messianic peace on his disciples, a peace that comes from his pierced hands and side. He shows us that the price he paid for our peace with God, with ourselves, and with all human beings was his sacrifice on the cross. But the peace he obtained for us is a gift we need actively to appropriate. Peace in this world always derives from embracing the cross; everyone must in some way suffer in this world, even though we should strive to alleviate the sufferings of our fellow human beings. But peace, ever new life and energy, and even unconquerable love come to us from uniting our small crosses to the sufferings of Christ. The water and blood flowing from Jesus' wounds and the Spirit he breathed upon us enable us to overcome our craving to kill our brother as Cain did and, instead, to love even our enemies.

6. However, we must acknowledge with our older brothers

and sisters that Jesus did not bring us a universal political peace. Universal cosmic peace will be the fruit of what Jews consider the first coming of the Messiah and what Christians see as his glorious manifestation. Even though universal peace will only be achieved at the end of history, it does not dispense us from working for it with all our energies, together with our older brothers and with every man and woman of good will. And here we Christians must confess with John Paul II our share of guilt. Throughout our 2000 years of history, we have not cooperated as we should have with the almighty power of God's Holy Spirit that the risen Christ has always offered to us. There were and there are pockets of true peace (with God and with each other) wherever a Christian community lives the teachings of Jesus. In fact, even where we find just one individual who radiates the peace of Jesus, the world changes around him. But a huge number of Christians have not allowed the leaven of Jesus' Spirit to permeate and change them. At such times, God humbles us by showing us examples of Jesus' peace and sacrificial attitude among our Jewish brothers and sisters, who do not even truly know him.

Chapter VII

COMMON PATTERNS IN RELIGIONS AND THE UNIQUENESS OF CHRISTIANITY

In this chapter we will begin explicitly to address the question that has motivated our study of world religions: how (if at all) do they manifest the Personal Absolute's Love for humankind? In order to respond to this question, first, we will attempt to classify into some basic types different religions' various beliefs in Divine Reality and their views on the nature and destiny of human beings. Second, we will identify the common patterns that we have found in all or most of these types. Third, we will describe the unique features that distinguish Christianity from all other religions.

1. Reduction of Religious Beliefs to Some Basic Types

With regard to the idea of God or Ultimate Reality, all religions belong in some way to one of three categories:

1. Monotheism that believes in one transcendent, personal God characterizes some of the primitive religions, Judaism, Christianity, and Islam.[116]

2. Polytheism is still practiced by the masses in India and in many tribal religions.

---

[116] Some studies classify the philosophical form of Hinduism monotheistic because it considers all particular gods (devas) manifestations of the one Brahman. Brahman, however, is ultimately impersonal and in the prevailing advaita interpretation of the Sacred Hindu texts Brahman is the only reality. Thus, its notion is closer to pantheism than to monotheism.

3. Pantheism develops as a result both of a rationalistic critique of polytheism and of mystical experience: the Divine cannot be fragmented into individual mythical figures, but it can become manifest in a multiplicity of divine forms. Ultimately, however, there is only one reality, the Divine: pan-theos, literally 'all is God.' The universe is seen only as a false appearance or certain form of the Divine, or at least it is perceived as a necessary complement to the Divine. In the ancient West we find a pantheistic vision in Neo-Platonism and Stoicism, while in the East we find it in the mainstream of philosophical Hinduism, the various forms of Buddhism and, to some extent, in Taoist philosophy.

A certain form of mystical experience lends itself easily to a pantheistic interpretation; the intoxicating feeling of oneness with the universe and with all that exists seems to confirm a pantheistic interpretation of all reality.

We have not dealt with atheism[117] in this study, but here we need to refer to it briefly in order to grasp the surprisingly consistent link between the understanding of the Divine and the self-understanding of the human being.[118]

In those religions in which one believes in a personal god (monotheism, polytheism), one also believes in an individual human self that transcends the limits of earthly life.

In a pantheistic system, there is no individual human self. What seems to be an individual is only the result of false perception, or is a part of or a manifestation of a Universal Divine Self (or of the universal Buddha nature).

In an atheistic system, the human self is not a reality in its

---

[117] Atheism can be either a theoretical system which denies God's existence (Marxism, atheistic existentialism, atheistic scientism) or practical atheism (many Christians or adherents of other religions). The practical atheist may admit in theory the existence of a divine being or many divine beings, but he lives and acts as if there were no divine reality.

[118] Contrary to a wide-spread popular belief, we should not label any form of Buddhism atheistic. While the gods or divine figures are irrelevant in obtaining enlightenment in original and in Theravada Buddhism, Nirvana is not simple nothingness but, as we have seen, some form of unnameable Absolute.

own right, but is simply the temporary function of highly organized living matter; therefore, the existence of the human person
does not transcend the limits of his biological life.

2. Common Patterns in Religions

Ultimate Reality

There is in humankind a spontaneous and necessary awareness of an 'Absolute.' Its forms vary, but even an atheist believes
in some Absolute (matter, nature, humankind) or, as we have seen,
at least implicitly intends an Absolute in his acts of thinking and
willing.

We have also seen a permanent struggle in the religious history of humankind to reconcile transcendence and immanence in
the experience and notion of God. This conflict between transcendence and immanence appears in various forms at different stages
in history. The heavenly god is transformed into a more immanent but less transcendent storm god or replaced by lesser gods.

In Hinduism it appears as the contradiction between the invisible, ineffable Brahman and the Brahman identical with everything in the world and manifesting itself in personal gods like
Vishnu who appears in visible forms such as the avatars Krishna
and Rama.

In Buddhism we encounter the universal, ungraspable Buddha nature, as well as the many savior Buddhas to whom one can
pray.

In Taoism there is a conflict between the gods and spirits in
popular Taoism and the one invisible and ineffable Tao.

Creation

In all religions the world depends on a divine reality. In
primitive religions, it is formed by God or by gods from some pre-

existent matter. Rarely is it seen as brought about by God's word, except in some stories about the heavenly god.

In a pantheistic system the world is either an illusion or it "flows out" from God as part of God or as another form of God.

The Human Being

In every religion, human beings are in some sense "divine": they either are created in God's image or are part of the divinity. Yet in a pantheistic system they lose their unique dignity, since all of nature is divine in a sense similar to that in which the human being is divine.

Redemption

All religions agree that the human race lives in a state from which it ought to be liberated. The differences concern only the causes of humankind's misery and the means of its liberation. The greatest difference consists in whether we can rescue ourselves by our own resources or must be rescued by some supernatural help.

All religions agree that we are capable of wrong-doing and that most of us have done some wrong either by free decision or by ignorance. Most religions also agree that, by doing what is wrong, human beings hurt themselves. But in a religion in which there is no personal god, we can right our wrongs by our own moral efforts. We may speak of sin in the full sense of the word only in a context in which the human being has offended a personal God (as in some primitive religions and the Abrahamic religions). Here moral effort at improvement is not sufficient; the sinner needs the forgiveness of the God he offended.

Sacrifice for obtaining forgiveness (animal or human sacrifice, voluntary or imposed) has been widely practiced in the past. Outside of Christianity, the bodhisattvas represent the noblest form of accepting suffering vicariously for the liberation of others.

Morality

In spite of many secondary differences in morality, most religions accept the Golden Rule: "Do unto others only as you would have them do unto you." Some control of passions, some form of love for the neighbor, honor for parents, respect for property and for human life, and the protection of the family are also widespread ideals.

At the same time, we have seen that the theoretical views of several religions are in logical contradiction to a morality that respects the inalienable dignity of the human person. We refer here not only to the Hindu caste system and to the belligerent interpretation of certain texts in the Qur'an, but first and foremost to the Hindu and Buddhist metaphysics that do not admit a qualitative distinction between human and subhuman sentient beings and ultimately deny the permanent value of the individual human person.

3. Unique Characteristics in the Abrahamic Religions and Christianity

God

As said before, besides some primitive religions, only the Abrahamic religions are fully monotheistic in the sense that they alone believe in one personal God who creates the world and manifests himself in it, but is also distinct from, and infinitely more perfect than, his creation.

Judaism and Islam, however, understand the unity of God in such terms that they exclude any plurality of persons in God. But this leads to the following dilemma: if God's supreme perfection consists in love, as some Jews and Muslims are inclined to admit, without a creation God's supreme perfection would not be actualized.[119] In other words, God would not be loving unless he

---

[119] Let us recall that all but one surah of the Qur'an begins with the phrase: "In the name of Allah the merciful." If there are no creatures, Allah cannot be merciful.

creates those whom he intends to love. Consequently, God would not be perfect without a creation. Therefore, in the context of Judaism and Islam, creation cannot logically be perceived as a gratuitous, free act of God, but as necessitated by God's divine perfection. If, then, God is not perfect without creation, creation becomes a necessary complement to God, which logically leads to a pantheistic system.[120] The alternative solution to the dilemma is to view something other than Pure Love as the supreme divine perfection. But this conception, professed at least tacitly by some Jews and Muslims alike, risks transforming the divinity into pure power, majesty, and aloofness.[121] It also contradicts the existential insight that cuts across all religious boundaries, that pure goodness must include love. If love is not essential to divine perfection, monotheism may easily become the source of terror and intolerance, as has often happened in history, and certainly even among Christians who ignored the central mystery of their own religion.

Only in Christianity is God love in himself, since the one God is a perfect communion of persons: Father, Son, and Holy Spirit. The Christian God is one in nature, essence, and being, but three persons or ontological subjects. In other words, the perfect unity of God results from the perfect love of the Divine Persons: the Father gives all that he has and is to the Son, and the Son returns all that he has and is to the Father. This mutual and total gift of self, however, is not closed and exclusive: their communication in love is fully shared by the Holy Spirit, in whom Father and Son are perfectly one.

In the Christian view, then, creation is not necessary for God to become perfect, that is, to become loving; he creates out of pure love rather than out of necessity. His motive is not the actualiza-

---

[120] Both Jewish and Islamic (Sufi) mysticism, as seen above, tends toward a pantheistic view of God.

[121] Think of those Muslims for whom the shari'ah, the Islamic Law in all its rigor, is the most proper expression of God's will.

tion of his own perfection but the sharing of his own goodness, life, and joy.

Creation

Besides a few primitive religions, only the Abrahamic religions believe that the world has been created out of nothing, rather than from some pre-existent matter or by "flowing out from God." According to Jewish, Christian, and Muslim beliefs, God created not by overcoming hostile deities or powers, but by his will: "He spoke and it was created." God causes the world to be real and have a value of its own which is distinct from God while entirely dependent on God. To put it simply, only the biblical God is believed to be so powerful as to bring about a reality that is other than himself and yet still good and valuable.

Humanity

According to the Judeo-Christian tradition and Islam, human beings are created in God's image and are called to eternal life with him even in their bodily reality.[122]

Only Christian revelation teaches that all people are called to share in God's own Trinitarian life: as result of Jesus' sacrificial death and resurrection, the Holy Spirit is offered to all human beings. If we accept him in faith (explicit or implicit), he shapes and transforms us so radically that we become united to the one Son. This relationship to the Son is so rich and manifold that we become his brothers and sisters, members of his Body, and even his virginal Bride. To the extent that we become conformed and united to the Son, we share in the unique relationship of the one Son to his Father in that we become children of the Father, not by nature and right as the Eternal Only-Begotten Son, but by grace

---

[122] We speak here about the original beliefs of these religions, excluding liberal Judaism.

alone. This adoption is infinitely more real than legal adoption, yet always remains an undeserved gift, a gratuitous "divinization" above the level of mere creatures and servants.

Incarnation

The religions of humankind are full of mediator figures who are either half-divine, half-human, or divine beings who take on human appearance. Yet, only Christianity believes that the one transcendent God has truly become a human being, not by changing his divine nature into human nature or vice versa (that would result in a logical absurdity). Without losing his divinity, and in fact by the power of his infinitely resourceful divine love, God the Son has taken on as his own our human nature, and has lived to its tragic end a human life, fully pure and holy, yet burdened by all the sins of our human race. Belief in the incarnation, understood in this sense, is unique to Christianity.

Redemption

As seen above, the religions of the world vacillate between building systems of self-redemption through magical, moral, ascetic or mental practices, and acknowledging systems of divine redemption through the intervention of some divine figure on behalf of needy humankind. However, only Christianity claims that the one transcendent God, the Father's coeternal and consubstantial Son himself, died in his human nature out of infinite, compassionate love in order to save all sinful men and women for eternal life.

Morality

Only in Christian morality do we claim to share in God's own love, with which we are to love all men and women. Moreover, through his Incarnation, the Son of God identified himself with every human being; thus, a service done to any of our neighbors is seen as a service done to God himself.

Even though Taoism preaches that we should be good to all men and women even if they are not good, only Christianity holds as a center of morality the commandment, based on God's personal love for his enemies, that human beings love their enemies as well.

Hinduism and Mahayana Buddhism also preach universal compassion and loving kindness, but that compassion is directed to all sentient beings and thereby fails to do justice to the unique dignity of men and women that Christianity upholds.

Hell

Hell in the sense of eternal damnation or definitive spiritual dying is taught unequivocally only in Christianity. The possibility of final damnation in its frightening reality has appeared only where God's love has been most clearly and most unambiguously revealed, namely in the cross of Christ. The greater the love we reject, the more serious are the consequences of our rejection; we cannot refuse the life-giving love of God and keep the life of our souls.

It is important to realize that the term "eternal" in eternal life and in eternal damnation are not used in a univocal sense. Eternal life means an eternal growth in knowing and loving God more and more deeply in the community of saints; it is eternal because God's infinite riches can never be exhausted. Eternal damnation, on the contrary, is the opposite of eternal growth; it is eternal only in the sense of being final or irreversible, not because God's mercy is limited, but because the persons in hell have definitively chosen to rebel against him. The one in hell is aware of being spiritually dead, and this awareness does not cease because a spiritual being cannot cease to exist. But there is no growth whatsoever. The book of Revelation speaks about hell as "second death"

(2:11; 20:14-15, 21:8); Jesus, however uses the image of everlasting fire (Mt 18:8; 25:41). The symbol of fire may mean that those in hell suffer by remaining opposed to the "fire" of divine love and to the order of a new universe in which their inordinate cravings remain definitively frustrated.

Having investigated the common patterns in world religions and the unique features of Christianity, we will inquire in the following chapters into its truth and the implications of that truth in relationship to other world religions.

PART III

Christianity, the Sacramental Presence of God's Saving Love in History

Chapter I

A PHENOMENOLOGICAL APPROACH

1. If Transcendent Reality is personal love, does it not seem "logical" that this Transcendent Lover wants to bridge the infinite gap between himself and sinful humankind so that he may become one of us? In other words, the mystery of the Incarnation, while infinitely exceeding our rational abilities, makes eminent sense if the Transcendent One intends to reveal to us the ultimate depth of his love.

2. If Transcendent Reality is personal love, then is it not reasonable to assume that he will not force us to worship him by terrifying threats or overwhelming heavenly signs? Does it not make sense that he will manifest himself through signs which can be deciphered only by those who are sensitive to true love?

3. If Transcendent Reality is personal love, why are we scandalized that we have no documents written directly by the Son of God made man? Is it not rather appropriate that he wanted to reveal himself in such a way that this revelation itself would create a community? We can accept Jesus as the Son of God only if we accept the testimony of the Church of today, which relies on the eyewitness testimony of the apostolic Church (that of the Twelve and those associated with them). We can have no trust in Jesus unless we trust a group of men and women who testify to him. Thus, communion with Jesus is mediated by communion with the Church.

4. If Transcendent Reality is personal love, the taking upon himself of our own guilt and our own dying appears as the un-

fathomable manifestation of ultimate love. It appears as profound wisdom that, once God becomes incarnate, he turns the natural consequences of our sins—suffering and death—into the means of overcoming our sinfulness and of surrendering lovingly to God.

5. If Transcendent Reality is personal love, it is most appropriate that he overcomes death, our most dreaded enemy, and turns it into the way to eternal life. Love wants the beloved to live forever. How could God be pure love and not want our eternal life?

These reflections show that Christianity appears as the *eidos* of the ultimate manifestation of divine love, i.e., its shape and form.[1] Here, however, a new question arises. Indeed, Christianity presents itself as the historically full revelation of God's love. But is this self-presentation true to reality? How can we make sure that this creed is not simply the projection of our own highest desires, the best myth ever produced by the best dreamers of humanity? At this point we must turn to history and ask: Does history support the truth of the Christian claim, and if so, how and to what extent? Again, we can only provide an outline here.

---

[1] This consideration is based on H. Urs von Balthasar's insight. See, for instance, *Love Alone* (New York: Herder & Herder, 1969).

Chapter II

HISTORICAL FOUNDATIONS FOR THE TRUTH OF THE CHRISTIAN CLAIM

First, we must clarify some methodological issues. If we start from the premise that historiography is merely a softer case of the natural sciences, and so each event and person must fit a pre-existing category, then we will inevitably follow the route of so many representatives of the two-centuries-old quest for the historical Jesus; we will manage to squeeze Jesus into a more or less clearly defined stereotype, such as the eschatological prophet, charismatic wisdom teacher, counter-cultural hero, or social revolutionary. Even though we may use a generally agreed group of historical criteria to highlight with more or less probability the "authentic" Jesus traditions that are historically verifiable, the results will nonetheless be different according to everyone's pre-conceived ideas; they will still display the usual pattern: part of the historical evidence will be either distorted or ignored so that the historians can neatly squeeze their reconstruction of Jesus into one of their own pre-existing categories.

If, however, we follow another model of historiography which (a) presupposes the freedom and uniqueness of every human being and tries to understand human actions and lives as expressing that personal uniqueness, and (b) moreover, allows for the possibility of Transcendent Reality manifesting itself in history, the results will be drastically different. Then we will try to read the writings of the New Testament in such a way that, bracketing our own ideological commitments and pre-conceived ideas,

133

we could enter the "world" of the biblical writers and their contemporaries by appropriating their presuppositions, expectations,
values, and experiences. We will, of course, succeed only to a limited degree, but we will still allow the person of Jesus to impress
us in his uniqueness as he impressed those whose experience and
testimony have been embedded in the Gospels and the other New
Testament writings. We will probably use the same criteria as the
first group of historians do in order to distinguish "authentic" Jesus
traditions[2] within these writings, but our conclusions will be different.[3] Even as we use a sound dose of what we call today the
'hermeneutics of suspicion' in order to discover rivalries and com-
petition among New Testament writers who compose and re-com-
pose the message of Jesus and the narrative of his life, death, and
resurrection, the sincerity and trustworthiness of the authors will
still come to light: they put into writing with an amazing combination of freedom and fidelity traditions received from eye-wit-
ness martyrs. The most important among them were Peter and
Paul. Peter was the chief witness to the earthly life of Jesus and to
the appearances of the Risen One, and Paul incorporated into his
First Letter to the Corinthians a very early summary of the appearances of the Risen Christ, an early creedal formula that goes
back to the first years after the crucifixion of Jesus, and he joins to
this list the appearance of the risen Lord to himself.[4] These two
chief apostles as well as James "the brother of the Lord" certainly
gave their lives for the truth of their preaching.

---

[2] I use "authentic" here in the sense of "demonstrably authentic" when employing the critical
method and I do not suggest that the "non-demonstrable data" would be inauthentic.

[3] The usual criteria of historical authenticity (such as multiple attestation, difference from
or opposition to existing trends in the cultural context of the writings, and embarrass-
ment) are able to "catch" only a part of the unique imprint of the person of Jesus in the
documents of the New Testament. For a discussion of the criteria of authenticity, see
J.P. Meier, *A Marginal Jew. Rethinking the Historical Jesus*, vol. I, *The Roots of the Problem
and the Person* (New York: Doubleday, 1991), 167-175. For a somewhat different treatment, see my *Jesus Christ*, 22-31.

[4] A full list of important witnesses includes also the women followers of Jesus; the discovery of the empty tomb and the risen Christ's first appearance are attested by them.

The good faith of the apostles appears also in the portrayal of their own behavior, in the candid description of their own cowardice, betrayal, and lack of understanding, as well as in the description of their hero's lack of success in converting his own people, his human weakness, and ignominious execution through crucifixion. The brutal honesty of the Gospels regarding the weaknesses of the first leaders of the Christian faith is unparalleled in world literature.

After these general considerations, we now come to outlining some basic facts regarding Jesus of Nazareth. Even if for the sake of seeking a more extensive consensus we use here only the most common sense criterion, that of multiple attestation,[5] we can reconstruct some historical events that defy any pre-existing historical pattern and thus resist any conventional explanation. Here only some of these facts will be outlined.

(1) There have been many prophets in Israel's history. The convergence of different traditions, however, points to a unique claim of the prophet Jesus: he teaches not in the name of Yahweh as the other prophets, but with his own authority, which is absolute. When introducing his teaching on the Kingdom, Jesus' formula is most unusual. Instead of using the customary address of the prophets: "Thus says the Lord" or "oracle of the Lord," he announces: "I (however) say to you," or "Amen, I say to you." He does not simply transmit the message of someone outside of himself as the prophets did, nor does he distinguish his own words from the word of God. His "I" speaks with an absolute divine authority that ranks above the divine Law mediated by Moses. His words are directly God's word.

(2) In the presence of his disciples, Jesus allows his unique

---

[5] This criterion admits as historical those features of Jesus which are common to at least three different, relatively independent channels of tradition, the Synoptics, the Fourth Gospel and the epistolary literature, in particular the proto-Pauline corpus. Of course, this critical approach to the Gospels is justified only for establishing the rational foundations for accepting the Christian faith. For the believer only the whole Bible reveals the full mystery of Christ.

relationship to the Father to become more manifest. In particular, he lets them see and hear his prayer. As J. Jeremias has rightly observed, it does not matter whether each and every instance of addressing God as "Father" ("Abba") in Jesus' prayer is historically authentic. Nor can we exclude evidence that some Jewish charismatic miracle workers may sometimes also have called God "Abba," Father. Nevertheless, no one can deny Jeremias' conclusion that Jesus uses the address "Abba," Father, in all his prayers, with the exception of the prayer on the cross in Matthew and Mark where he quotes Psalm 22:2.[6] This fact is unique in the history of Israel. Israel as a whole considered itself the son of God, so some prayers were addressed to God as "Father in heaven" or "our Father" at the time of Jesus. Yet it never became the prevailing form of calling upon God. "King," "ruler of the universe," "my Lord and my God" were much more frequent and more characteristic addresses for Jewish prayer in the time of Jesus. The word "abba" was primarily a family word, meaning "father" in the emphatic and vocative case or "my father." In using this address in all his prayers, Jesus shows an awareness of a unique intimacy with God. He distances himself from his disciples in this respect. He does not address God together with them as "our Father." Yet he bestows on them a share in his own unique relationship with his Father. For the first Christians the word "abba" was so expressive of the unique relationship of Jesus to God in which they were all given a share in the Spirit that even the Hellenistic communities of Galatia and Rome preserved the Aramaic word in their Greek liturgy (Gal 4:6; Rm 8:15). So did the Gospel of Mark, which was meant for a Gentile Christian audience. It is remarkable that, of all possible scenes, Mark quotes the address of Jesus to his Father in the original Aramaic precisely at the moment of his agony:

---

[6] See Joachim Jeremias, *The Prayers of Jesus* (Philadelphia: Fortress Press, 1978), 55. For possible Jewish parallels (which Jeremias denies) see David Flusser, *Jesus* (New York: Herder & Herder, 1969), 93-98.

"Abba, Father, all things are possible to you. Take this
cup away from me, but not what I will but what you
will" (14:36).

Only in the agony of Gethsemane and of the cross does the
full depth and strength of the relationship between Jesus and his
Father come to the fore; Jesus is abandoned by everyone and is
supported only by an unbounded trust in his Abba.[7]

(3) Yet this Jesus who demands unconditional loyalty, a loyalty that prevails even against the most sacred family ties, spends
his life in humble service and absolute obedience to God. He is
among his disciples as the one who serves (Lk 22:27; cf. Mk 10:45,
Mt 20:28 & Ph 2:5-8). In the Last Supper he sums up his life
and anticipates his crucifixion when he gives his disciples his body
and blood as food and drink (1 Cor 11:23-26; Mt 26:26-28; Mk
14:22-24, Lk 22:19-20 & Rm 12:14-21).[8]

(4) Human culture accumulated many lofty moral teachings;
the sayings of Confucius (Kung-Fu-Tzu) and the Book of Tao
(Tao-Te-Ching) certainly belong to its best. But no other teacher
but Jesus centered his moral message on the love of the enemy
and the forgiveness of those who sin against us (Mt 5:38-48, Lk
6:27-28, 32-36). This teaching is not based on the Hindu or Buddhist metaphysics that by loving others we love ourselves since we
are individuals only in appearance but are, in fact, one and the same
Absolute Reality. According to Christ, we should love our enemies, since God the Father loves us, sinners who are his enemies.
Even David Flusser, a Jewish historian, who otherwise minimizes
the originality of Jesus' teaching, claims that the commandment
to love one's enemies is Jesus' "definitive characteristic."[9]

---

[7] Numbers (1) & (2) are somewhat modified excerpts from my *Jesus Christ*, 139, 146. For
    more details on the uniqueness of Jesus see 136-147.

[8] See on this theme more in my *Wedding Feast of the Lamb. Eucharistic Theology from a His-
    torical, Biblical and Systematic Perspective* (Chicago: Hillenbrand Books, 2004), 19-37.

[9] *Jesus*, 70.

(5) Many myths of dying and rising gods have been born and cultivated in the history of religions. But there is no parallel to the appearance list of First Corinthians 15:1-10 or to the appearance and empty tomb accounts of the gospels. No historical person has ever been claimed by his own contemporaries including his closest disciples and one of his chief enemies, to have been raised back to immortal, divine life in such a way that his appearances changed the disciples' lives and gave rise to a world-wide missionary movement.

Moreover, these same disciples gave their lives for their belief in the resurrection of this crucified, alleged criminal.[10]

(6) There are many human beings who were raised to divine status in the history of religions: kings and emperors already during their lifetimes, Siddhartha Gautama (Buddha) several hundred years after his death by a certain branch of Buddhism, and even Muhammad was given divine attributes by some of his followers centuries after his death. However, the fact that adherents to a strict monotheistic religion such as the faith of Israel would attribute divine status to a crucified human being so shortly after his shameful execution is without parallel in history (cf. 1 Cor 16:22; Ph 2:6-11).[11] If this had happened in India where every human being is believed to be divine by nature, it should not surprise us. But in Israel idolatry was at the time of Jesus the most heinous crime. Thus, the fact that the Jewish disciples of Jesus came to believe, so shortly after his death, in Jesus' transcendent lordship in the same absolute sense as Yahweh is the Lord of his people points to some weighty evidence in their experience. They must have had solid reasons to believe in Jesus' divine power and dignity in spite of the culture in which they lived.

---

[10] See more on the appearances of the risen Christ in my *Jesus Christ*, 34-71.

[11] "Maranatha" in 1 Cor 16:22 is an Aramaic liturgical exclamation: "The Lord comes" or "Come, Lord!" It is not Paul's invention but must have originated in the earliest Aramaic speaking community. Its use in the liturgy implies the divine dignity and lordship of the risen Christ.

A historian, then, who, by using the method of his discipline, is led to admit these facts, cannot go any further without transgressing the boundaries of his discipline. His search will end in an insoluble puzzle: the historical Jesus as he was able to reconstruct him explodes the usual categories of historiography and remains inexplicable within the realm of the historian's competence: he is more than a rabbi, a prophet, charismatic healer, or teacher of a new morality.[12]

On the one hand, the historians' perplexed conclusions cannot, by themselves, generate faith. Yet, they can prepare faith by compelling them to ask the question, "Who is this man?" and by suggesting to them the principle that a unique phenomenon calls for a unique cause.

On the other hand, if the historians' study of the historical Jesus is coupled with their existential search for the manifestation of Perfect Love in history, the response of the Christian faith that transcends their boldest desires for Infinite Love will appear to them eminently reasonable. Thus, the conclusions of our philosophical inquiry, in particular, our "incipient insight" about the reality of a Transcendent Lover, combined with the results of the quest for the historical Jesus, provide a convergence of probabilities in favor of the truth of Christian faith. However, no accumulation of probabilities or even rational certainties could lead us to faith unless God's grace enlightens our mind and enables us freely to decide to believe in the truth of Christianity as the self-revelation of God in Jesus Christ. Then in the very act of faith, we no longer rely primarily on the convergent probabilities or practical certainties that we have assembled, but on the authority of the

---

[12] Martin Buber, the great Jewish philosopher, theologian and historian, expressed a similar conclusion in these terms: "I am more than ever certain that a great place belongs to him [Jesus] in Israel's history of faith and that this place cannot be described by any of the usual categories" (*Two Types of Faith: A Study of Interpenetration of Judaism and Christianity*, New York: Harper Torchbooks, 1961), 13.

Word of Jesus Christ himself.[13] We will believe in his Word, entrust our lives to his Word and thereby participate in the absolute solidity and certainty of God's Word itself.[14]

The analogy of faith in human beings can shed some light on the nature of the act of faith in God. If you accept as true about your fiancée only that which can be ascertained by the sum total of your rational inquiries, you still don't have faith in her, since you trust only the reliability of your own investigation. As long as you remain at this stage, no real trust and communion can exist between you and her. But once you take the risk of deciding to trust her word, accept her self-revelation, and entrust your life to her, you have transcended the results of even the most rigorous rational investigation. From that point on, your knowledge of her rests primarily not on the results of your own quest but on her words of self-revelation. This knowledge of her through self-revelation, then, is as solid as her own word, whose reliability can be very weak or very strong. But regardless of the weakness or strength of her truthfulness, you have chosen to depend on her word, and thus you build your life on something or rather someone who is false or truthful, fickle or consistent. The similarities and differences between the genesis of trust in a human being and that of trust in God's Word are rather obvious.

---

[13] The Word of Jesus Christ is inaccessible to us unless we accept the Bible as preparing him (Old Testament) and as testifying to his presence (New Testament). However, we cannot accept the Bible as God's authentic testimony unless we accept the Church that produced and authenticated the Bible. Thus the paradox arises that our faith can rely on the Word of God only through relying on the Church, or more concretely, on the uninterrupted chain of witnesses that goes back to Peter and Paul and James (and the other apostles), the eyewitnesses who gave their lives for their testimony. This inseparable ecclesial dimension of our faith in the Son needs some further elaboration. Suffice it to say here that we cannot believe in Jesus Christ unless we believe his Church.

[14] Yet as long as we live by faith rather than by seeing God face to face, our faith may be buffeted by ever new doubts and difficulties. But it will not be shaken as long as we live the truth of our faith and rely on the joint light of faith and reason.

PART IV

The Christian View on the Relationship
Between Christianity and Other Religions

Once we have accepted the truth claim of Christianity, we need to examine its relationship to other religions. To anticipate our conclusions, this relationship is characterized by two different—although not adequately distinguishable—activities, dialogue and evangelization. Dialogue is based on the shared conviction that the non-Christian religions and Christianity can mutually enrich each other's understanding of divine truth; evangelization, on the other hand, derives from the Christian conviction that Jesus Christ is the sole mediator of salvation for all the world and that his Word contains the fullness of God's self-revelation. The goal of the former is elimination of misunderstandings and mutual enrichment; the goal of the latter is conversion to Christianity. The two activities, however, overlap to some extent. Evangelization must be pursued in a dialogical mode, that is, by acknowledging the hidden operation of God's grace and truth in the non-Christian religion; dialogue, in turn, if it is to be conducted in an honest way, will result in the exposition of the fullness of Christian truth, which claims the adherence of all human beings.

Before dealing with these two activities in the present context, an historical outline is in order. While explicit dialogue with other religions is a recent development, the apologetics of the Fathers in general and the *De Pace Fidei* (1453) of Nicolaus Cusanus in particular include elements of dialogue in their works of polemic and evangelization. Following the lead of Paul, the early Fathers judged very harshly the popular polytheistic religions of their own times but saw a divinely inspired preparation for Christianity in the religious philosophies of Platonism and Stoicism. While they transformed the key notions of these philosophies (for instance, the notion of "logos or reason," "world soul," "natural law"), the Church also gained much from the encounter with Hellenistic culture: the transformed notions of Platonism and Stoicism helped the Church to articulate more precisely its central mysteries.[1]

Ratzinger remarks that we can distinguish two phases in the relationship between Christianity and other religions. In the first phase Christianity allied itself with philosophy, the movement toward rationality that ultimately destroyed the polytheistic, idol-worshiping religions. But with Gregory the Great a second phase began: Gregory instructd St. Augustine of Canterbury not to destroy the pagan temples, but only the idols. The newly converted pagans could even continue their sacred meals, as long as it was done in honor of the saints rather than their gods. Thus,

> The gods are no longer gods. As such, they have been overthrown: the question of truth has itself deprived them of divinity and brought about their downfall. Yet at the same time their truth has emerged: that they were a reflection of divinity, a presentiment of figures in which their hidden significance was purified and fulfilled. In that sense, there is such a thing as the "transposition" of the gods, who, as intimations, as steps in the search for the true God and for his reflection in creation, may become messengers of the one God.[2]

Nicolaus Cusanus, this multi-talented renaissance theologian, is perhaps the first to recommend a dialogue among all religions with the goal outlined by Ratzinger above: to find the one true God behind the multiple representations of the many gods.

---

[1] Cf. Ratzinger, *Truth and Tolerance*, 202-203.

[2] *Truth and Tolerance*, 228-230.

Chapter I

TOWARD A CHRISTIAN THEOLOGY OF INTER-RELIGIOUS DIALOGUE

Dialogue between Christianity and other religions has become a most fashionable activity, practiced by dilettantes and theologians, contemplative monks and skeptical scholars alike. Indeed, it has achieved some remarkable results, such as a growth in mutual respect, elimination of misunderstandings and prejudices, and an appreciation of, and empathy towards, each other's religion or religious philosophy.

Yet, in today's climate, ambiguity and confusion prevail regarding the rationale and tasks for a genuine dialogue between Christian theologians and those of other religions. For instance, the demand for the recognition of the personal equality of the partners is often confused with the demand to acknowledge the equal value of their respective positions; the open-minded readiness to learn from one's dialogue partners is instinctively equated with relativizing one's own position vis-à-vis that of the dialogue partner. Thus, anyone who dares to represent the absolute and universal claim of his/her religion will most likely incur the charge of cultural imperialism.

We must then face two main issues, of which the first includes two related questions: (a) Why should Christians, who believe that Jesus Christ is the fullness of God's revelation, enter a genuine dialogue with representatives of other religions? How can those who claim to have the fullness of truth learn from others? (b) If genuine dialogue is possible, or rather imperative, what are its tasks and benefits?

Building on the work of many others, in particular, the encyclicals of Popes Paul VI and John Paul II and a recent article by Cardinal Walter Kasper, I will attempt to provide a partial answer in which reasons for the necessity and the requirements for the integrity of dialogue will be treated in their close interrelationships.[3]

My reflections will primarily be based on a dialogical anthropology and on the self-understanding of the Catholic Christian faith.[4]

I. The Rationale for Dialogue

1. The dialogical nature of humankind

The process of coming to know any truth is always a dialogical process, a most personal but also eminently communal exercise. Suppose that I have discovered "the light of being," the intelligibility of something that is real. This light calls for sharing and confirmation by other knowing subjects. It invites sharing because I want to share the joy of "seeing the truth"; I also want to share the discovered truth in order to be confirmed by those who see the same light and perceive the same intelligibility. How-

---

[3]   See especially Paul VI, *Ecclesiam Suam*, 1963; John Paul II, *Redemptoris Missio*, 1991 (You can easily access these encyclicals from the website: www.vatican.va); W. Kasper, "The Nature and Purpose of Ecumenical Dialogue," *Harvard Divinity Bulletin*, Winter 2001-02, 19-23.

[4]   I assume here the knowledge of the Church's teaching on salvation outside the visible boundaries of the Church and on the relationship of Christianity to other religions. See especially Francis Sullivan, *Salvation Outside the Church. Tracing the History of the Catholic Response* (New York: Paulist, 1992). For the teaching of the Fathers see Henri de Lubac, "The Pagan Religions and the Fathers of the Church," *The Church: Paradox and Mystery* (Staten Island, NY: Alba House, 1969), 68-95. For a detailed bibliography and for the various theological positions, see J. Dupuis, *Toward a Christian Theology of Religious Pluralism* (Maryknoll, NY: Orbis, 1997).

ever, even the truth of finite realities is inexhaustible, let alone that of the Infinite, Transcendent Reality. Moreover, although our intellects are by nature ordained towards the Infinite, in their categorical operation[5] they can only handle finite truths. Therefore, progress in the knowledge of truth also necessitates a dialogical cooperation: each one of us has a special angle from which he sees an aspect of truth that others do not see with the same clarity or depth. Regarding the face-to-face vision of God, St. Thomas asserts that we obtain the fullness of joy by our sharing in the vision and joy of all those in heaven.[6] If this complementarity is an essential ingredient of our experience in heaven, it is even more necessary in earthly knowledge. Thus, if God's revelation intends to adjust to human nature, it makes eminent sense that his plan calls for dialogue and cooperation to include all humankind.

Such a dialogical process of discovering truth and progressing in the truth requires that we acknowledge the equality of our dialogue partners. Unless we accept and respect their personal dignity and integrity, we cannot learn from them. Without learning from one another, however, no dialogue exists.

The mutual recognition of the partners' personal equality and our readiness to learn from each other are necessary conditions for dialogue. On the other hand, the assumption that genuine dialogue requires that none of the dialogue partners should claim possession of absolute truth needs some clarification.

To claim possession of truth is to distort both the nature of truth and the process of knowing it. Such a misconception derives from a popularized Kantian epistemology according to which the mind imposes its own (transcendental) categories on the object of knowledge and thus acquires for the knowing subject some useful information. The thing in itself remains unknown; we know

---

[5] I use the term "categorical" in a Rahnerian sense as opposed to the transcendental orientation of the intellect towards the Infinite. In other words in forming a propositional truth, we always do it against the global, unobjectified background knowledge of Infinite Truth.

[6] *Credo in Deum*, Opuscula Theologica 2 (Torino, 1954), 217.

only how to use or manipulate reality for technological purposes whereby we try to dominate the empirical world.

If, however, our understanding of knowing is not an extrapolation of the domineering, technological model, but that of critical realism, knowledge is seen not to result in the possession but (to use an ornate word broadly) in the contemplation of truth. As long as we only form concepts regarding an object, we do not know the reality of the object, but only a sum of intelligible thought patterns. In the act of judgment, however, as we affirm a certain intelligible thought pattern to apply to the object, we come to know a truth. When we say that this state of affairs is so, the copula "is" of our affirmation participates in the actual being, in the "is," of the thing we come to know. Thus, while maintaining their distinct identity, the knowing subjects transcend their own limitations as they receive into themselves, and are enriched by, the objects of knowledge. In this view, then, the truth is perceived as being above the knowing subject and calling for respect and love from the subject rather than legitimizing an attitude of possession and manipulation.

If this is so, then in no dialogue may the truth be used as a weapon to assert one's superiority over the other; rather, truth is always (potentially at least) a common treasure we both acknowledge as transcending, enriching, and even governing us. At the moment we abuse the truth as a means of domination, we have already distorted it. Thus, we can never "possess" the truth: should we try, it will slip away from us and we will be left only with its distorted caricature.

This understanding of truth, however, excludes any relativist approach. If my dialogue partner's affirmation of a truth can be valid only for him/her but not for myself, and vice versa, as we have discussed at the beginning of our study, the dialogue cannot enrich either of us; it will degenerate into a double monologue that may call for mutual sympathy but renders any exchange of views ultimately meaningless.

2. The Self-Understanding of Christianity in Relationship to Other Religions

If God has in fact adjusted his mode of revelation to our dialogical nature, it should become manifest from its dialogical structure. Moreover, not only the nature of the human being but also that of the Trinitarian God himself makes the dialogical structure of revelation highly intelligible a priori.[7]

In this essay I presuppose, rather than expose or justify, the doctrine of the Magisterium on God's revelation. My goal is to perceive its inner coherence and its implications for inter-religious dialogue.

(a) From all eternity God (the Father in union with the Son and the Holy Spirit) has decided to enter into full communion with fallen humankind through the Incarnation and redemptive work of the Son so that humankind may enter into full communion with the Triune God.

This plan corresponds to both human nature and God's Trinitarian being. In order to enter into the most intimate solidarity with humankind, God the Son had to become one of us, and this climax had to be prepared by a slow education of a people so that they would be ready for a direct encounter with God through Jesus Christ. Since humankind can reach fullness and completion only through the unity of its members and since human nature is both spiritual and corporal, it was appropriate to achieve this unity in the one Incarnation. Several incarnations of the one Son would have obscured rather than revealed the Son's oneness and would not have achieved the unity of humankind on a visible, corporal level. If the Son had established several incar-

---

[7] Being created in the image of God, the dialogical character of human nature reflects that of the Trinitarian God. Not in the individual's need for communal confirmation of his/her insight does this analogy appear but in the free decision of the individual to share with others the joy of discovery. The Father fully shares his joy in the Son with the Holy Spirit and, in the act of knowing the Father, the Son rejoices in the Holy Spirit (cf. Lk 3:21-22; 10:21-22).

nations in history, the unity of humankind would have been restricted to the level of the spirit rather than include the level of the flesh as well. Thus, it is the specifically human intimacy of communion between God and humanity that calls for historically contingent and temporally and spatially limited events of a Salvation History that culminates in the one Jesus Christ. Since God educated one people and became eventually a member of that one people, a Jew from the stock of David, this most intimate communion resulted in historical particularity and limitation: the Son of God could not be simultaneously a Hindu, Chinese, or contemporary Jew. Hence the scandal of the one Incarnation: a contingent human being at a given point in history is the absolute center of history and the fullness of God's revelation. The Church has always clung to this truth in spite of its apparent absurdity.

Most recently, apropos of J. Dupuis' carefully reasoned though somewhat ambiguous work, *Toward a Christian Theology of Religious Pluralism*, the Doctrinal Congregation insisted that it is not the eternal disincarnate Logos, but the incarnate eternal Son, Jesus Christ, who mediated the fullness of revelation and redeemed all humankind.[8] We can make sense out of this teaching by considering the peculiar transcendence of human nature: it is finite yet tends toward the Infinite. As spirit, the human being is a priori oriented towards Infinite Being, Truth, and Goodness; therefore it does not appear impossible for the Son, who is Infinite Being, Truth, and Goodness, to elevate an individual human nature to

---

[8]   See the "Notification" on Dupuis' book by the Congregation for the Doctrine of the Faith, Rome, January 24, 2001. The same Congregation issued earlier a "Declaration '*Dominus Jesus*' On The Unicity And Salvific Universality of Jesus Christ And The Church" (August 6, 2000) which rejects a pluralistic approach to religions. See conflicting reactions to it in *"Dominus Jesus." Anstößige Wahrheit oder anstößige Kirche?* Ed. M.J. Rainer (Münster: Lit Verlag, 2001).

[9]   R. Haight's book, *Jesus, the Symbol of God* (Maryknoll: Orbis, 1999), fails to do justice to the Church's faith not by calling Jesus the symbol of God but by not seeing the ontological depth of what it means that Jesus is the perfect symbol of God. He is such a perfect self-expression of God that the man Jesus is God.

the point of making it into his own self-expression, his own per-fect symbol.[9] The Infinite does express itself so perfectly in the man Jesus that this man Jesus is rightly called God the Son. Yet, since the human spirit remains finite and expresses itself in a finite body, this finite expression of the Infinite calls by its very nature for an unfolding in all humankind.

Such an apparent contradiction needs some further expla-nation. In everyday life, when we truly encounter a person, we en-counter an indivisible whole; we always face the whole person in some sense, even though on varying levels of intensity and from different angles. This is so because no human being is simply an aggregate of different characteristics, but is a more or less unified whole: simplicity, indivisibility, and wholeness are hallmarks of every spiritual being. Obviously, their realization even in the most integrated human person pales in comparison to the analogous simplicity, indivisibility, and wholeness of a Divine Person. Since it is the Divine Person of the Son (identical with the fullness of divinity) who expresses himself in the human nature and exist-ence of Jesus, we always encounter in him the fullness of divinity. Jesus' personal presence, even if he says only a brief word and per-forms only one gesture, in some sense always contains the whole of divinity. Yet this fullness is condensed and implicit. Any single word or deed of Jesus needs not only the elucidation provided by all his other words and deeds, but should also be seen in the con-text of all the events of Salvation History as reflected in the Scrip-tures and explained by the Church. One more step is needed: the whole of Salvation History will obtain its full meaning and the Word of God will be fully explicated only at the end of history, when all human beings who accepted God's grace will have per-fected the manifestation of Christ in their lives.

To put this into traditional terms: the Incarnation, begun in Bethlehem and consummated on Calvary, will achieve its God-intended purpose only when the whole mystical body of Christ (the multitude of those who express Jesus' words, deeds, and passion in their own unique words, deeds, and sufferings) enters the Father's presence in the heavenly Jerusalem.

This growing understanding and manifestation of the mystery of Christ in and through all humankind is the work of the Holy Spirit. While the Son's intimate presence requires its finite expression in the one man Jesus Christ, the Holy Spirit, breathed forth by the crucified and risen Christ, draws all humankind to Jesus and carves out the features of Jesus in all those who receive him.

Thus, the document *Dominus Jesus* and the Notification added to Dupuis' book call attention to a central mystery of faith: the incarnate Word does contain the fullness of revelation and all graces of redemption. But *Dominus Jesus* and the Notification do not deny that the teachings of this one man and the graces emanating from the one redemptive event are destined to reveal their riches only through the whole of history and through all redeemed humankind. This is true not in the sense that every human being or at least several of them would become a new incarnation of the one Logos, but rather in the sense that all the saved will reflect and unfold the infinite riches present in the one man Jesus Christ.

(b) What has been said so far explains the theological context but not the status of non-Christian religions in God's plan of salvation. First, however, we need to pin down two oversimplified views. One assumes that the major non-Christian religions hide an anonymous Christianity, which waits only to be unveiled and articulated in explicit Christian terms.[10] This position offends the representatives of other religions and ignores the constant tradi-

---

[10] Many of his followers simplified Rahner's position on anonymous Christianity in this way. While Rahner himself is more nuanced, he himself does not sufficiently recognize the negative effects of sin in so many structures of world religions. See K. Rahner, "Christianity and the Non-Christian Religions," *Theol. Invest.* 5 (Baltimore, MD: Helicon, 1966), 115-134; "Church, Churches and Religions," *Theol. Invest.* 10 (New York: Herder & Herder, 1973), 30-49; "Anonymous Christianity and the Missionary Task of the Church," *Theol. Invest.* 12 (New York: Seabury, 1974), 161-180; "The Religions for Salvation," *Theo. Invest.* 18 (New York: Crossroad, 1983), 288-295.

tion of the Catholic Church. The second view claims that all major religions are equally valid ways to reach communion with God and that their great founders (Buddha and Muhammad) are such significant mediators of God's revelation for their own culture as Jesus is for ours.[11] Again, this hypothesis substantially falsifies the perennial self-understanding of Christianity.

I assume here a Christian evaluation of other religions that has developed with solid scriptural bases in the Catholic Church; it can be summarized in the following points:

(1) Created in the image of God and for personal communion with God, the human race distorted this relationship into an attempt at self-divinization. Our ancestors wanted to be "like gods" by their own efforts, which resulted in the obscuring of religious and moral knowledge: "They exchanged the glory of the immortal God for images resembling mortal man or birds or animals or reptiles" (Rm 1:23). Thus, the influence of original sin and personal sins, as well as the ignorance resulting from the accumulation of sins, had a significant distorting effect on the shaping of cultures and in particular on the structures (beliefs, rituals, and moral teachings) of all religions.

(2) At the same time, however, God has not abandoned fallen humankind. The Church has always rejected as heresy those views which claimed that God would offer his grace only to Christians. In every place and time of human history, the Father has always offered sufficient grace for salvation to everyone. This grace has always been a grace of Christ, resulting from, and prefiguring, the sacrifice of Christ. Christ died for everyone, even for those who lived before him, and obtained the grace of salvation for all. The Holy Spirit calls every human being and molds those who accept his invitation into the likeness of Christ.

---

[11] The most emphatic voice to proclaim this kind of religious pluralism is Paul Knitter's. Of his many publications see especially *No Other Name? A Critical Survey of Christian Attitudes to World Religions* (Maryknoll: Orbis, 1985); *One Earth Many Religions: Multifaith Dialogue and Global Responsibility* (Maryknoll: Orbis, 1995).

The Fathers of the Church understood the words of John's Gospel about "the real Light which enlightens every man" (1:9) in the sense that even the pagans were exposed to the Light, who is the eternal Son and Word of God. Some of them accepted this light and thus, according to St. Justin, possess a "seed of the Word of God" in themselves. St. Justin even insists that the people who taught and lived according to the Word of God (such as Heraclitus and Socrates, who taught and lived according to the values their conscience presented to them), should be called Christians.[12]

If, then, the grace of Christ has been offered to everyone by the Holy Spirit, it may have influenced some of those individuals who shaped the structures (the sacred books, beliefs, rituals, and moral teachings) of non-Christian religions. For instance, this grace of God calling everyone to become like Christ may have inspired some of the moral teachings in Taoism, Confucianism, and Buddhism that seem so strikingly similar to Christian morality. The grace of God may also explain the loving devotion of Arjuna for Krishna in the Bhagavad Gita and the worship of the compassionate Buddha in the writings of Mahayana Buddhism.

These two contradictory influences on the formation of religious structures outside of Christianity, the influence of sin and ignorance on the one hand, and grace on the other, account for the ambiguity of these structures. For instance, one and the same religious text may be interpreted as the expression of a fundamentally sinful attitude (an effort at self-deification) or a loving union with God through the very gift of God. A ritual may be used as an acknowledgment of one's dependence on a higher power but also as magic, that is, as an attempt to control the Sacred Power, an attempt which is sinful from a Christian perspective.

(c) Even though the structures of non-Christian religions are most often the mixture and/or ambiguous result of the contradictory influences of these two contrasting "magnetic fields," sin and

---

[12] *First Apology* 46.

grace, individual members of a non-Christian religion may become "saints." The biblical example for sainthood outside Israel and the Church is Job. Historical examples may be Confucius and Gandhi. Confucius' ideal was the superior man who keeps the heart of a child, is not power-hungry, and works for justice and goodness in all human relationships. Gandhi urged the love of truth and the love of the enemy in his struggle for India's independence. Both died as failures. Confucius was dismissed as chief justice by his prince and spent the rest of his life wandering from place to place in search of a prince who would be ready to put his ethical principles into practice. Gandhi was killed by one of his fellow Hindus who could not endure Gandhi's opposition to the war between Hindus and Muslims. It is important to note, however, that Gandhi, unlike the Christian saints, became a saint partly through his Hindu religion but partly also by going against his own religion. He rejected the caste system, a fundamental tenet of orthodox Hinduism, and showed a special love for the "outcastes"[13] as Jesus did for the poor and rejected of his own society.

(d) If grace is offered also to non-Christians and some accept and cooperate with this grace to the point of becoming saints, and if sin is active not only among non-Christians but also among Christians, what, then, is the difference between Christianity and non-Christian religions?

The difference does not lie on the level of personal acceptance or rejection of grace; both are possible within and without Christianity. The basic difference concerns the mystery of Incarnation in a broad sense, that is, the expression of grace in visible structures. The person and work of Jesus Christ himself is the pure and full self-expression of God for us. In fact, Jesus Christ is God made visible, tangible, audible: everything in Jesus expresses God without the slightest distortion. It is from the perspective of this climax that everything else before and after Christ as recorded in

---

[13] He affectionately called the outcastes "children of God."

the books of both Testaments needs to be interpreted. The history and experience of Israel as commented upon by her Scriptures are authenticated by God himself as a preparation, prefiguration, and actual anticipation of the event of Jesus Christ. The Church, on the other hand, in its essential structures, extends to peoples of all times and places the teachings, the actions, and the very person of Christ. For this reason these structures (the books of the Old and New Testaments, the teachings of the Magisterium, and the sacraments of the Church) are guaranteed by God—to varying degrees and in various ways—to be the authentic expression of Christ's grace. Even though individual popes, bishops, priests, and lay-Christians may sin gravely, they cannot destroy the Church of Christ, her Bible, her teaching, and her sacraments.

At the same time, although individuals may reach not only salvation but even holiness outside the visible boundaries of the Church, the beliefs, writings, rituals, and moral teachings of other religions are not guaranteed by God; they are the products of both graced insights as well as human sinfulness and ignorance. These conflicting influences often produce ambivalent expressions that may be interpreted in contradictory ways. The non-Christian religion, however, does not carry within itself a sufficient criterion of discernment.

One example might illustrate this point. Once I asked a Muslim acquaintance of mine: "Why did you invite this gentleman for our Muslim-Christian dialogue? Why not professor X.Y.? X.Y. has the highest academic credentials and is widely respected by both Muslims and Christians; he would have been a more effective catalyst for dialogue than your gentleman was." He responded: "We don't like people like X.Y. He cares only about the love of God and love of neighbor." I had to learn my lesson: Islam lacks an adequate criterion within itself to discern what is authentic and what is inauthentic Islam.

(e) Can other religions, then, be called means of salvation, analogous in some way to non-Catholic Christian denominations? While the Magisterium explicitly stated this only about the latter, it did not exclude it about the former. The most significant statement of John Paul II in this regard, as F. Sullivan has pointed out, refers to the manifold participations in the one mediation of Christ:

> Although participated forms of mediation of different kinds and degrees are not excluded, they acquire meaning and value only from Christ's own mediation, and they cannot be understood as parallel or complementary to his.[14]

However, if we keep in mind the conflicting and ambiguous religious forms in non-Christian religions, no single, universally valid answer appears possible. Every belief, every sacred writing—or rather each and every literary unit of a sacred writing, every ritual or moral principle—has to be evaluated on its own. For instance, can the worship of a fertility god such as Indra who is powerful when drunk on soma juice be a salvific act?[15] Is it not rather a classic case of idolatry, a divinization of our own vital powers? On the other hand, meditating on a text of the Upanishads that speaks about our fusion with Brahman may become both a boost

---

[14] *Redemptoris Missio*, 5. On the role of non-Catholic Christian churches and ecclesial communities in salvation, see *Unitatis Redintegratio*, 3.

[15] On this point I disagree with Rahner. Even though he acknowledges that non-Christian religions are "a mixture of disparate elements" consisting of the effects of grace, religious instinct and sinfulness, he still maintains that "even in the most primitive, corrupt or grotesque forms this grace still offers to man the ultimate possibility of activating in some way or other [...] that orientation towards the mystery of God which is implanted in him by grace" ("Church, Churches and Religions," *Theol. Invest.*, Vol. 10, 30-49, at 46-47). Pace Rahner the cult of certain gods expresses the anti-religious tendency of the fallen human race which worships itself instead of a Transcendent Absolute. Similarly, certain magic rites are a clear expression of the human effort to dominate rather than worship the Transcendent. To those who practice these religions grace still may be offered through visible, social structures (as Rahner rightly emphasizes), but through encounter with one's neighbor rather than through an explicit religious structure.

to our efforts of self-divinization or an expression of grace-inspired love for the Absolute. In the first case it becomes a means of sin; in the other, a means of salvation. At the opposite end of the spectrum we find some texts that can hardly be used for anything else than expressing and fostering a grace-inspired attitude. For instance, some texts on the bodhisattvas who want to take upon themselves the burden of others to save them fall into this last category.

That some religious structures cannot be means of grace because of their objectively sinful nature, such as worshiping a fertility god or practicing black magic, does not mean that people who belong to this kind of religion in good faith are necessarily doomed to damnation. Obeying the absolute commands of one's conscience, especially in matters of loving one's neighbor, may be for these people the means of receiving God's grace. After all, even the salvation of Christians who have the fullness of Christ's revelation and all his means of grace depends ultimately on serving Christ in our neighbors (Mt 25:31-46).

II. The Tasks and Benefits of Dialogue

The above considerations help define the nature and the tasks of inter-religious dialogue. Since the Holy Spirit may have influenced some expressions of a given religion, we need to identify and acknowledge these "seeds of the Word." Some features of a non-Christian religion may indeed providentially bring to light hitherto unperceived or half-forgotten truths of Christ's revelation, truths that are particularly relevant in our age. As Pope John Paul II explained, they may help the Church to realize more deeply her own identity and her own teaching.[16]

The learning from other religions, however, must be accompanied by a process of discerning: the Catholic participants in the

---

[16] See *Redemptoris Missio*, 56.

dialogue should separate truth from error and resolve the ambivalence of a doctrine or ritual by articulating it in the light of the Christian mystery. Those adherents of a given religion who are open to the Holy Spirit (even though their awareness of the Holy Spirit may not be conceptualized at all) will find that the Christian interpretation of their own ambivalent doctrines or practices does not distort but rather illuminates the deepest truth of what they have already intuited in their own religion[17] (provided, of course, that the cultural barriers and misunderstandings are successfully overcome).

The process of learning and discerning calls for a third task, that of integration. The critically evaluated and articulated truth or practice derived from another religion needs to be integrated into the whole of the Christian mystery, whereby this truth or practice will appear in a new perspective, and will in turn shed new light on the Christian mystery itself.

When discussing the individual religions, I tried to evaluate each of them from this threefold perspective. In what follows, I will highlight the most important examples to which this threefold process of learning, discerning, and integrating can be applied, examples that, I hope, will show the providential role of religions in the contemporary understanding and living of the totality of the Christian mystery.

a) Hinduism

(1) Even though it has for the time being become strangely ignored in Hindu politics, the Hindu doctrine of ahimsa, non-violence, has already proved itself by inspiring a colonized India

---

[17] A Buddhist university student told the priest who prepared him for baptism: "Father, I have believed all these truths from my youth. It is only when I studied Buddhism at the university level that I learned the doctrines which are incompatible with Christian faith" (from an oral communication from Professor P. Nemeshegyi, a Jesuit who taught at the Sophia University in Japan for several decades). Indeed, if all grace comes from Christ and leads to Christ, how could this be otherwise?

to resist the oppressor not by violence but by peaceful, non-violent resistance. By means of ahimsa India obtained independence from Britain and Martin Luther King promoted the civil rights of Black Americans. If ahimsa is separated from its original Hindu context of pantheism and the eternal cycle of creation and re-absorption into Brahman, and is combined with the love of all human beings, a love that is based on their God-given dignity and the redemptive sacrifice of Christ, it receives a new perspective, but also a new urgency. If a whole nation or country can be persuaded and educated to practice ahimsa, such peaceful resistance coupled with the love of the enemy is to be preferred to a just war. We need to learn this fundamentally evangelical form of responding to evil from another religion.

(2) Hatha Yoga serves as another example. This combined series of mental and physical exercises was originally designed to actualize the energies of the Divine Self (Atman). However, if we detach it from its original objective, we can use it as a powerful means of enlisting the body's help in developing a readiness to pray and meditate on the Word of God. So many Christians have tried to develop a spiritual life by attempting to suppress rather than master and sublimate the cravings of the flesh, and they have failed miserably. Yoga does help in integrating our life energies into the service of the spirit. Placed in a Christian context, yoga obtains a new perspective. The body is no longer viewed as a husk for the Spiritual Self but as an integral constituent of a body-soul unity destined for eternal life.

b) Buddhism

(1) According to Christian faith, every human self was created by God in his own image and likeness and the Son of God died for every individual human being. Therefore, we cannot accept the unreality of the individual self as every form of Buddhism teaches in one way or another. But if the metaphysical doctrine

of selflessness is transformed into an ethical imperative of selflessness, it reinforces a basic Christian conviction: our inflated egos are unreal and the source of illusory cravings. Stressing a "positive Christian outlook on life," we rarely take seriously the words of Jesus: "Whoever wants to keep his life will lose it. And whoever loses his life for my sake and for that of Gospel will save it" (Mk 8:35). Denying oneself and taking up the cross cannot mean for us a denial of our metaphysical self but a dying to the "false self." Integrated into a Christian context, then, the teaching on Anatman (no self) confirms a crucial aspect of Christ's call to discipleship.

(2) The need to deflate our oversized egos is certainly not a popular Christian doctrine. But even less understood is the truth of vicarious atonement. Ever since Abelard, many "cutting edge" theologians rejected the idea of vicarious sacrifice for sin as part of an unhealthy myth, a distorted interpretation of the meaning of Christ's death.

Here again, a Buddhist belief can help us re-learn the value of vicarious suffering for others: we should compare the Mahayana texts on bodhisattvas with the Songs of the Suffering Servant. The Holy Spirit has powerfully prepared the understanding of the sacrifice of Christ by inspiring the ideal of the bodhisattvas, who burn with the desire to take upon themselves all human sufferings and faults in order to rescue all living beings into Nirvana. Again, the context blurs the distinction between human suffering and that of all living beings; moreover, Nirvana cannot be equated with heaven. Yet, those Buddhist monks who vow to carry the burdens of others are—unconsciously—manifesting the features of Christ to the world and reaffirming for us a central truth of our faith, a truth that we are inclined to reject, forget, or minimize.

c) Taoism

(1) Tao is the ultimate and ineffable source of all beings and the law that governs the universe. One's happiness, according to the Taoist view, is to live in harmony with the cosmic order that manifests Tao. While Christians cannot accept Tao's impersonal character, living in harmony with the cosmic order may become a providential corrective to our craving for the manipulation of our own nature and that of the cosmos. Instead of preserving the Earth and improving conditions for a more just and humane social order and for a more healthy society, we are in danger of subverting nature's ecological balance and destroying ourselves as we claim absolute control over human life. Taoist philosophy can help us restore respect for what is known in Christianity as the natural law.

(2) The classic book of Tao, the Tao-Te-Ching, knows that the sage is whole even though he has not experienced the union of man and woman (#55). In other words, the author of this classic was aware that celibacy for the sake of wisdom can successfully integrate the yin (female, passive) and yang (male, active) aspects of human nature. At a time when even committed Catholics question the value of celibacy for the sake of the Kingdom, the Taoist sage, the Hindu holy man, and the Buddhist monk help us rediscover the importance of pure, integrated celibacy. Again, the Christian context for celibacy is very different from that of these religions. It brooks no low esteem of sexuality, and the motive for celibacy is undivided virginal union with a personal God who in Christ comes for the Messianic wedding feast. But the Oriental emphasis can strengthen our appreciation for celibacy as a way of enriching rather than impoverishing human life.

d) Islam

A fallen away Catholic officer observed the devout prayers of his Muslim soldiers in colonial Algeria in the first years of the 20th century. He marveled at their deep faith, their awareness of God's majesty and glory, as they prostrated themselves no matter where they were in adoration, praise, and thanksgiving five times every day. Through their prayers, the young French officer, Charles de Foucauld, came to realize that God is real and found his way back to his Catholic faith. Brother Charles, as he came to be called, spent the rest of his life as a hermit priest among the poorest of the poor in Africa. The role Islam played in his conversion will, I hope, prove paradigmatic for many post-Christian agnostics and even for believing Christians who tend to reduce God to a sweet and harmless grandfather figure. For us all Islam is a providential warning and educational tool to rediscover the majesty and greatness of God, which ought to shake up our complacent familiarity with or haughty indifference towards him. Only if we are first awed by God's holiness can we appreciate the undeserved intimacy that the incarnate Son grants to his brothers and sisters.

e) Judaism

The very existence of a believing Jewish remnant confirms our Christian faith in God's fidelity and our hope in the eschatological fulfillment of Salvation History. We are gradually discovering what it means that we Gentile Christians are like wild branches grafted into the cultivated olive tree which is historic Israel. "We do not support the root (the sacred beginnings of Israel) but the root supports us." Unless we share in the rich sap of the root, we will wither away (Rm 11:11-24). Christian faith loses its own identity and becomes the Marcionite heresy if cut off from its Old Testament roots. Without it the person and teaching of Christ, our whole New Testament, becomes unintelligible and distorted.

Moreover, if we take seriously its Old Testament preparation, the Incarnation appears in a new light. In embracing all humankind, God has embraced first of all his own chosen people, his adopted son (Ex 4:22-23): he chose to become man by becoming the new, eschatological Israel. As the canticles of Mary and Simeon sing out in joy, the Jesus event is first an exaltation of Israel and only through Israel the exaltation of all humankind (Lk 1:54-55; 2:29-32).

After surveying the tasks and benefits of dialogue for Christianity, we should at least begin to explore the other side: what benefits, if any, derive for adherents of other religions from a dialogue with Christians? From a Christian perspective the most important benefit seems to be a shift toward a personal relationship with the Transcendent and universal love of neighbor within many religions. That representatives of almost all religions accepted John Paul II's call to pray for universal peace in 1986 and once again after the destruction of the Twin Towers in 2001 is a case in point. You can pray only to a Personal Reality of some kind, and you pray for universal peace only if you care for all humankind. However, this shift is welcomed by some and rejected by other members within the same religion. Ironically, the move towards a Personal Absolute and universal love seems to bring about a division within the religions themselves.

These ominous fault lines have recently come to light most clearly in Islam. Muslims who concentrate on love of God and love of neighbor seem marginalized by the fundamentalists for whom the shari'ah, the Islamic law, overrules the emphasis on love.[18]

---

[18] The life and death of the Trappist Cistercian, Christian de Chergé, illustrates this point most eloquently. Prior of a Cistercian monastery in Thiberine, Algeria, Fr. Christian admired and loved the faith and piety of his Muslim neighbors to the point of dedicating his whole life to praying for and with them. When Islamic radicals demanded that all foreigners leave Algeria, their Muslim neighbors begged Fr. Christian and his fellow monks to stay. They did so and in a short time they were kidnapped by Islamic terrorists and executed in 1996. The encounters between Muslims and Christians have brought to light and strengthened the love of God and love of neighbor in some Muslims and provoked hatred in others.

Conclusions

The anthropological basis for inter-religious dialogue derives from the dialogical structure of human knowing and its necessity from the different but interrelated roles of the Son and Holy Spirit in our salvation. On the one hand, in his incarnate Son, Jesus Christ, God has condensed his Word, the fullness of revelation that had been prepared and prefigured by the Old Testament and was extended through the Church to all times and places. On the other, the Holy Spirit's universally offered grace has been accepted by some adherents of "other religions" and found a more or less ambiguous yet enlightening expression in their structures (writings, rites, and moral code). The Holy Spirit comes from the Father through Christ's death and resurrection, engraves in whomever welcomes him the features of Christ, and leaves his imprint in their actions and writings. These elements of Christic revelation that bring forth Christ-like features in adherents of other religions need to be acknowledged, purified, and integrated into an ever-growing understanding of the mystery of Christ.

There is no contradiction between affirming the fullness of revelation in Jesus Christ and the need for integrating truths of other religions into our understanding of this revelation. Since the man Jesus Christ is God the Son, his personal presence reveals the indivisible fullness of him who is the Word of God. Truths recovered from other religions are not parallel or complementary to this revelation but rather bring to light its hidden or forgotten treasures.

However, integration must be preceded by critical discernment. In today's theological climate it is unpopular and yet imperative to recall that the Fall (including original sin and the avalanche of personal sins that followed) has thoroughly affected the religious structures of non-Christian religions. The mixture of truth and falsehood, the results of the contradictory influences of sin and grace need to be sorted out carefully before other religions can enrich Christianity.

Yet, this enrichment is willed by Providence and even in our own times God wants to teach his Church some of her own half-forgotten or never fully appropriated truths by using other religions. Thus, genuine learning can and should take place: the condensed fullness of God's revelation is destined to unfold also by an ongoing dialogue with other religions.

Finally, we have seen that inter-religious dialogue is beneficial also for the "other religions." The encounter with Christ's teachings brings to light and strengthens the Christic elements in these religions. Even though they may cause divisions within a given religion, such rays of light and seeds of truth will comfort and strengthen those members who are obedient to the operation of the Holy Spirit.

Chapter II

EVANGELIZATION

Dialogue cannot replace the Church's duty to proclaim the Gospel to all human beings; it must, however, remain an intrinsic element of announcing the Christian message. In other words, we must always respect what is true in the religion of those whom we evangelize and remain open to learn from them such truths that we in the Church at a given time and place in history have forgotten or have actually never discovered. The Holy Spirit may want to teach us also through other religions!

However, in today's theological climate I sense a wide-spread uneasiness about this dialogical form of evangelization. Many feel that only a fundamentalist approach to evangelization could reasonably argue for its urgency. At first glance, only those who believe that no one can be saved without an explicit faith in Jesus as Savior could identify today with St. Francis Xavier's anguished cry from India:

> Many, many people hereabouts are not becoming Christians for one reason only: there is nobody to make them Christians. Again and again I have thought of going round the universities of Europe, especially Paris, and everywhere crying out like a madman, riveting the attention of those with more learning than charity: "What a tragedy: how many souls are being shut out of heaven and falling into hell, thanks to you."[19]

---

[19] H. Tursellini, *Vita Francisci Xaverii*, Rome, 1956, *Liber* 4, *Epist.* 4, quoted in the *Liturgy of the Hours*, vol. I, p. 1211.

Today no Catholic theologian would accept Francis's desperate conclusion without at least some qualifications. In the 20th century we have gradually recovered a more ancient, patristic tradition which, after the Middle Ages, the mainstream of Catholic theology had forgotten. St. Justin had no difficulty in arguing that there were Christians before Christ, people like Socrates, who had the seeds of the Word in their souls and lived according to the Word. St. Irenaeus and St. Hilary insisted that the Word of God had been shining throughout the whole duration of human history and illumined all those who opened the windows of their souls to him. In the 12th century St. Bernard still allowed for the salvation of even the infants of pagans in virtue of their parents' faith, a faith that manifested itself in offering sacrifices to God. Thus, according to a patristic and medieval tradition salvation cannot be restricted to the visible boundaries of the Church. Beginning with the excommunication of Fr. L. Feeney (who maintained that only baptized Catholics and Catholic catechumens with an explicit desire for baptism may be saved),[20] through the conciliar documents *Lumen Gentium* and *Gaudium et Spes*, up to the recent encyclical *Redemptoris Missio* (1990), the Magisterium itself began to emphasize the real possibility of salvation not only for non-Catholic Christians but also for all human beings, including some kinds of atheists.[21]

However, this renewed emphasis on the possibility of universal salvation has made it difficult for many Catholics to believe in the urgency of evangelization. If *Gaudium et Spes* and *Redemptoris Missio* are right in asserting that the gift of the Holy Spirit is offered to all humankind, if through the Spirit all human

---

[20] See Henricus Denzinger & Adolphus Schönmetzer, *Enchiridion Symbolorum Definitionum et Declarationum de Rebus Fidei et Morum*, 36th revised ed. (Freiburg: Herder, 1976), 3866-3873.

[21] See *Lumen Gentium*, nn. 14-17; *Ad Gentes*, n. 3; *Gaudium et Spes*, n. 22, all recalled in *Redemptoris Missio* nn. 9-11, 28-29. From now on *Redemptoris Missio* will be referred to as RM.

beings may participate in the Paschal mystery of Christ, why is evangelization necessary at all? In spite of his own intention, K. Rahner's writings about anonymous Christianity have led a number of his disciples to conclusions Rahner himself had never intended, conclusions that have seriously undermined the importance of evangelization.[22] One conspicuous example is the essay of H.R. Schlette. While stressing the incomparable superiority of Christianity above all other religions and the importance of missions in order to reveal the definitive eschatological self-revelation of God in Jesus Christ, he calls non-Christian religions the ordinary way of salvation and Christianity the extraordinary way.[23] In spite of Schlette's personal emphasis on evangelization, the reader may easily draw the opposite conclusion: why should everybody belong to the "elite" to whom the visible, social, historical manifestation of grace has been granted if this grace is anonymously yet truly operative in every religion? Giving a name to what one already possesses seems to be like cosmetic surgery: it may embellish one's faith, but does not seem to add anything essential to what the non-Christian does already have, namely the direction of his whole existence towards God and God's immediate,

---

[22] Rahner's most important articles on this issue are "Christianity and the Non-Christian Religions," *Theol. Invest.* 5 (Baltimore, MD: Helicon, 1966), 115-134; "Anonymous Christians," *Theol. Invest.* 6 (Baltimore, MD: Helicon, 1969), 390-398; "Anonymous Christianity and the Missionary Task of the Church," *Theol. Invest.* 12 (New York: Seabury, 1974), 161-180; "The One Christ and the Universality of Salvation," *Theol. Invest.* 16 (New York: Seabury, 1979), 199-224. We must admit that Rahner's works lend themselves to an ambiguous interpretation. For instance, he was unable to comprehend the importance of the distinction of H. de Lubac, who accepted the existence of anonymous Christians but rejected the possibility of anonymous Christianity ("anonymes Christentum"). See H. de Lubac, *The Church: Paradox and Mystery* (New York: Alba House, 1969), 68-95. For Rahner, the two expressions refer to the same reality, either a group of anonymous Christians or that reality by which people become anonymous Christians. He does not seem to perceive the danger of a third interpretation, which many of his followers have adopted: all major religions are basically equivalent expressions of God's one transcendental self-revelation; Christianity only uncovers the true identity of these religions (see "Anonymous Christianity and the Missionary Task of the Church," 163-170).

[23] *Towards a Theology of Religions* (New York: Herder & Herder, 1966), 79-81.

transforming presence in his heart. If the vast majority of humankind reaches God through other religions, for a democratic mentality the conclusion is quite obvious: why bother about the extraordinary way of a minority?

Add to this misunderstood interpretation of anonymous
Christianity the recent insistence on cultural pluralism, and you
will be drawn to what Paul Knitter calls a "genuine pluralistic
Christology."[24] If Christianity has remained the way of a minority for two millennia, it must be providential. We then have every
right, affirm Knitter and other Christological pluralists, to question the grounds, historical or theological, on the basis of which
Christianity has traditionally been called the definitive and complete self-revelation of God. Knitter would admit the validity of
this claim only for Christians. For those raised in non-Christian
religions there may be and there actually are other definitive
revealers, in particular, Mohammed and Buddha. They all reveal
the same God; they are all "Christs" in this sense. As P. Knitter
has put it: "The totality of Jesus is the Christ but the totality of
the Christ not Jesus."[25] For a pluralist Christology, evangelization
among the adherents of other religions makes no sense whatsoever. It calls only for a dialogue in which every partner is led to
recognize the equivalence of a variety of definitive revealers and
the infinite riches of God's revelation is to be discovered under
new aspects and modalities in different religions. In the pluralist
perspective, evangelization could easily be perceived as a form of
cultural aggression, an attempt to subjugate and oppress another
religious culture. In the first perspective, that of a distorted
Rahnerian ecclesiology, evangelization is legitimate and useful, but

---

[24] See P. Knitter, "Christianity as Religion: True and Absolute? A Roman Catholic Perspective," *Concilium*, 136 (New York: Seabury Press, 1980), 12-21; L. Swidler, editor,
Toward a Universal Theology of Religion (New York: Orbis, 1987). For a full bibliography on the various theologies of religions see J.A. Dinoia, *The Diversity of Religions. A
Christian Perspective* (Washington: CUA, 1992), 171-194. Dinoia himself argues for a
more nuanced position than the alternatives listed above.

[25] "Christianity as Religion: True and Absolute?", 18.

not necessary. In the logic of the second, that of pluralist Christologies, evangelization becomes an illegitimate, in fact morally questionable, activity.[26] If evangelization among the adherents of non-Christian religions in general is unimportant or illegitimate, then a new evangelization appears even more so.

In the present chapter I will not deal with the "anti-mission" implication of pluralist Christologies, since their position is manifestly opposed to the essentials of Catholic faith. My goal is to dialogue with the representatives of the first view, with those who emphasize so much the real possibility of universal salvation that they fail to perceive the urgent need for a universal evangelization. I intend to show that the real possibility of salvation outside the visible boundaries of the Church and the necessity of evangelization are not only not contradictory but interdependent and complementary truths.

Summing up both patristic tradition and the doctrine of Vatican II, *Redemptoris Missio* contains up to now the most explicit statement of the Magisterium about the universal offer of the grace of Christ in the Holy Spirit to all human beings throughout the entire duration of human history. At the same time, *Redemptoris Missio* is also the most comprehensive magisterial statement about the theological necessity and urgency of evangelization. However, *Redemptoris Missio* only hints at how the above two truths are interdependent and complementary (cf. RM 11). My goal here is to attempt to explain this connection in greater detail and to point out some reasons why we can rightly speak about a new evangelization.

First, we need to understand the meaning and theological grounds for evangelization, then the meaning and theological

---

[26] I must confess that I have not found any explicit anti-mission statement in any of the works of the pluralist Christologists. The above are simply my conclusions that I believe follow logically from the premises of a pluralist Christology. In a personal conversation with me, however, P. Knitter has emphatically affirmed the desirability of Christian evangelization.

grounds for the universal possibility of salvation; if this job is well done, their conjunction should appear as a necessity.

1. Evangelization

The two mysteries which show evangelization as constitutive of the Church are the Trinitarian missions and the social and physical-spiritual nature of man.[27] Both mysteries find their ultimate intelligibility in the one divine plan of salvation: it is the one and the same Triune God who has decided to create humans as social beings and as psychosomatic unities and to save them in accord with their created nature.

The Father's love is universal: Beyond relating to human beings as their Creator, he has adopted us so that we may become, not only by legal title but in reality, his very children. In his infinite generosity the Father wants "an innumerable multitude" to share in the very being of his only Son and in the Son's relationship to his Father.

The Father's love respects our social and physical-spiritual nature, which he has created. Thus, he has communicated the fullness of his divinity to humankind in such a way that his own perfect, consubstantial self-expression, the Son himself, has become a flesh and blood human being. The Father's will is that all human beings should participate in the being and existence of the man Jesus, in whom the fullness of divinity dwells. In order to conform to the demands of human nature, this participation has to be both physical and spiritual. Since the human being is the substantial unity of body and soul, or using a contemporary expression in the same sense, he is a psychosomatic unity, the human spirit comes to itself, expressing and perfecting all spiritual

---

[27] In addition to the documents of the Magisterium, I am most indebted in this section to Y. Congar, "Die katholische Kirche," *Mysterium Salutis*, vol. 4/1 (Einsiedeln: Benziger, 1972), 478-502.

activities, in and through the body; moreover, communication with other human beings and communion with them in love are also perfected in the body. These same laws must then apply to our communication with Christ and to our communion with him and with one another in him.

The Son's mission is also universal: while his historical life and activity were as limited as that of any other human being and purposely restricted to the "lost sheep of Israel," he offered his life as sacrifice for the many (for all) and intercedes with his Father for the forgiveness of all sins and for the unity of all in him and in the Father.

The goal of the Son's mission is not only a universal spiritual bond with us, but a union both physical and spiritual, since he himself is God made man and wants to unite to himself the whole man, soul and body. Just as he has given his flesh for the life of the world, so does he want to unite all human beings to his crucified and risen "body-person," whose presence and activity is extended throughout the ages by means of the sacramental signs, teachings, and the community of the Church.

In order to accomplish this task of uniting us to himself in his Church, the Son sends both the apostles and the Holy Spirit from the Father. The apostles testify to the mystery of Christ crucified and risen by human words and actions and, ultimately, by giving up their lives for him. The Spirit accompanies their testimony and makes it effective. He does not remain outside the hearers but enters their innermost being: in everyone who receives him, the Holy Spirit himself is directly present and enables the hearer to receive the human words of the apostles as the divinely guaranteed Word of God (1 Th 2:13). He becomes in the recipient a principle of new life and action. Since the Spirit is both the Spirit of the Father and the Son, his activity has no other purpose than to carve out in us the features of Christ, conform us to his dying and rising, and thereby perfect our filial relationship to the Father. In other words, the Spirit does not offer an alternative to

Christ (RM 29) but rather—in different ways and to different degrees—he offers all men and women everywhere and at all times a participation in the paschal mystery of the crucified and risen Christ (GS 22, RM 10). To the extent that this one transcendent subject becomes personally present and active in people, he will draw them into a spiritual and visible communion that conforms to human nature and to the nature of the incarnate Son. This communion is infinitely more spiritual than any mere human communion of souls and minds could be, since one and the same Divine Spirit is the transcendent subject who acts in all members and joins all members together. Yet the communion of the Church is also essentially visible since in her sacraments, preaching, and service of love she continues to carry out and manifest the actions and sufferings of Christ in this world.

In summary, then, the Church's universal mission of evangelization derives from the universal love of the Father, Son, and Holy Spirit, and from the Triune God's respect for the laws of human nature in its physical and social dimensions.

If we understand by catholicity both universality and totality as patristic theology does, we might define the theological foundation of evangelization in these terms: the catholicity of Trinitarian love calls for the catholicity of the Church so that she may extend this love to all humankind, transform the totality of every human being, not only his soul but also his body, and create a universal community which embodies in itself the universal love of the Holy Trinity. Briefly put, the Church's evangelizing mission is a necessary actualization of her catholicity.

2. The Universal Possibility of Salvation

From what has been proposed above regarding the foundations, nature, and scope of the mission of the Church (Trinitarian love respecting the structure of human nature and existence), the reasons for the universal possibility of salvation have also become manifest. If God's love indeed embraces all human beings without exception, if the incarnate Son died for all, if the operation of the Holy Spirit transcends the limitations of space and time as well as social and cultural barriers, and if human nature as it concretely exists is everywhere and always ordained to a supernatural fulfillment, then salvation must be available always and everywhere. At the same time, however, it has also become evident that the Father's universal love wants to gather all God's children into one visible and spiritual community. That is salvation in the full sense of the word, a salvation already available here on earth. The Church's visible mission, however, going from Christ to the apostles and their successors (while including in this task the whole Church, every local community, and every individual member) is necessarily limited by space and time, by the inertia and sinful negligence of her individual members and communities. The work of evangelization is also hindered by the missionaries' inability to overcome the cultural and sociological barriers which separate them from the peoples to whom they are sent. Also, the listeners are often prevented by their own cultural limitations to perceive God's Word in the language of an alien culture. Unlike the many limitations of the Church's visible mission, "the Spirit blows where he wills," all hearts and thoughts are open to him; sin alone closes one off to his life-giving activity. Hence according to Vatican II and *Redemptoris Missio*, the Spirit has sown the "seeds of the Word" not only in individual non-Christians but also in non-Christian cultures and religions. *Redemptoris Missio* insists on this universal effectiveness of the Holy Spirit to the extent that it does not hesitate to speak about the "incipiens Regnum" (beginnings of the Kingdom of God) outside the visible boundaries of the Church (RM 20).

Taking the lead from the same magisterial documents we can also provide examples of the many activities of the Spirit among non-Christians; all forms of self-sacrificing love, all efforts to promote the dignity of the human person, the unconditional obedience to the voice of one's conscience, all genuine prayer, and the desire for true goodness come from the same Holy Spirit whose fullness dwells in Christ and in the Church. Even when one is not reflexively aware of the work of the Holy Spirit in himself, and does not have an explicit knowledge of Christ, the Spirit still leads him to participate in the Paschal mystery. To the extent that he is inspired by the Holy Spirit, he will seek to die to selfishness, affirm and do what is good, and especially practice the Golden Rule. By living in this way, he will call forth opposition and persecution by those who reject the Holy Spirit, but in the midst of his sufferings he will in some way experience the power of love and goodness that comes from the risen Christ. This experience may not be anything else than the conviction that love is worth any suffering or a longing for the triumph of justice and goodness, a longing which contains within itself a glimmer of hope for its fulfillment. To put it simply, the Spirit, at least in some initial way, conforms to the pattern of Christ the living, acting, and dying of those who are open to his promptings, even if they lack an explicit knowledge of Christ or the Holy Spirit.[28]

3. The Link between the Universal Possibility of Salvation and the Church

If the Holy Spirit leads us always and everywhere to Christ, if Christ is available in his Word and in his crucified and risen Body only in the Church, and if human encounter can be perfected only in a visible and tangible way, then being on the way to salvation is the same as being on the way towards the Church.

---

[28] The pagan Job of the Old Testament has been presented by the Fathers, especially Gregory the Great, as a saint who foreshadowed in his destiny the suffering of the innocent Christ. From among non-Christians of our times, the life and death of Mohandas Gandhi stands out for me as a prime illustration of this universal Christic pattern of holiness. Gandhi taught his people to love their enemies, the British colonists; he persisted in preaching non-violence in spite of violent opposition, and was murdered by one of his fellow Hindus since he refused to endorse the war against the Muslims.

There can be many historical and cultural obstacles because of which someone moved by the Spirit will never formally join the Church, yet grace always and everywhere impels one towards it.

Thus, neglecting or opposing evangelization is neglecting or opposing the will of the Triune God: one ignores the Father, who sent his Son so that all may know him in the fullest way possible; one ignores the love of Christ, who died for all human beings so that they may eat his flesh and drink his blood; and one ignores the Holy Spirit, who impels everyone open to his grace towards finding that community where the Spirit is explicitly recognized and his all-embracing love is acknowledged and appreciated.

Moreover, to the extent that a society becomes closed to the Gospel, the spiritual and moral quality of life in that society is seriously jeopardized: the inviolable dignity of the human person (especially the unborn, the poor, and the terminally ill) as well as love for one's enemies will lack a sufficient foundation. Without the Judeo-Christian tradition, scientific and technological progress could easily turn destructive. On the other hand, if the awareness that every human being is a child of God, redeemed by the blood of the Son of God, and is called to intimate communion with the Father transforms the general atmosphere of society, a high appreciation of the individual human beings will make life qualitatively happier and more peaceful.

In a non-Christian society, if a non-Christian, moved by the grace of the Holy Spirit, wants to translate into words and action his grace-given intuition, he has to oppose, at least partly, the express beliefs of his culture or religious community.[29] Thus, entering the Church means for a grace-inspired non-Christian[30] to take a critical stance towards his cultural milieu and come home.

---

[29] Again, a foremost example is Mohandas Gandhi who, by showing a preferential love for the pariahs, the outcastes, turned against a major tenet of his Hindu heritage, the religiously sanctioned caste system.

[30] I purposely use this expression instead of Rahner's "Anonymous Christian." The latter was rightly criticized for attributing Christianity to those who expressly deny being Christians.

He enters a community where he is supported in his life of grace, where he can participate in the building of a Christian society and culture so that God's grace may permeate and transform every aspect of human life.

In summary, the salvation of every human being is necessarily directed toward the Church, insofar as she is the goal to which every human being tends by the very dynamism of the grace received, even though his formal entering into the Church may often be prevented by causes beyond the individual's personal responsibility (RM 10). We should do everything in our power to remove these obstacles so that the grace-inspired non-Christian may come home in the Church. By entering the Church through (explicit) faith and baptism, the individual's "quality of life" will be immensely enhanced, and he or she, in turn, will be able to contribute to the building of Christian culture, an improvement of the quality of life for all humanity.

However, it would be naïve to think that everyone who hears the preaching of the Gospel has already accepted God's sanctifying grace beforehand. Those who are already in the state of sanctifying grace when hearing the Gospel would merely discover their true identity and that reality for which, or rather for whom, they have already longed for. However, in real life many people have long resisted the grace that has been offered to them. For these, the hearing of the Word of Christ preached by the Church may become that providential impulse which would break the sinner's resistance to the inward working of grace. In other words, the hearing of the external word of preaching combined with the inner voice of grace may become the privileged moment of conversion, the passage from death to life. In such cases the mysterious connection (RM 10) between salvation and the Church includes also the explicit mediation of salvation by an ecclesial act.

Here, however, a further question arises: beyond the simple cases of conversion when listening to ecclesial preaching, and beyond the *ex opere operato* bestowal of grace through the sacraments, how can one explain the traditional teaching that all grace comes in some sense through the mediation of the Church? *Redemptoris Missio* and the conciliar documents of Vatican II affirm or imply but do not explain that the Church is not only the anticipation of the eschatological goal and form of salvation, but also "the instrument of the redemption of all."[31] How can this universal instrumentality be maintained in face of the massive evidence that the majority of human beings have not heard the Gospel, let alone received any of the Church's sacraments?

For lack of space I cannot survey the whole tradition on this matter; I can only summarize what I consider its main points of emphasis.

The Church's universal mediation can be considered on two levels, connected yet distinct. We might call them Eucharistic and existential mediation. Both are rooted in the same mystery: Christ has associated the Church to himself in the work of salvation. As Blessed Isaac of Stella declares: "The humble and faithful Bridegroom does not want to do anything without his Bride."[32] Thus, just as all saving grace comes from Christ, all saving grace must also include the mediating role of the Church. In a Catholic context it needs no explanation that even this active cooperation of the Church is the gift of Christ: Christ grants his Bride not only to be united to him but also to cooperate with him in extending the bridal union to an ever greater multitude. Thereby the Bride becomes mother: she truly gives birth to Christ in all who open themselves up to his grace.[33]

---

[31] LG 9, quoted by RM 9. See also LG 1: "The Church is in Christ as it were a sacrament, that is, the sign and instrument of intimate union with God and of the unity of the entire human race." Cf. LG 48.

[32] Isaac applies this general principle: "Nihil vult sine Sponsa humilis et fidelis Sponsus" (Sermon 11, 14) to the forgiveness of sins; no sin is remitted without the Church. Obviously, Isaac does not think that sins are remitted only in the actual reception of the sacrament of penance, yet he does not hesitate to make such a general statement. Thus, if no forgiveness of sins may occur without some role of the Church, neither can any saving grace be received without her.

[33] See H. de Lubac, *The Motherhood of the Church* (San Francisco: Ignatius, 1982).

The level of Eucharistic mediation means that Christ has given over to his Church his crucified and risen Body and Blood, the sacrifice he has once and for all offered on the Cross for all humankind. Thus, wherever the Holy Eucharist is offered, the ecclesial act of offering by the priest and community truly participates in Christ's once and for all act of self-offering, which has given shape and form to his glorified existence in heaven.[34]

This sacramental participation in the self-offering of Christ calls for an existential appropriation: those who have sacramentally shared in the sacrifice of Christ for all the living and the dead, the sacrifice which "advances the peace and salvation of all the world," are invited to offer "through Christ, with Christ, and in Christ" their own personal lives for all. The most perfect existential appropriation of the universal sacrifice of Christ is that of Mary who—inspired by God's grace—has given her free consent not only to the Incarnation but also to the life-long self-offering of her Son, which has been brought to perfection on the cross.[35] In other words, she has given Christ to the world not only physically, but also spiritually, and in Christ she has also given the fullness of grace. Her motherhood is truly universal, since she wants to share with all human beings the fullness of divine life that she has received for all of us. Every member of the Church is called to share in the motherhood of Mary: the grace one receives is received not only for oneself, but also for sharing with others, by action and prayer, by the offering of one's living and dying.[36]

The awareness of this universal mediation of the Church and of every member of the Church for all human beings is today at a very low ebb in the Church. Yet, unless we rediscover it, the new em-

---

[34] The risen Christ retains his wounds and stands "in the midst of the throne as if slain" (Rv 5:6; cf. Jn 20:20, 27).

[35] See the scriptural foundations for it in A. Feuillet, "L'heure de la femme (Jn 16,21) et l'heure de la Mère de Jésus (Jn 19,25-27)," *Biblica* 47 (1966), 169-84, 361-80, 557-73; the data of patristic tradition combined with those of Scripture are built into LG chapter VIII and the discourse of Paul VI at the closing of Vatican II.

[36] See H. de Lubac, *The Motherhood of the Church* (San Francisco: Ignatius Press, 1982).

phasis on evangelization will remain nothing but a catchy slogan.

Once all members of the Church become aware of their responsibility for the salvation of all, even for those whom they do not know, this missionary awareness will give a new dimension to every act and suffering in their lives. St. Thérèse of Lisieux, terminally ill with tuberculosis and hardly able to move, said matter of factly: "I am walking for a missionary." We are all called to walk and live for other people, and through those people, in some way, always for everybody else, for all humankind; charity is either universal or non-existent. Only if I accept all my fellow human beings as brothers and sisters, can I truly love that person whom Providence places next to me. Only if we all become "universal brothers and sisters" will we heed God's voice in case he calls us to an explicit missionary vocation.[37]

Today, then, a new Francis Xavier's cry for help would not be less urgent but only somewhat different from that of the saint in the 16th century. He might call attention to the fact that there are souls among the adherents of other religions and among non-religious people who are so sensitive to pure love and truth that they seem to obey already an impulse of grace. How would one dare to deny them the Christ towards whom the Holy Spirit is leading them? How could one deny them access to the knowledge of the Truth and the fullness of God's gift who is Christ in the Eucharist? Rejection of a missionary vocation is indeed an act of opposing the Holy Spirit, who wants all human beings to embrace the fullness of Christ in the Church where alone this fullness of joy can be found. Could we justify our refusal by pointing out that this person already loves God (at least) implicitly, so he might be saved without our cooperation?[38] One worries today so much about

---

[37] RM 89 borrowed this expression from the spirituality of Bl. Charles de Foucauld: the members of the religious communities inspired by his Rule like to call themselves "universal brothers or sisters."

[38] This would be tantamount to justifying our refusal to re-unite a lost child with his family on the flimsy ground: "Why worry about bringing this child home? He is already close to his family since he loves them in his heart. Physical closeness is not that important."

the quality of life; but what quality of life is it to possess all the material comforts and not to know about a heavenly Father who gave us his only Son so that we might all live forever with him?

Our new Francis Xavier would also call attention to those people, religious, irreligious, or agnostic, who show all the signs of resisting grace: they are hardened by hatred, trying to control the divine through the magic use of the rites of non-Christian religions, or striving to achieve self-deification through meditation and other spiritual exercises. In God's plan the way to conversion for them may be precisely the encounter with a community in whom Christ is truly present. But even if these people would not turn to Christ, our duty to preach the Gospel to them is the same. The terrible words of the Lord to Ezekiel remain in effect also for the Christian missionary:

> You, son of man, I have appointed watchman for the house of Israel; when you hear me say anything, you shall warn them for me. If I tell the wicked man that he shall surely die, and you do not speak out to dissuade the wicked man from his way, he shall die for his guilt, but I will hold you responsible for his death! (Ezk 33:7-8)

Evangelization, then, even today, or perhaps more than ever today,[39] is a matter of life and death, eternal life and eternal death, both for some of those to be evangelized and certainly for the evangelizer. In some way each one of us should echo St. Paul's cry that John Paul II felt obliged to repeat in the name of the whole Church: "Woe to me if I do not preach the Gospel!"[40]

---

[39] The duty to evangelize is more urgent today than ever before since the human situation is becoming more critical and we have learned more about the right way of evangelizing which includes inculturation and dialogue. In the past, missionaries in good faith often tried to impose their own culture upon the natives as part of the Gospel and thereby created unnecessary obstacles to conversion.

[40] 1 Cor 9:16 (quoted in RM 1).

READER'S GUIDE

The ensuing selective bibliography is aimed at increasing and deepening the knowledge the readers have obtained from reading the preceding chapters, while the Review Questions are designed to help their understanding of both the text and the recommended literature.

Part I: A Philosophical Approach to Reality and its Meaning

Further Readings

Berger, Peter. *A Rumor of Angels. Modern Society and the Rediscovery of the Supernatural.* New York: Anchor Books, 1990. Berger shows the transcendent dimension of the many facets of everyday human experience. It can powerfully awaken the secularized reader.

Davies, Brian. *An Introduction to the Philosophy of Religion.* 3rd ed. New York: Oxford Univ. Press, 2004. It summarizes and ponders the various arguments for the existence of God through the history of philosophy.

Hick, John, ed. *Classical and Contemporary Readings in the Philosophy of Religion.* 2nd ed. Englewood Cliffs: Prentice Hall, 1970. A very informative collection of original texts proving and disproving the existence of God from Plato to the modern age. Especially relevant for contemporary readers is chapter 20: "The Existence of God. A Debate between Bertrand Russell and Father F. C. Copleston," 282-301.

Lonergan, Bernard J.F. *Insight: A Study of Human Understanding.* New York: Harper & Row, 1978. Lonergan shows God's existence within a post-Kantian epistemological and metaphysical synthesis. Read especially "General Transcendent Knowledge," 637-686.

de Lubac, Henri. *The Discovery of God.* Edinburgh: T & T Clark, 1996. This classic contains both philosophical insights and religious meditations. It served as a major source for my reflections in this chapter.

Nichols, Aidan. *A Grammar of Consent: The Existence of God in Christian Tradition.* Notre Dame: Univ. of Notre Dame Press, 1991. Starting from the "illative sense" of Newman, Nichols examines the many different approaches of the Christian tradition in order to build his case for a reasonable assent to the existence of God.

Weissmahr, Bela. *Philosophische Gotteslehre.* Stuttgart: 1994. A lucid transcendental Thomist approach to a philosophy of God. My approach in this chapter owes much to Weissmahr.

Review Questions

1. Show the inconsistency of the principle that only empirically verifiable statements can be accepted as true.
2. Why is cultural relativism or perspectivism inconsistent and self-destructive?
3. Show the self-contradictory character of the view according to which only religious experience matters and contradictory religious doctrines should be acceptable.
4. In our approach, what is the starting point of philosophical reflection?
5. How does the method of philosophy relate to that of the natural sciences?
6. Develop one argument for the existence of God in detail.
7. Show briefly that every aspect of reality points to an Absolute Reality.

Part II: A Survey of World Religions

Further Readings on Religions in General

Brandon, S.G.F., ed. *A Dictionary of Comparative Religion.* New York: Scribner, 1970. A somewhat dated yet informative reference work.

Burke, T. Patrick. *The Major Religions: An Introduction with Texts.* Cambridge: Blackwell Publisher, 1995. A reliable guide with a good selection of sacred texts from religions of Indian, Chinese, and Semitic Origin.

Eliade, Mircea. *Essential Sacred Writings from Around the World.* San Francisco: HarperSanFrancisco, 1992. A rich anthology of primary texts and of ancient oral traditions from most of the religions, beginning with the sky gods of primitive religions and ending with the Qur'an.

Eliade, Mircea. *Patterns in Comparative Religion.* 1958. Rpt. Lincoln: Univ. of Nebraska Press, 1996. Although dated, this work is still the best introduction to understanding the religious history of humankind.

Eliade, Mircea. *A History of Religious Ideas:* vol. I, *From the Stone Age to the Eleusian Mysteries;* vol. 2, *From Gautama Buddha to the Triumph of Christianity.* Chicago: Univ. of Chicago Press, 1978-82. Though less insightful than his *Patterns in Comparative Religion,* this book is still a rich storehouse of encyclopedic knowledge.

Esposito John L., Darrell J. Fasching, and Todd Lewis. *World Religions Today.* New York: Oxford Univ. Press, 2002. The book's strength constitutes also its weakness: it emphasizes the encounter of world religions with modernity rather than analyzing in depth their sacred writings.

Chapter I: Primitive Religions

Further Readings

Eliade, Mircea. *Patterns in Comparative Religion,* 38-366. In addition to other sources, Eliade draws also on the research of W. Schmidt and associates, but he understands the symbolic character of primitive religious sensitivity better than Schmidt.

_____. *The Sacred and the Profane: the Nature of Religion.* New York: Harcourt, Brace and World, 1959. Although less rich in data than *Patterns in Comparative Religion,* this book shows both primitive religions' links with, and differences from, modern sensitivity.

Schmidt, Wilhelm, et al. *Ursprung der Gottesidee.* 12 vols. Münster: 1926-
55. It contains a meticulously collected database for all primitive
religions. Its thoroughness remains unsurpassed up to this day. See
a one volume summary in English: Schmidt, *The Origin and
Growth of Religion: Facts and Theories.* tr. H.J. Rose. New York:
The Dial Press, 1931.

Review Questions

1. Describe the evidence for the probable first stage in the history of
   religions on the basis of the studies of M. Eliade and W. Schmidt.
2. Describe the conflict between the idea of divine transcendence and
   divine immanence in the history of religions.
3. What "happens" (in the imagination of peoples) to the sky-gods
   in the history of religions?
4. Compare the sky god to the biblical God.
5. Illustrate the definition of myth according to Eliade by explaining
   the Babylonian myth of creation, the "Enuma Elish."
6. Is Genesis 1-3 a myth? Answer this question by comparing the
   story in Genesis 1-3 to the "Enuma Elish."
7. How does the rest of biblical revelation (beginning with chapter
   12 of Genesis) differ from the world view of primitive myths?
8. Explain the meaning of primitive rites.
9. Compare the meaning of primitive rites to that of Christian rites.
   Use the example of immersion into water and that of a ritual killing of a god and compare the first to Christian baptism and the
   second to the Eucharist. Show both similarity and difference.

Chapter II: Hinduism

Further Readings

SACRED TEXTS:

Sarup, Laksman, ed., *Rgveda-Samhita with Rgarthadipika of Venkatamad-
hava.* 6 vols. Lahore: Motilal Banarasi Dass, 1939. English translation with commentary by R.T.H. Griffith, 2 vols. *Chowkhamba
Sanskrit Series,* 5th ed. Varanasi, 1971.

Weber, A., ed., *Yajurveda Vajasaneyi Samhita*. London: 1852. *Texts of the Yajurveda*, tr. R.T.H. Griffith, Benares, 1889.

Bandhu, Visva, ed., *Atharava-Veda-Samhita (Sauhaka) With Sayanacharya's commentary*. Hoshiarpur: Vishveshvarand Vedic Research Institute, 1960. Translation with commentary by R.T.H. Griffith. *Chowkhamba Sanskrit Series*. Reprint. Varanasi, 1968.

Samasrami, Satyavrata, ed., *Sama-Veda-Samhita, with Sayanacharya's Commentary*. Calcutta: Asiatic Society of Bengal, 1976. Translation with commentary by R.T.H. Griffith. *Chowkhamba Sanskrit Series*, 4th ed. Varanasi, 1963.

Nikhilananda, Swami, trans., *The Upanishads*, vols. 1-4. 2nd ed. New York: Vivekananda Center, 1975.

Radhakrishnan, S., trans., *The Principal Upanishads*. London: Allen & Unwin, 1951.

Rhadakrishnan, S., trans. *The Bhagavadgita*. London: Allen & Unwin, 1949.

Gambhirananda, Swami, trans. *Bhagavad Gita*. Commentary by Madhusudana Sarasvati. Calcutta: Advaita Ashrama, 1998.

STUDIES ON HINDUISM:

Griffiths, Bede. *River of Compassion: a Christian Commentary on the Bhagavad Gita*. Warwick: Amity House, 1987. Griffiths, a Benedictine monk who dedicated his life to Christian-Hindu dialogue, comments on the *Bhagavad Gita* from the viewpoint of Christian mysticism.

Pandit, Bansi. *The Hindu Mind: Fundamentals of Hindu Religion and Philosophy for Children Under Ninety*. Glen Ellyn: B & V Enterprises, 1992. It is a clear summary of contemporary mainline Hindu religion and religious philosophy.

Panikkar, Raimundo. *The Unknown Christ of Hinduism: Towards an Ecumenical Christophany*. Maryknoll: Orbis Books, 1981. Panikkar's Christian evaluation of Hinduism needs to be critically examined in the light of authentic Christian tradition and the teaching of the Magisterium.

Review Questions

1. Explain briefly the sacred Hindu writings: name, time of composition, content.
2. Describe the main features of classic Hinduism: polytheism (Dyaus Pita, Varuna, Indra, Brahma, Vishnu, Shiva, Krishna, Rama) 'karma,' 'samsara,' caste system.
3. Explain the notion of Brahman and the relationship between Brahman, man, and the world in Sankara, Ramanuja, and Madhva.
4. Explain the figure of Krishna in the Bhagavad Gita. Compare this figure to the notion of Brahman.
5. Explain the ways of "liberation" in the Bhagavad Gita: meditation, yoga, unselfish performance of duty, 'bhakti.'
6. Give a Hindu evaluation of Christianity.
7. Give a Christian evaluation of Hinduism: what can a Christian accept or interpret in a positive sense and what can he not accept?

Chapter III: Buddhism

Further Readings

SACRED TEXTS:

The oldest Buddhist texts are contained in the Pali Canon called Tipitaka (Three Baskets). An incomplete translation (50 volumes, approximately 12,000 pages) is available from the Pali Text Society.
    Some other important editions of sacred Buddhist texts:

The Connected Discourses of the Buddha: A New Translation of Samyutta Nikaya. tr. Bhikku Nikaya. 2 vols. Boston: Wisdom Publications, 2000.

The Middle Length Discourses of the Buddha: A New Translation of the Majjhina Nikaya. tr. Bhikku Nanomoli and Bhikku Bodhi. Boston: Wisdom Publications, 1995.

The Long Discourses of the Buddha: A Translation of the Digha Nikaya. tr. Maurice Walsh. Boston: Wisdom Publ., 1996.

Buddhist Texts Through the Ages, eds. Edward Conze, et al. Rpt Oxford: Oneworld Publ., 1995.

The Religions of Tibet in Practice. Princeton: Princeton Univ. Press, 1997.

CLASSIC ZEN TEXTS:

The Bodhidharma Anthology: The Earliest Records of Zen. ed. Jeffrey L. Broughton. Berkeley: University of California Press, 1999.

Classics of Buddhism and Zen. tr. Thomas Cleary & J.C. Cleary. 4 vols. Boston: Shambhala, 2002.

The Heart of Dogen's Shobogenzo. tr. Norman Waddell & Masao Abe. New York: SUNY, 2002.

STUDIES ON BUDDHISM:

Buddhist Spirituality. Vol. I: *Indian, Southeast Asian, Tibetan and Early Chinese*; vol. II: *Later China, Korea, Japan and the Modern World.* New York: Crossroad Publishing, 1993, 1999. The single most insightful study of the various branches of Buddhism.

A Dictionary of Buddhism. ed. Damien Keown. New York: Oxford Univ. Press, 2003. It is a most comprehensive guide to every form of Buddhism.

The Zen Canon: Understanding the Classic Texts. ed. Steven Heine. New York: Oxford University Press, 2004.

The Dalai Lama. *Ethics for the New Millennium.* New York: Riverhead Books/Penguin Putnam Inc., 1999. Without engaging in an explicit ecumenical dialogue, the book formulates an ethics of universal responsibility and concern in such general terms that it could be embraced by Buddhists, Hindus, Christians, Jews and by peace-loving Muslims as well.

Dumoulin, Heinrich. *Zen Buddhism: A History.* 2 vols. Rpt. New York: Oxford University Press, 1994. This is one of the most reliable comprehensive histories of Zen.

Habito, Ruben L.F. *Healing Breath: Zen Spirituality for a Wounded Earth.* 2nd ed. Dallas: Maria Kannon Zen Center Publications, 2001. In its attempt to show the universal healing power of Zen spirituality, the book blurs the differences between the Christian and Zen vision of reality.

Hanh, Thich Nhat. *Living Buddha, Living Christ.* New York: Riverhead Books/Penguin Putnam Inc., 1995. The famous Zen Buddhist monk attempts to show the essential identity between the teachings of Jesus and the Buddha, but his insights apply mostly to the Gnostic Christ of the Nag Hammadi manuscripts.

Harvey, Peter. *An Introduction to Buddhism: Teachings, History, and Practices*. Cambridge: Cambridge Univ. Press, 1990.

Kapstein, Matthew T. *The Tibetan Assimilation of Buddhism: Conversion, Contestation and Memory*. New York: Oxford University Press, 2002.

de Lubac, Henri. *Aspects of Buddhism*. London: Sheed and Ward, 1953. This short work remains the best Christian evaluation of Buddhism.

Machida, Soho. *Renegade Monk: Honen and Japanese Pure Land Buddhism*. tr. Ioannis Mentzas. Berkeley: University of California Press, 1999.

Suzuki, D.T. *Zen and Japanese Culture*. Rpt. Princeton: Princeton University Press, 1993. An important bridge between Zen and Western culture.

Review Questions

1. Summarize the life of Buddha.
2. Explain in detail the Four Noble Truths.
3. What indicates that even original Buddhism has some understanding of Absolute Reality?
4. Describe Theravada (Hinayana) Buddhism, in particular
   (a) its understanding of the figure of Buddha,
   (b) its understanding of Nirvana,
   (c) their ideal lifestyle.
5. Describe Mahayana Buddhism, in particular
   (a) the re-appearance of Absolute Reality (=universal Buddha-nature)
   (b) karuna: compassion
   (c) the bodhisattva.
6. Give a Christian evaluation of each of the Four Noble Truths of original Buddhism.
7. Compare the Christian doctrine of compassion to that of Mahayana Buddhism.

8. Analyze the similarities and differences between the figure of a bodhisattva and the Suffering Servant of Isaiah 52:13-53:12.
9. Concerning Zen Buddhism, explain:
   (a) zazen
   (b) koan
   (c) satori
   (d) Does Zen Buddhism believe in God?
10. How could one differentiate between various experiences of Zen enlightenment from a Christian perspective?
11. Why is experience itself in need of discursive knowledge?

Chapter IV: The Religious Philosophies of Taoism and Confucianism

Further Readings

Wing-Tsit Chan. *A Sourcebook in Chinese Philosophy*. Princeton, NJ: Princeton Univ. Press, 1973. A comprehensive introduction with selected original texts and extensive bibliography (793-811).

LAO-TZU. *TAO TE CHING, THE BOOK OF THE WAY AND ITS VIRTUE.*
TRANSLATIONS:

Chen, Ellen M. New York: Paragon House, 1989. It contains also a good commentary and glossary.

Cleary, Thomas. *The Essential Tao*. New York: Harper Collins, 1993. It includes also the teachings of Chuang Tzu.

Fu-Feng, Gia and Jane English. New York: Random House, Vintage Books, 1972. A poetic, easily accessible translation.

McNaughton, William, ed. *The Taoist Vision*. Ann Arbor: The University of Michigan Press, 1971.

Waley, Arthur. *The Way and Its Power*. London: Allen and Unwin, 1935.

CONFUCIUS, *THE ANALECTS.*
TRANSLATION, INTRODUCTION AND ANNOTATIONS:

Brooks, E. Bruce and A. Taeko Brooks. *The Original Analects: Sayings of Confucius and His Successors.* New York: Columbia University Press, 1998.

Cleary, Thomas. *The Essential Confucius.* New York: Harper Collins, 1992.

Dawson, Raymond. Oxford: Oxford Univ. Press, 1993.

McNaughton, William, ed. *The Confucian Vision.* Ann Arbor: University of Michigan Press, 1974. It organizes the Confucian sayings according to topics.

Van Norden, Bryan W., ed. *Confucius and the Analects: New Essays.* New York: Oxford Univ. Press, 2002. It evaluates Confucian thought from various viewpoints by a variety of experts.

Waley, Arthur. New York: Random House, Vintage Books, 1989.

Review Questions

    1. Regarding Taoism, explain:
- (a) the concept of Tao,
- (b) yin and yang,
- (c) the qualities of the sage according to Taoism.
- (d) Comment on the similarities between Christian and Taoist morality
- (e) How does the metaphysical foundation of Taoism distance it from Christian morality?
- (f) How does the ambiguous meaning of te lead to magic in Taoist religion?

    2. Regarding Confucianism, explain:
- (a) life of Kung-Fu-Tzu,
- (b) the role of Heaven in Confucius' life and philosophy,
- (c) the Analects,
- (d) the basis tenets of Confucianist morality, in particular the notions of: te, chün-tzu, jen, shu and the five relationships.
- (e) What shows the absolute value of morality in Confucius' thought?
- (f) How does Confucius characterize a chün-tzu?
- (g) How does Christian ethics differ from Confucianism?

Chapter V: Islam

Further Readings

The Meaning of the Holy Qur'an. New edition with revised translation and commentary by Abdullah Yusuf Ali. Brentwood: Amana Corporation, 1993. It contains both the original Arabic text and a translation widely used by Muslims in the U.S. and equipped with a detailed commentary.

The Concise Encyclopedia of Islam. ed. Cyril Glassé. San Francisco: HarperSanFrancisco, 1991. A most informative encyclopedia written from an Islamic perspective.

The Oxford History of Islam. ed. John L. Esposito. New York: Oxford Univ. Press, 1999. A comprehensive and well-informed summary of Islamic history.

The Oxford Dictionary of Islam. ed. John L. Esposito. New York: Oxford University Press, 2002.

Islamic Spirituality, vol. I: *Foundations.* ed. Seyyed Hossein Nasr. New York: Crossroad, 1987.

Islamic Spirituality, vol. II: *Manifestations.* ed. Seyyed Hossein Nasr. New York: Crossroad, 1991/97. The two volumes of *Islamic Spirituality* are indispensable for understanding the sources and the spiritual dimension of Islam; they are also most fruitful sources for Islamic-Christian dialogue.

Firestone, Reuven. *Jihad: the Origin of Holy War in Islam.* New York: Oxford University Press, 2002. The author provides a plausible explanation for the origin of jihad.

Lings, Martin. *What Is Sufism?* London: George Allen and Unwen Ltd., 1975. An introduction to the mystical tradition in Islam.

Nasr, Seyyed Hossein. *The Heart of Islam.* San Francisco: HarperSan Francisco, 2002. Nasr is perhaps the most prominent representative of the spiritual dimension of Islam who is at the same time very cognizant of, and sympathetic to, the Christian tradition.

Nasr, Seyyed Hossein. "The Tariqah - The Spiritual Path and Its Quranic Roots." *Ideals and Realities of Islam*, 121-146. London: Allen and Unwin, 1985.

Ray, Marie-Christine. *Christian de Chergé Prieur de Tibhirine.* Paris: Bayard Editions, 1998. The fascinating history of the Trappist Cistercian, Fr. Christian, and his monks in Tibhirine, Algeria, their friendship with the neighboring Muslims, and their martyrdom at the hands of Islamic terrorists.

Rumi: A Spiritual Treasury. ed. Juliet Mabey. Oxford: Oneworld, 2002. A collection of beautiful religious poetry by one of the most prominent representatives of Sufi mysticism.

Review Questions

1. What makes it difficult to write a biography of Muhammad?
2. What can be known about him with a reasonable degree of certainty?
3. Describe the essential message of Muhammad.
4. Characterize the Qur'an by comparing it to the Bible.
5. Explain the Five Pillars of Islam.
6. Comment on the different interpretations of jihad.
7. Show similarities and differences between Sufi and Christian mysticism.
8. Explain in detail what the Qur'an says about Jesus, Mary, and the Trinity.
9. How is the Muslim conception of state and Islam different from the Christian understanding of the relationship between state and religion? How can you show that the Islamic conception derives from Muhammad himself?

Chapter VI: Judaism

Further Readings

Jewish Study Bible. Jewish Publication Society. 2nd ed. New York: Oxford University Press, 1999. Contains an introduction to each book and ample annotations.

Neusner, Jacob. *The Classics of Judaism: a Textbook and Reader.* Louisville: Westminster John Knox Press, 1995. A most helpful introduction into the documents of the "Written and the Oral Torah" of Judaism with reading selections by one of the most prominent authorities in Judaic studies. It contains a list of the English translations of the classics of Judaism.

Neusner, Jacob. *Introduction to Rabbinic Literature.* New York: Doubleday, 1994. A scholarly introduction to the classics of Judaism.

A Concise Companion to the Jewish Religion. ed. Louis Jacobs. New York: Oxford University Press, 1999. One of the best short reference works on Judaism.

Jewish Spirituality, vol. I: *From the Bible through the Middle Ages;* vol. II: *From the Sixteenth-Century Revival to the Present.* ed. Arthur Green. New York: Crossroad, 1986-87. An indispensable tool for going beyond mere facts in order to understand the many historical forms of Jewish spirituality.

Zohar: the Book of Enlightenment. tr. Daniel Chanan Matt. New York: Paulist Press, 1983. *Zohar* is the most important work of medieval Jewish mysticism.

Jesus' Jewishness. Exploring the Place of Jesus in Early Judaism. ed. James H. Charlesworth. New York: Crossroad Publishing Company, 1996. One of the best books on Jesus' relationship to early Judaism.

Buber, Martin. *Two Types of Faith.* Macmillan, 1951. Even today this is one of the most profound appraisals of Judaism and Christianity from a Jewish perspective.

Christian-Jewish Dialogue: a Reader. ed. Helen P. Fry. Exeter: University of Exeter Press, 1996. A representative although incomplete selection of excerpts from the ongoing dialogue between Christians and Jews.

Christianity in Jewish Terms. ed. Tikva Frymer-Kensky, et al. Boulder: Westview Press, 2000. Major theological themes are addressed by both Jewish and Christian theologians attempting to find a mutually understandable language. It is an indispensable tool in Jewish-Christian dialogue, even though the Catholic perspective is not adequately represented.

Zolli, Eugenio. *Before the Dawn: Autobiographical Reflections.* New York: Sheed and Ward, 1954. It is the story of the conversion of the former Chief Rabbi of Rome while shedding light also on the effective support of the Jews by Pope Pius XII during World War II.

Hocken, Peter and Daniel Juster. *The Messianic Jewish Movement: an Introduction*. TJII Booklet Series. Ventura, CA: 2004. It describes the rapidly growing Messianic Jewish Movement that acknowledges Jesus as the Messiah, fully human and fully divine, but keeps also the Torah and the Jewish feasts. Their goal is full union with Christians while preserving a clear Jewish identity.

Review Questions

1. Why do the Pharisees, the Sadducees and, eventually, even the crowds turn against Jesus?
2. Describe the formation of rabbinical Judaism after 70 AD.
3. Show some similarities between certain passages in the Talmud and in the New Testament.
4. Give a short outline of the history of Jewish-Christian relations beginning with the "Council of Yavneh" up to the present. In particular:
   a. Discriminatory practices against Jews during the Middle Ages.
   b. What does the Council of Trent say about the guilt of Jews and Christians regarding the death of Jesus?
5. What influence did the Enlightenment have on Judaism?
6. How can you show that the Incarnation has been prepared (although not revealed) in the Old Testament?
7. How would you answer the Jewish statement: "Jesus does not fit the job description of the Messiah"?
8. How is our Christian faith enriched by the study of the Old Testament?

Chapter VII: Common Patterns in Religions and the Uniqueness of Christianity

Further Readings

Eliade, Mircea. *A History of Religious Ideas*, vol. I: *From the Stone Age to the Eleusian Mysteries*; vol. 2: *From Gautama Buddha to the Triumph of Christianity.* Chicago: Univ. of Chicago Press, 1978-82. In spite of its concision, this comprehensive survey is helpful for discerning common patterns and the dynamics of development in the history of religious ideas.

Eliade, Mircea. *Patterns in Comparative Religion.* 1958. Rpt. Lincoln: Univ. of Nebraska Press, 1996. Eliade describes primarily the common features within primitive religions.

Ratzinger, Josef. *Truth and Tolerance: Christian Belief and World Religions.* San Francisco: Ignatius Press, 2004. Especially Part I of this book contains seminal insights for understanding the unity and diversity of religions as well as the unique place of Christianity among the religions of the world.

Review Questions

1. Reduce religious beliefs in God and man to four basic types.
2. Define pantheism (not the word, but the religious system).
3. Which religions are or tend to be pantheistic?
4. There is a correspondence between the idea of God and that of man in a given religion. Explain this relationship
   (a) in a religion that believes in a personal God (or gods),
   (b) in a pantheistic religious philosophy,
   (c) in an atheistic system.
5. How could a Christian explain this interesting correspondence?
6. Show that human beings cannot live and act without some form of Absolute. As Luther said: "One believes either in God or in an idol" ("entweder Gott oder Abgott"). Explain the various forms of a spontaneous and necessary idea of the Absolute in humankind.
7. The conflict between transcendence and immanence is a widely recognizable feature in the development of religions. Explain how it appears in primitive religions, in Hinduism, and in Mahayana Buddhism.
8. What are the common elements in the notion of creation, man, redemption, and morality in most religions?
9. On what ideas do most religions agree concerning the notion of sin?

10. In what religions is there no need for divine forgiveness?
11. Mention at least three common features of moral teaching that appear in most religions.
12. With regard to the notion of God, what is unique to the three Abrahamic religions?
13. With regard to the notion of God, what is unique to Christianity?
14. With regard to the notion of creation, what is unique to the Abrahamic religions?
15. With regard to the notion of incarnation, what is unique to Christianity?
16. With regard to the notion of redemption, what is unique to Christianity?
17. Describe briefly three unique features of Christian moral teaching.

Part III: Christianity, the Sacramental Presence of God's Saving Love in History

Chapter I: A Phenomenological Approach

Chapter II: Historical Foundations for the Truth of the Christian Claim

Further Readings

von Balthasar, Hans Urs. *The Glory of the Lord: A Theological Aesthetics*, Vol. I: *Seeing the Form*. San Francisco: Ignatius Press, 1982.

_____. *Love Alone*. New York: Herder & Herder, 1969. These two books by Balthasar explain—the first in detail, the second in a masterfully condensed way—how all the mysteries of the Christian Faith are ultimately credible only as the self-authenticating revelation of God's Trinitarian love.

Kasper, Walter. *The God of Jesus Christ*. New York: Crossroad, 1986. A masterful treatment of the mystery of the Trinity providing also solid apologetic foundations.

_____. *Transcending All Understanding: The Meaning of Christian Faith Today*. San Francisco: Ignatius Press, 1989. A short contemporary apologetics mainly for a European audience.

Kereszty, Roch. *Jesus Christ: Fundamentals of Christology*, 3-147. Revised 2nd ed. New York: Alba House, 2002. The book provides a detailed treatment of what is summarized in Part III, Chapter II of the present work.

Kreeft, Peter and Ronald K. Tacelli. *Handbook of Christian Apologetics: Hundreds of Answers to Crucial Questions*. Downers Grove: InterVarsity Press, 1994. A clearly written, helpful, popular apologetics.

Rahner, Karl. *Foundations of Christian Faith: An Introduction to the Idea of Christianity*. New York: Seabury Press, 1978. Although the presentation of the Christian mysteries calls for a serious critique, Rahner shows well the supernatural orientation of the human person towards Christian revelation.

Review Questions

1. On what basis can you say that Christianity presents itself as the full self-communication of Absolute Love in history?
2. Explain briefly some of the historical facts that are unique regarding Jesus and the origins of Christianity, facts for which the historian cannot find a natural explanation.
3. How can this historical puzzle of the Jesus phenomenon lead to faith?

Part IV: The Christian View on the Relationship Between Christianity and Other Religions

Chapter I: Toward a Christian Theology of Inter-religious Dialogue

Further Readings

Dupuis, Jacques. *Toward a Christian Theology of Religious Pluralism*. Maryknoll: Orbis Books, 1997. This book is a valiant attempt to sketch out a theology of religious pluralism while maintaining the universality of the saving work of Christ. It does not lack ambiguous formulations, hence it should be read along with the "Notification" by the Congregation for the Doctrine of the Faith, 2001. It contains a comprehensive bibliography.

Dupuis, Jacques. *Christianity and the Religions: From Confrontation to Dialogue*. Maryknoll: Orbis Books, 2002. This book does not seem to register any major development in the author's thinking since his previous work on the subject.

In Many and Diverse Ways: in Honor of Jacques Dupuis. ed. Daniel Kendall and Gerald O'Collins. Maryknoll: Orbis Books, 2003. The essays in honor of Dupuis contain a variety of perspectives on inter-religious dialogue.

Hick, John, and Paul F. Knitter, ed. *The Myth of Christian Uniqueness: Toward a Pluralistic Theology of Religions*. Maryknoll: Orbis Books, 1987. John Hick and Paul F. Knitter are the most well known representatives of an unambiguously pluralistic theology of religions in which Jesus Christ is only one of the many mediators of salvation.

Ratzinger, Josef. *Truth and Tolerance: Christian Belief and World Religions*. San Francisco: Ignatius Press, 2004. The book is a collection of essays that deal in a most nuanced way with the relationship of Christianity to other religions and religious cultures. It is in the light of these insights that one should read the "Declaration '*Dominus Jesus*' on the Unicity and Salvific Universality of Jesus Christ and the Church" of the Congregation for the Doctrine of the Faith, August 6, 2000 (Vatican website).

The Uniqueness and Universality of Christianity. In Dialogue with the Religions. ed. Massimo Serretti. Grand Rapids: Eerdmans Publishing, 2004. Some of the best insights of European theologians are here made available to English-speaking readers.

Review Questions

1. What are the anthropological and Trinitarian foundations for a theology of inter-religious dialogue?

2. How does Christianity evaluate non-Christian religions?

3. How does Christianity understand itself with regard to non-Christian religions?

4. What are the tasks of Christianity with regard to dialogue with non-Christian religions?

5. Give as many examples as you can find to show a possible influence of grace in a non-Christian (non-Abrahamic) religious belief or moral teaching.

6. Give as many examples as you can find to show a possible influence of sin and ignorance in a non-Christian (non-Abrahamic) religious belief, moral teaching, or practice.

7. Describe an ambiguous text in a non-Christian (non-Abrahamic) religion ("ambiguous" in the sense that it can be interpreted both ways, either as expressing a sinful distortion of the man-God relationship or as an expression of genuine knowledge and love of God).

8. Why is genuine holiness possible outside the visible boundaries of Christianity?

9. Show by concrete examples what a Christian can learn from Hinduism, Buddhism (original Buddhism, Mahayana, and Zen Buddhism), Taoism, Confucianism, Islam, and Judaism. ("To learn" means to see a Christian teaching or practice in a new light or to "remember" what has always been part of Christian revelation but had been forgotten by most Christians.)

Chapter II: Evangelization

Further Readings

"*Ad Gentes*. Decree on the Missionary Activity of the Church." *Decrees of the Ecumenical Councils*, vol. II, 1011-1042. ed. Norman P. Tanner. Washington: Georgetown Univ. Press, 1990. It provides a comprehensive outline of a profound Trinitarian theology of the missions and it also deals with concrete pastoral problems, in particular, inculturation.

Pope Paul VI. Apostolic Exhortation *Evangelii Nuntiandi*, "On Evangelization in the Modern World." Washington: USCCB, 1975. The pope's exhortation signals the Papal Magisterium's turn from focusing on internal reform to universal evangelization.

Pope John Paul II. *Redemptoris Missio*, "Encyclical Letter on the Permanent Validity of the Church's Missionary Mandate." Washington: USCCB, 1990. While acknowledging the saving work of the Holy Spirit even outside the visible boundaries of the Church, John Paul shows the urgency of the "new evangelization."

The Church As Mission: "The New Evangelization and Western Culture." articles by A. Scola, R. Kereszty, L. Albacete, M.L. Lamb, R. Royal, F. Javier Martinez, D.L. Schindler, K.L. Schmitz, C.A. Anderson, J.A. Little, M. Ouellet, S. Caldecott. *Communio*, 21 Winter (1994), 567-821.

"*Mission for the 21st Century*: Papers from the Symposium and Consultation Celebrating the 100th Anniversary of the Foundation of Techny and the 125th Anniversary of the Foundation of the Society of the Divine Word." ed. Stephen B. Bevans and Roger Schroeder. Chicago: Chicago Center for Global Ministries Publications, 2001. The Symposium contains both a Catholic and a Protestant perspective on evangelization as well as the issues of inculturation in Europe, Asia, and Africa.

Review Questions

1. Explain the Trinitarian basis for evangelization.
2. Explain the anthropological basis for evangelization.
3. How is the "quality of life" in individuals and in society enhanced by evangelization?
4. In what sense is Francis Xavier's plea for missionary activity true even today?
5. In what sense does every Church member have a missionary vocation?

Appendix

THE MEANING AND FUNCTION OF LOGOS IN JUSTIN'S "CHRISTIAN PHILOSOPHY"

Instead of providing a complete history of the self-understanding of Christianity with regard to other religions and religious philosophies, I include here only a representative sample of this history, the insights of the first Christian philosopher-theologian who reflected extensively on this question.

My intent is to provide an outline of the central role of the notion of Logos in Justin's attempt to sketch out for the first time a universally relevant Christian philosophy in relationship to the Hellenistic religious philosophies and popular religions of his age.[1] I understand here by Christian philosophy not a system of knowledge obtained by mere philosophical reasoning, as distinct from a body of knowledge based on principles gained by faith in God's revelation.[2] Rather, philosophy is meant here in the same undifferentiated sense in which Justin (and other Fathers) use the word: it aims at presenting an integral view of God, the cosmos, the drama of universal human history, the moral order, the history of Israel, the mystery of Incarnation and Redemption, Christian initiation through baptism and Eucharist, the role of Christians in the preservation of the cosmos, and eschatology.

---

[1] As H. Chadwick put it, Justin "is the first Christian to make a serious attempt to determine the relations between Christianity and philosophy, between faith and reason." (Henry Chadwick, "Justin Martyr's Defense of Christianity," *Bulletin of the John Ryland Library* 47 [1965], 275-297 at 275).

[2] See more on the notion of Christian philosophy in the sense in which it does not apply to Justin in E. Gilson, *The Spirit of Mediaeval Philosophy* (New York: Scribner, 1936).

Instead of analyzing all these aspects in detail, I plan to focus on one key notion, that of the Logos, in order to investigate its range of meanings and their function within Justin's thought and, in particular, the role of "Logos" in defining the relationship between Christianity and contemporary non-Christian philosophies and religions.[3]

Context

The first chapters of Justin's *Dialogue with Trypho* provide some personal background for Justin's quest. Even though the dialogue between Justin and the mysterious old man who represents Christian faith may be a literary device, it nonetheless reveals some basic facts about Justin's personal history. He has been involved in a philosophical quest all his life, searching for what is and what is true (*epistehmeh tou ontos kai tou alehthous epignosis*) (D 3).[4] He found in Christianity the only "solid and helpful philosophy" (D 8), and it changed his whole outlook on reality. He saw, however, no reason to reject all his previous philosophical convictions; rather, he corrected and inserted their partial insights into his Christian synthesis. Even as a Christian, he retained the pallium of a philosopher and desired to be known and treated as a philosopher.

Although we cannot be sure to what extent he reinterpreted his pagan past according to the convictions of his later Christian philosophy, the dialogue with the mysterious old man provides us with a probable glimpse into his pre-Christian views, a mixture of Stoic and Middle-Platonist notions. Hence, we can at least conjecture how the acceptance of Christian faith changed his philosophy.

It is intriguing that the first theme of the conversation between Justin and the mysterious old man, the spokesperson for Christianity, revolves around the Logos:

---

[3]   The most important monograph on Justin's theology is Eric Francis Osborn, *Justin Martyr* (J.C.B. Mohr: Tübingen, 1973). See also by the same author *The Beginning of Christian Philosophy* (Cambridge University Press: Cambridge, New York, 1981).

[4]   "D" stands for "Dialogue with Trypho" and "A" for "Apology."

What greater work could one perform than to show that
the Logos rules all things and that the one who, grasping
(the Logos) and being sustained by it, evaluates the errors
and undertakings of others (and sees) that they do nothing which is sound or pleasing to God? (D 3)

This text reveals that the Logos had been a fundamental tenet
of the pagan Justin's philosophy.

The conversation with Trypho and his companions also reveals
the reason that the doctrine of the Logos was so important for Justin:
it constituted a crucial part of his quest for acquiring the knowledge
of God. He left his Stoic teacher because the Stoic philosopher could
no longer teach him anything about God nor did this teacher consider learning about God necessary. After experimenting with a Peri-
patetic (of the Aristotelian school) and a Pythagorean teacher, Justin
thought he found what he was looking for in a teacher that belonged
to the "Platonists" (Middle Platonists). Justin was fascinated by learning about non-corporeal realities and ideas and was expecting to see
God soon (D 2). He knew at that point that God is "that which is
always the same and exists in the same way and is the cause of everything else" (*to kata ta auta kai hosautos aei ekhon kai tou einai pasi tois
allois aition*) (D 3).

However, only from his Christian teacher, the mysterious old
man, did Justin learn the fundamental ontological distinction between
creature and creator and the authentic way of knowing God: human
souls can see God not because their mind is a particle of the divinity
(D 4) but only if, and to the extent that, they are adorned with the
Holy Spirit and live a virtuous life (D 4).

The pre-Christian Justin had sympathized with the opinion of
some Platonists that the soul is unbegotten and immortal (D 5). Now
he learns that outside of God everything is begotten and corruptible;
even the soul dies if God wills it (D 5). The soul is not life itself; if it
were, it would make others alive. Rather, our souls participate in life
and live because God wants them to participate in life. The Christian
Justin's position here is not quite consistent, since he both affirms that

God does not want the soul to die but he also states in the same con-text that souls do die (D5).[5] Yet, the philosophical principle he has formulated remains foundational for the future of Christian philoso-phy: the soul lives "not because it is life but because it participates in life" (*ou zoeh ousa zeh, alla metalambanousa tehs zoehs*) (D 6). Thus not only the cosmos but also souls are creatures totally dependent on God for their existence; they do not transmigrate to another body, but their one earthly life decides their eternal destiny of punishment or vision of God (D 4-5).

While Justin's Christian formation teaches him to establish the fundamental ontological divide between Creator and creature, with particular emphasis on the creatureliness of the human soul, and to attribute the vision of God to the grace of the Holy Spirit rather than to the soul's divine nature, he also learns that the human soul is above the necessity of fate (*eimarmeneh*): the soul freely (by itself: *aph' heautou*) chooses evil or good. Necessity then does not cause the evil or good human act but rather governs the relationship between the good act and its reward as well as the evil act and its punishment (A I 43). Note that Justin attributes even the philosophical doctrine on human free-dom to the "holy prophetic Spirit" who spoke through Moses and Isaiah (Dt 30:15, 19; Is 1:16-20). In fact, according to Justin when-ever the philosophers and poets spoke about the immortality of the soul, about punishments after death, and about the contemplation of heavenly realities, they borrowed "these seeds of truth" from the proph-ets who had lived before all the Greek authors (A I 44).

The truth, then, is not with the philosophers—since they have fallen into so many errors—but with the prophets. These blessed and just men, beloved by God, lived a long time before those who are con-sidered philosophers, and they alone have known the truth and an-nounced it to the human race:

---

[5]   A possible way to reconcile this apparent contradiction is to interpret Justin's statement: "For this reason souls die and are punished" in the same sense as Irenaeus explains the eternal punishment of souls as spiritual death (*Against Heresies*, II, 34:3).

They feared no one, deferred to no one, did not crave for glory; filled with the Holy Spirit, they said only what they have heard and seen.[6] Their writings are still extant and whoever reads them with faith will profit greatly in his knowledge of the origin and end of things and of any other matter that a philosopher should know about. For they did not use (philosophical) proof (*apodeiksis*), since as trustworthy witnesses of the truth (*martures tehs alehtheias*) they were far above all proofs. But what have taken place and what are taking place compel us to agree with what has been said by them. They also are worthy of belief because of the powerful signs they performed for they glorified God, the Father and Creator of all things, and made known Christ, his Son who was sent by Him. (D 7)

Justin narrates the above speech of the mysterious old man to his Jewish interlocutors. This might explain why the only source of knowledge he mentions are the prophets and why he describes the prophetic mission by the terminology of apostolic preaching: being filled with the Holy Spirit the apostles testify to what they have seen and heard, while in Justin the prophets testify to what they have heard and seen. For the Jews the prophets fulfill the role of the apostolic witness. In addition, it seems plausible that at the beginning of the *Dialogue* Justin explains his own coming to the faith in which the fulfillment of the Old Testament prophecies have in fact played the decisive role. At any rate, Justin's previous perspective on gaining knowledge of God has changed dramatically through his initiation into Christianity. The philosophical proofs have been transcended by trustworthy testimony that calls for faith; instead of analyzing the abstract issue of truth and being, Justin's attention has turned to the past and present events of Salvation History, events that have already been fulfilled and are being fulfilled at the time of his writing, such as the sending of the Son of God, the conversion of the Gentiles, and the

---

[6] Remarkably, Justin characterizes the mission of the prophets by what defines the apostolic mission in Acts and in First John (Cf. Ac 4:20, 2:4 & 1 Jn 1:3).

destruction of Jerusalem as a punishment for the unbelief of the Jews. Moreover, Justin has realized that he can obtain this knowledge not by his own resources but only by prayer, that is, only if God and his Christ give him understanding. (D 7, 8)

In the following chapters of the *Dialogue*, Justin explains the fulfillment of the Old Testament in the events and person of Jesus Christ, and by doing so he paints a wide panorama of the entire Christian faith.

As we have seen so far, in the *Dialogue* Justin sets up a sharp contrast between the erroneous teachings of non-Christian philosophers and the one solid and true philosophy of Christians. The object of Christian philosophy and pagan philosophies partially overlap: both deal with God, the cosmos, the nature and destiny of man, but Christianity corrects the philosophers' errors and adds the new dimension of Salvation History: God chooses himself a people, educates and prepares it for the coming of the Messiah, his Son, who is to suffer and to die for our salvation while our attitude toward him decides our eternal destiny of salvation or condemnation. The method of developing the pagan world view and obtaining the Christian one seems to be totally different: in the former you use *apodeixis*: rational philosophical proof; for the latter you need faith in the *martyria*, the testimony of the prophets and ultimately faith in God who spoke through his Holy Spirit in the prophets. You acquire the former through mere human achievement, the latter, through the grace of the Holy Spirit for which you should pray because you cannot obtain it by your own resources.

The Logos in Justin's Philosophy

While the *Dialogue* declares categorically that the truth is not with the philosophers, the *First Apology*, to the contrary, states that some of the philosophers like Socrates and Heraclitus, who lived in accord with the Logos, were in fact Christians before Christ. At first reading both the *First* and *Second Apologies* contradict the view of the Dialogue on philosophers and their method of arriving at the truth. The *Apologies* appear to be pure rhetoric which, for the purpose of

proving the ancient age of the Christian religion (a requirement for
the credibility of a religion in the antique world), dilute the very essence of Christian identity. We quote the entire controversial passage
of the *First Apology*:

> Lest some should unreasonably (*alogistainontes*) assert, in
> order to turn men from our teaching, that we affirm that
> Christ was born one hundred and fifty years ago under
> Quirinius, and then afterward, under Pontius Pilate, taught
> what we claim he did, and should accuse us as if (we said)
> that all men born before (that time) were unaccountable
> (for their actions), we shall anticipate and answer such
> difficulty. We have been taught that Christ was First-be-
> gotten of God and we have indicated above that he is the
> Word (Logos) in whom the whole human race has par-
> ticipated (*metesche*). Those who lived in accord with rea-
> son (*meta logou*) are Christians even though they have been
> considered atheists: such as, among the Greeks, Socrates,
> Heraclitus and others like them; among the Barbarians,
> Abraham, Ananias, Azarias, Misael and Elias and many
> others whose deeds or names we now omit for we think it
> would be too long to enumerate them. Therefore, also
> those who existed (before Christ) and lived without rea-
> son (*aneu logou*) were harmful (*achrehstoi*) people, enemies
> of Christ and murderers of those who lived in accord with
> reason (*meta logou*). Those, however, who lived and live in
> accord with reason (*meta logou*) are Christians, fearless and
> unshaken. From what has been said an intelligent man will
> be able to understand why, through the power of the Word
> (Logos), in accordance with the will of the Father of all
> and the Lord God, he (the Logos) was born as a man
> through a virgin, was named Jesus, was crucified, and hav-
> ing died he rose up and ascended into heaven (A I 46).[7]

---

[7]   In the following quotes I used with more or less modifications the translation of Thomas B.
Falls, *Saint Justin Martyr*, The Fathers of the Church (Washington: CUA, 1948), 83-84.

Justin's character, in particular, his ardent search and service of the truth, attested to by his writings and the Acts of his martyrdom, militates against the hypothesis that the above-mentioned apparent contradictions result from mere rhetorical accommodation to two different audiences.[8] Nor should we assume inconsistencies in his thought before attempting to find a coherent explication. In fact, Justin's Logos doctrine, I believe, provides the clue to the basic coherence of his thought, and to the comprehensive synthesizing potential of his Christian philosophy. We should now examine his Logos doctrine in more detail.

For the Christian Justin, the Logos is no longer identical with what he described in his conversation with the mysterious old man before his conversion. It is not the impersonal Divine Reason or Mind (*nous*) of the Stoics and Middle Platonists that rules all, a particle of which constitutes the human being's highest identity and governs one's judgments and actions. The Logos is the Son, the firstborn of the unbegotten, invisible God, the Father of all. He is on the divine side of the ontological divide, he is not a creature, but the Father's own Son (*idios huios*: A I 23) born from God outside the common way of becoming (*para tehn koinehn genesin*: A I 22); he is the Father's offspring, *gennehma*, a word Justin reserves for Christ alone. He is personal and he is rational, he is God whom Christians worship and love in second place after the Father. He is also God's wisdom who was begotten before all creatures but was active in creation (A I 13). He is a different God (*Theos heteros*) but different only in number not in mind or will (*gnomeh*: D 56; cf. A I 21, D 62, 129). Evidently, Justin has not found the precise articulation of the Trinitarian mystery that will result only from the Arian controversy. Even though he was struggling

---

[8]   In both of his works the truth is put on the highest pedestal. He adopts Plato's dictum: "No man must be honored before the truth" (*Republic* 10.595C quoted in A II 3). Read Chadwick's assessment: "Justin is a propagandist, writing to defend Christianity from outside attack and addressing himself, at least in the *Apologies*, to a prospective pagan audience. Yet there is singularly little in Justin of the uncandid salesman who pushes his wares with high-pressure advertising and is silent about those features which are unlikely to appeal to the public" ("Justin Martyr's Defense of Christianity," 275-276).

to uphold the divinity of the Son and the unity of God by stressing that the Son is of one mind with the Father and born from the Father in a unique way (*idios*), he could not avoid a certain subordinationism by placing the Son in the second place after the Father (A I 13).

Although the Logos does not constitute our identity, all human beings are given a participation in him. This participated Logos is called the "seed of the Logos" (*sperma tou Logou*), *Logos spermatikos*, or part (*meros*) of the Logos. Every human being is given the choice to live *meta logou or kata logon*, in that he can live in accord with the Logos by refusing the worship of demons, and by worshiping the true God and practicing virtues. While the expression *meta logou* is a Stoic formula, Justin transforms its meaning.[9] Since the Logos for Justin is personal, with a personal name, Christ who is the Son of God, the Father of all, living *meta logou* also has at least a vague personal connotation: it means living with the Word, following the Word, following Christ. Conversely, living *alogos*, or *aneu logou*, without the Logos, means going against the personal will of God, being under the dominion of demons so as to persecute those who follow the Logos. The entire course of human history is characterized by the struggle between those people who are under the influence of demons and those who live according to the Logos. This conflict is not restricted in time and space but extends to the universal history of humankind. It is in the context of these two warring camps that Justin's statement becomes intelligible, viz., that all those who lived and live in accord with the Logos (whether before or after the Incarnation) were and are Christians and those who opposed and now oppose them are *achrehstoi*, evil or harmful.[10] When considering this universal battle, Justin does not perceive any difference between the pagan philosophers, such as Socrates and Heraclitus and the great men of God in the Old Testament, such as Abraham, Ananias, Azarias, Misael, Elias and many

---

[9] See, for instance, Marcus Aurelius, *Meditations* VIII, 48.

[10] There might be here an implicit allusion to the opposition *Christianoi - chrehstoi* (A I 4) the enemies of Christos are *achrehstoi* (A I, 46).

others. Both groups followed Christ and were hated and persecuted by the enemies of Christ.[11]

Even the way of justification for the just men in the Old Testament, in particular for Abraham (whose faith is the paradigm of the faith of Christians, so that Christians are all children of Abraham) and the way to holiness for the philosophers is analogous. On the one hand, Abraham was justified by faith in the Logos who spoke to him, a faith that resulted in obedience as he left the land where he lived (D 23, 92, 119). Likewise, some philosophers became truly holy because they dedicated their mind to philosophy, the study of the wisdom of the Logos (D 38, 61, 62, 100, 126). This true philosophy has been sent down from heaven (*katepemphtheh*), it is the greatest possession of (the human race), and is of the greatest value in the sight of God. It leads us to God, and this alone commends us to him (D 2). However, the purpose and nature of philosophy, which in itself always remains one and the same (*mias ousehs tautehs epistehmehs*), has remained hidden from most people (D 2). Thus, philosophy developed into different and contradictory views because, as people followed famous philosophers, they became fascinated by the individual philosophers' personality and by the novelty of their teachings. As a result, they gave up the search for truth (D 2). Yet, true philosophers, like Socrates, remained faithful to the original gift of the seed of the Logos and lived in accord with him (or it). While Justin never applies the term "justification," or its correlates to philosophers, he implies that the way they became holy (by partaking of and living in accord with the Logos) is analogous to the faith of the just ones in the Old Testament and of Christians. The common element in both cases is obedience to, or living in accord with the Logos.

In spite of this profound analogy we have observed, Justin does not lose sight of the difference between the situation of the just men in the Old Testament and that of the 'true philosophers' in the Hellenistic world. Abraham, Moses, and others did not only participate in

---

[11] On the figure of Socrates in Justin's works see especially Michel Fédou, "La figure de Socrate selon Justin," *Les Apologistes chrétiens et la culture grecque*, ed. B. Pouderon & J. Doré (Beauchesne: Paris, 1998), 51-66.

the Logos, but also encountered the Logos in some form (such as angel or fire) and conversed with him. According to Justin the theophanies of the Old Testament are theophanies of the Son and Word of God. Moreover, the prophets, inspired by the Holy Spirit, have revealed the integral mystery of Christ that has included his role in the work of creation, his appearances in different forms in the Old Testament, and the mysteries of his birth, life, passion, and resurrection. Justin presents the prophetic revelation in close parallelism with the apostolic testimony. The prophets, filled with the Holy Spirit, testified to what they have seen and heard (D 7. Cf. Ac 4:8, 20; 1 Jn 1:1).[12]

On the contrary, the philosophers, writers and legislators had only a partial knowledge of the Logos that has come not from a special revelation by the Holy Spirit or Logos but from the seed of the Logos that has been implanted in them (*dia tehs emphutou tou logou sporas*).[13] Without prophetic revelation human souls may know only "that God exists and that justice and piety, in other words, the virtuous life is valuable" (D 4). This knowledge, however partial and obscure, enabled them to live a moral life so that Justin does not hesitate

---

[12] Even here a certain parallelism is presented between the Jews and the philosophers: just as only a few philosophers pursued the search for truth who is the Logos, only a few Jews believed the testimony of the prophets.

[13] Even though the knowledge of the "true philosophers" derives from humanity's common participation in the Logos, the participation cannot be simply opposed to participation by grace. The later distinction between nature and grace must not be retrojected into Justin's works. Justin indeed distinguishes participation by the pagan from participation by the Christian: "For the seed of something and its copy (*mimehma*) given according to one's capacity is one thing but the thing itself whose participation and imitation (occur) according to His grace is another" (A II 13). However, even the implanted logos is a real participation in the Logos, analogous to the situation of "explicit Christians" in whom the "seed from God, the Logos dwells" (A I 32). The analogy is so close that Justin dares to call Socrates and others like him Christians and their persecutors enemies of Christ. For this reason I cannot accept the sharp contrast that Osborn sees between the believer and the pagan philosopher. "The pagan has the shadow. The Christian has the reality" (*Justin Martyr*, p. 38). According to Justin both the "Christian" pagan and the "explicit Christian" participate in the same Logos, but the former only by partial knowledge and by living according to that partial knowledge, while the latter receives the grace to live according to the knowledge of the fullness of the Logos who is Christ himself (*kata tehn tou pantos logon, ho esti Christou gnosin*).

to call some of them Christians. And as a result of living in accord with the Logos, they became the target of demonic persecution.

Whatever other truths the philosophers and other pagan writers knew about the immortality of the soul and judgment after death they learned from the prophetic writings of the Old Testament. Moreover, their teaching was always mixed with errors.

What, then, according to Justin, is the advantage of becoming an (explicit) Christian if the object of faith for the true philosophers and for the explicit Christians is one and the same, the Logos?

For the pagan philosophers the adoption of the Christian faith would mean the realization that the one whom they had followed with only an obscure and partial knowledge they would now encounter as the personal Logos, the Son of the invisible and unnamable God, the Logos who has become a concrete human being, reason, soul, and flesh. He is the *logikon to holon* (A II 10), the *pas Logos* (A II 8) the totality of the rational principle that governs the universe while transcending it. He is the firstborn of all creation, its archetype (*archeh*) and meaning (D 61, 129); he provides his followers with a teaching, a model to follow, and a power that enables them to live the life based on the Sermon on the Mount and to be ready to face persecutions much fiercer than the philosophers had encountered. However, the beatitude that follows this life and is anticipated in this life dwarfs even the suffering of martyrdom (A I 11-17).

To know the fullness of the Logos includes the discovery of the mystery of the cross, which neither the philosophers nor the demons understood. This mystery is "the greatest symbol of (God's) power and rule," it has been announced by the prophets and its symbols appear everywhere around us, the cross is inscribed into the very fabric of the universe[14]; even the shape of the human body reflects it (A I 55, 60).

---

[14] According to Justin's interpretation of Numbers 21:9 (which does not correspond either to the Septuagint or to the Hebrew text), "Moses through the inspiration and impulse of God, took some brass, shaped it into the figure of a cross and placed it over the holy tabernacle" (A I 60). Justin then claims that Plato understood the tabernacle to be the symbol of the universe and placed the sign of the cross in the universe in the form of the letter X, a sign he did not understand to be the cross of Christ (Cf. *Timaeus* 36 B-C).

Christ as Lord reigns from the cross as Justin's version of Psalm 96:10 has prophesied (A I 41, D 73). The cross of Christ provides the pattern for the suffering of his disciples and the power which inspires them to follow his example.

While some of the religious philosophies disclose a partial similarity with the Logos that derives from the philosophers' "living according to the Logos," the popular religions surrounding Justin display a similarity of an entirely different kind. The demons who listened to the prophecies and understood them partially, invented the myths of these religions in conscious similarity to the future history of the Logos made man. The purpose of such activity, however, was to discredit the story of Christ in the eyes of intelligent pagans: since these pagans considered the myths of the pagan gods fables, they would be tempted to consider the true story of Christ that resembles the pagan myths just a similar fable (A I 23, 54).

For a more precise understanding of Justin's Logos we need to discuss its relationship to the pagan philosophies and explore its scriptural roots.

Sources

As we have seen, the mature Justin does not owe allegiance to any philosophy but one, to the solid and helpful philosophy of Christians. At the same time, he uses and transforms elements from Stoic and Middle Platonic philosophy with remarkable freedom.[15] While the stated intent of such critical appropriation in his *Apologies* is apologetical, viz., to defend the legitimate and reasonable nature of Christian faith for a loyal and educated citizen of the Empire, it has also an underlying philosophical purpose. By a transformed use of Stoic

---

Regardless of the convoluted and arbitrary nature of such an interpretation, Justin is struggling to express the fundamental Christian conviction that the mystery of the cross lies at the very center of human history and of the entire cosmos.

[15] On the influence of Middle Platonism in Justin's thought see especially Carl Andersen, "Justin und der mittlere Platonismus," *Zeitschrift für die neutestamentliche Wissenschaft und die Kunde des Urchristentums* 44 (1952/53), 157-195.

and Middle Platonic notions Justin strives better to understand his Christian faith and to articulate this faith's relationship to other religious philosophies.

Under the impact of Middle Platonism and, later, through the decisive influence of the Johannine tradition[16], Justin's Logos is transformed from the Stoics' purely immanent cosmic principle, which accounts for the rationality of Nature, into a personal God, the Son of the unbegotten, invisible, and ineffable Father. This personal God is the one through whom God creates everything and, consequently, it fulfills also the role of the Stoic Logos by explaining the rationality of the cosmos. The *zoon logikon*, the rational (human) being's mind, is a copy (*mimehma*) and seed (*sperma*) of the Logos-Son; therefore, just as the Stoics would teach, the human being must act rationally. This Stoic dimension of the meaning of the Logos enables Justin to defend the Christian faith against its Stoic detractors on its own terms: if they persecute the Christians, they act *alogos or aneu logou*, irrationally or without rationality and consequently, immorally.

At the same time Justin shows the Stoics in their own terms that their Logos-based morality is incompatible with their own teaching on the necessity of fate (*eimarmeneh*). A responsible human act presupposes the freedom of the will. Praise or reproach for a human act done according to the Logos or against the Logos may be considered reasonable only if the respective human act has indeed been performed freely rather than out of necessity (A I 43, II 7).

Similarly, Justin also shows that the moral order based on the Logos presupposes rewards and punishments. If the good or evil act has no necessary consequences for its perpetrator, there is no real difference between good and evil; such notions, then, are but mere human opinions (A I 43).

---

[16] The masterly master thesis of C.R. Helms, "St. Justin, St. John and the Logos-Christ," University of Dallas, Dallas, 1985 and the valuable article of R. Holte, "Logos Spermatikos. Christianity and Ancient Philosophy According to Justin's Apologies," *Studio Theologica* 12 (1958), 109-168 at 125 do convincingly prove the influence of Johannine tradition on Justin's works but they cannot establish his dependence on the Fourth Gospel in its final form.

However, Justin's moral doctrine cannot be reduced to its Stoic elements. To act *meta logou* means for him much more than observing the Stoic principles of justice toward human beings and piety toward the Divine. For the Christian, who is in possession of the teachings of the whole Logos, Jesus Christ, to live in accord with the whole Logos means to follow all his teachings, in particular the Sermon on the Mount, with special emphasis on enduring persecutions with a loving and forgiving heart. The practice of this morality is made possible only by grace for those who participate and imitate the fullness of the Logos, Jesus Christ (A I 14-17). The central function of the Logos in morality assures the anchoring of the whole of Christian morality in the order of creation and, at the same time, its transcending of the natural order.

The notion of the Logos understood as the Son of the Father of all, his first offspring (*gennehma*), the firstborn (*prototokos*) of all creation, intends to make intelligible the role of the Son in creation and salvation history for those intellectuals, Christians and pagans, who were imbued with Middle Platonist notions. While in Middle Platonism God is absolutely and onesidedly transcendent, invisible, and ineffable, the nous-Logos is an intermediary being, not fully divine nor simply a creature. In contrast, Justin makes a great effort to show that the Son-Logos is God. Yet he is God in the second order or rank (A I 12, 13, A II 13, D 56).[17] He alone makes the invisible Father visible and he alone reveals him. And as we have seen, he makes the Father known in different ways to all human beings. Through the partial knowledge of his existence and of basic morality he makes the Father known to the pagans, while through the prophets he reveals the whole mystery to Israel (even though only a remnant of Israel has accepted this revelation).

The decisive influence of the Johannine Logos doctrine appears especially in Justin's approach to the Incarnation and the Eucharist.

---

[17] *Taxis* (A I 13) means both order, which does not necessarily imply higher or lower grade of being, and also rank, which does imply that.

We find only one direct quote or, more precisely, a loose conflation of two Johannine verses (Jn 3:3, 5) in Justin's works. Yet the influence of the Johannine Logos-Son doctrine is palpable in Justin's conception of revelation. In the Gospel of John, God always reveals himself through the Logos-Son. The Word has been coming into the world throughout history (Jn 1:9) so that God has revealed himself through the Word even in the Old Testament: Isaiah saw in the Temple the glory of the Son (Jn 8:41), and the identity of the One who revealed his name I AM to Moses will be unveiled only when they lift up the Son of Man (Jn 8:28). Then they will know that they crucified the One who revealed himself to them through Moses (A I 63). Justin expands on this Johannine theme and shows that in the encounter of Abraham with the three angels the one who spoke was the Logos (D 56). Likewise, the angel walking in the fiery furnace with the three young men was also the Logos (A I 46).

The Johannine influence is even more explicit in Justin's Eucharistic doctrine. He not only further develops the Johannine theme that the Eucharist is the goal of the Incarnation, but he also uses some of John's key terms: *Logos, sarx,* and *haima* (word, flesh, blood):

> We call this food *Eucharistia* of which no one is allowed to partake except the one who believes to be true what we teach and who has been washed in a bath for the forgiveness of sins and for a new birth[18] and who lives according to the pattern Christ has handed on to us. For we do not receive these things as common bread or common drink. But as Jesus Christ, our Savior incarnate, by the Word of God took both flesh and blood for our salvation, so we are also taught that the food made Eucharist by the word of prayer that comes from him, the food which nourishes by transformation our flesh and blood, is the flesh and blood of that incarnate Jesus (A I 66:2).

---

[18] *anagennehsin* is also close to *gennehthehnai anothen* (to be born again) in Jn 3:7.

Besides the *Logos sarkopoiehtheis* that reflects Jn 1:14, the word pair *sarx, haima* (flesh and blood) so characteristic of John 6, dominates the text: it occurs three times, marking three crucial turning points in God's plan of salvation. Its first occurrence designates our humanity taken up by Jesus as his own. The second designates our humanity to be nourished and transformed by the Eucharist; the third refers to the food that has become Eucharist, the flesh and blood of the incarnate Jesus. This Eucharistic flesh and blood of Jesus achieves the eschatological transformation of our humanity. The agent of both the Incarnation and Eucharistic transformation is analogous: in the first case it is the Word of God (*Logos theou*); in the second it is the word of prayer (*euchehs Logos*) coming, ultimately, from the Logos himself. Thus, in Johannine terms the whole mystery of Christ is summarized here with admirable simplicity: the goal of the saving Incarnation is the Eucharist, and the goal of the Eucharist is humankind's eschatological transformation.[19]

Luke's presentation of Paul's speech on the Areopagus in Acts 17:16-34 seems to have influenced Justin's approach to the educated pagans: in spite of the pagan philosophers' partial knowledge of the Logos, he proclaims to them "the unknown God" while quoting their own philosophers to support Christian doctrine, just as Paul quoted one of their poets in his speech.[20]

At the beginning of the *Dialogue with Trypho*, Justin describes what could be called the "fall of philosophers," in which we may detect a mitigated version of Romans 1. According to Paul, at the be-

---

[19] That for Justin the Eucharist is also a sacrifice which both fulfills the sacrificial acts of the Old Law and serves as a memorial of the Lord's Passion, we cannot establish from the words of the institution account he quotes in the *First Apology*. In his *Dialogue with Trypho* (41, 70), however, the latter is the predominant theme. The Eucharist appears as a commemorative sacrificial celebration which takes place *eis anamnehsin tou pathous*: "unto the remembrance of the passion that he (Christ) suffered in order to purify the souls of men from all evil" (41:1. cf. also 117:3). That the remembrance itself is not a simple psychological recalling but actual participation is assured, as seen above, by the real presence of the flesh and blood of the incarnate Jesus Christ (A I 66:2).

[20] Cf. Ac 17:23 to A II 10 and Ac 17:28 to the many passages about the partial knowledge of the Logos in the two *Apologies*.

ginning of history all humankind has suppressed the truth (about God) by their wickedness (1:18) and exchanged truth for a lie, in that they worshiped the creature instead of the Creator (1:25). Claiming to be wise, in reality they became fools (1:22). In Justin's *Dialogue*, those early philosophers who truly dedicated themselves to philosophy, that is, to the search for the truth that unites us to God, were truly holy men. Their successors, however, misled by the glorious reputation of these first philosophers, neglected the search for truth, the one truth, the Logos (A I 6,12, 44, 68[21]), and diverged into different philosophical groups that developed errors and thus contradicted one another.

We could summarize the analogous elements between the views of Justin and Paul in three parallelisms:

(a) Humankind's original ability to know the true God to some extent (Paul) — philosophy's original goal to lead us to God as practiced by the first philosophers (Justin).

(b) Humankind exchanged the truth about God for a lie (Paul) — the philosophers neglected their search for the truth that leads to God (Justin).

(c) The refusal to give glory to God resulted in various forms of moral depravity (Paul) — the neglect of the search for God and the following of glorious philosophers instead led to many conflicting philosophical schools with erroneous notions regarding God and the meaning of life.[22]

While here the Pauline influence is only possible, it is most probable in the description of Abraham's faith as the paradigm for the faith of all believers:

"Abraham himself, while he was not yet circumcised, was justified and blessed because of the faith by which he believed God. [...] He received circumcision for a sign not for justification" (D 23).[23]

---

[21] According to a lost fragment (TLG 13:2) to live according to the truth is synonymous with living according to the Logos.

[22] Holte shows the influence of Rm 1:18 & 20 also on A I 28 (p. 130, fn. 77).

[23] *"Kai gar autos ho Abraham en akrobustia on dia tehn pistin, hehn episteuse to theo edikaiotheh kai eulogehtheh [...]Tehn de peritomehn eis sehmeion, all' ouk eis dikaiosunehn elabe."*

We find here key elements of Paul's reasoning in Romans 4:2-11 as well as Paul's favorite Old Testament text, Genesis 15:6. Further on in the *Dialogue* we are also told that Abraham's justification through faith rather than through circumcision is the model for our justification (D 92) and we Christians are "children of Abraham because of a similar faith" (D 119).[24]

The role of Christ in creation and in the eschatological, risen human race is also expressed by a combination of Johannine and Pauline terminology: The Logos is also the first born of the Father of all (A I 23, 33, 63) and "the first born of all creation" (*prototokos pasehs ktiseos*) and became also the principle (*archeh*) of the new [human] race that has been regenerated by him through water, faith, and wood which contains the mystery of the cross" (D 138).[25]

An Evaluation

Our brief description of the meaning and function of the notion of Logos in Justin's thought helped us better to grasp his attempt at outlining a comprehensive Christian philosophy. This philosophy includes a metaphysics of the Father-Son relationship and of the cosmos, a theology of universal salvation history which includes the entire history of humankind and the special Salvation History that centers on Israel, the Incarnation, and the mystery of the Cross; it lays down the foundation of an anthropology of freedom and the moral order and explains the basic sacraments of initiation and eschatology. Even though it has many lacunae and ambiguous formulations, it provides some valuable insights for a contemporary Christian systematic theology. Here I plan to show in some detail both his lasting contributions and its limits from the perspective of the mainline Christian tradition.

---

[24] Cf. Gal 3:7.

[25] Cf. *prototokos pasehs ktiseos* (Col 1:15) and *archeh, prototokos ek ton nekron* (Col 1:18).

1. While Justin affirms the divinity of the Son-Logos unambiguously, he is unable to articulate an adequate expression of the mystery of the Trinity. He inserts the Trinitarian formula into his works as part of his Christian faith, but speaks only about the relationship of the Father and the Son (A 13, 61). In explaining the revelatory function of the Son-Logos, he remains too dependent on the Middle Platonic understanding of the Absolute.

God the Father is described as so unspeakable (*arrhehtos*) and so unilaterally transcendent that he does not leave heaven; only the Son does. Following Middle-Platonic usage, Justin characterizes only the Son-Logos as *ho On*, the one who is. Only the later Fathers work out the notion of the transcendent fullness of being to be applied to the Trinity as such.

Moreover, the Son-Logos is *heteros theos*, a different god from God the Father of all, and he is God in the second place (*en deutera chora*), a formulation that does not fully safeguard either monotheism or the full equality of Father and Son (A I 13).[26]

2. Rather than in Trinitarian theology, Justin's lasting contributions lie in other areas, and they are relevant even today for building an integral Christian "philosophy." In particular, by means of the notion of Logos he shows the unity of what certain later theological trends separated and even opposed,[27] the unity of the "God of philosophers and the God of Abraham, Isaac and Jacob," while maintaining and explaining the qualitative difference between a philosophical knowledge of God and the revelation conveyed through the prophets by the Spirit. Unlike Bonhoeffer and his school of thought, Justin does not view the Logos of man as the denial of the divine Logos, but a copy (*mimehma*) and seed (*sperma*) of that Logos. While Justin describes a qualitative difference between these two forms of knowledge,

---

[26] Yet, Justin's text does allow also for an orthodox interpretation in which *chora* (place) and *taxis* (order) would simply mean a logical order in the procession of the three Divine Persons, an order that has always remained part of the classic formulation of Trinitarian doctrine.

[27] Cf. B. Pascal, *Pensees.*

he also implies a certain continuity. The same Son-Logos is the principle of the intelligibility of creation and of human history; he is the guiding principle in the life of the true philosophers and the one who has appeared in various forms and spoken to the people in the Old Testament; finally he has been made man, Jesus Christ, in whom (explicit) Christians possess the fullness of the Logos.

3. It is on this basis that Justin is able to sketch out a universal Salvation History that is coextensive with the history of the human race. He presents the historical revelation of the Logos (beginning with Abraham, continuing through the prophets and culminating in the Incarnation of the Logos) in a relationship of parallelism and qualitative difference vis-à-vis the universal history of salvation.

He articulates a parallelism in the sense that both some philosophers, historians, poets, and writers, and the prophets lived in accord with the Logos. However, to the beneficiaries of prophetic revelation the whole mystery of the Logos was gradually revealed and the Logos himself manifested himself in various forms to the just men and women of the Old Testament even before his becoming man in Jesus Christ. On the contrary, whatever specific knowledge the philosophers received about creation, God's punishment, and reward after this life, derived from their reading of the prophets. From the seed of the Logos implanted in them they have known only the existence of God and the value of justice and piety. Thus they could live only according to a partial knowledge of the Logos.

4. Justin's Logos doctrine contains also the beginnings of a radically Christo-centric theology of Scripture. The same Logos, the Son of the Father of all, reveals the Father in both Testaments through the same prophetic Spirit. Even when the inspired prophet speaks in the name of the Father or in the name of a human being or the people, he does not speak by himself but he is always moved by the divine Logos (A I 36). Yet the prophets and the apostles are not passive instruments, but witnesses to what they have heard and seen. From the writings of the New Testament Justin quotes explicitly only the sayings of Christ, even though, as we have seen, he must have known the Acts and at least some of the Pauline epistles. But if everything is re-

vealed by the Son and centers on the Son who reveals the Father, and if the role of the apostles is only witnessing to the Son's revelation, Justin's practice of quoting only the *logoi* of the Logos becomes intelligible. The words of Christ are short and concise, but just as the Logos is the power of God, so are his words (A I 14, 23, 32, D 18).[28] They have in themselves such ground for godly fear that they can move to shame those who have deviated from the right path while they provide a most enjoyable refreshment for those who practice them (A I 8).

5. The conflict between the universally available presence of the Logos in human history on the one hand, and the universally active machination of the demons on the other, defines the dynamics of human history, two centuries before Augustine's *De Civitate Dei*.[29] Justin characterizes the whole of human history by the all-pervading struggle of two opposing forces: wherever someone lives according to the Logos, he is persecuted by those who are without the Logos and act under demonic influence. This universal struggle intensified as the Logos himself becomes man and Christians are able to live in possession of the whole Logos.

6. On the one hand, the Logos doctrine of Justin provides a foundation for a universally obligatory morality which serves as a common basis for dialogue with his Stoic adversaries. He argues that his opponents should not act *alogos*, that is, irrationally, without the Logos but rather *meta logou*, that is, rationally. On this basis Justin hopes for a rational dialogue with those cultured pagans, including possibly the Emperor, who live according to a partial knowledge of the Logos. We have here the beginnings of what will later be called the natural moral law. On the other hand, the possession of the fullness of the Logos

---

[28] Justin quotes the words of Jesus freely either from memory of a written gospel or from oral tradition. See, for example, Mt 5:32, 19:12; Mk 10:18 23:23 in A I 15, 16, D 17.

[29] The difference, of course, between the two conceptions of history is enormous. While Augustine restricts the working of grace even within the Old Testament and within the Church to those predestined to glory, Justin attributes the potential to live according to the Logos to every human being and admits the existence of Christians even before Christ and outside the confines of biblical history.

also explains a specific Christian morality which is labeled impossibly hard by Justin's opponents but affirmed by Justin to be fully consistent with that rational morality which Christians and the true philosophers hold in common.

7. The most intriguing aspect of Justin's thought seems to be his understanding of Christianity's relationship to other philosophies and religions. In some philosophies, as we stressed repeatedly, Justin points to a similarity with Christianity as the result of the working of the *Logos spermatikos*, or seed of the Logos, a similarity to such an extent that on that basis Justin calls these philosophers Christians. Yet, contrary to most contemporary theological writings that stress only the 'positive' similarities between Christianity and other religions, Justin sees in the polytheistic popular religions of his age 'negative' similarities which are not the work of the Logos but of demons. While we may disagree about whether this principle should be applied to a given myth or religious practice, Justin's insistence on deceptive similarities to Christianity in other religions is an opportune corrective to many contemporary systematic theologies.

It is customary to exaggerate the parallelism between Rahner's notion of anonymous Christians and Justin's reference to Christians before Christ. However, the criterion of identification in Justin is strikingly different from that of Rahner. Rahner considers an anonymous Christian any human being who fully actualizes his humanity since this fully actualized humanity presupposes the grace-inspired acceptance of our supernatural destiny. In Justin's theology the criterion for recognizing the Christian who lives according to the Logos is some form of martyrdom: even the Christians before Christ suffered persecution for the sake of the truth from people under demonic influence. Ultimately then, Justin's criterion for the anonymous Christian is the eighth beatitude, the person's share in the destiny of Christ. The mystery of the cross, as we have seen, is for Justin the deepest mystery of Christianity, the greatest demonstration of divine power, inscribed into the very fabric of the universe, although not even the true philosophers were able to recognize it. Yet, unknowingly they did share in the fate of the persecuted Christ. Remarkably, Justin's criterion comes close to what a contemporary Protestant theologian proposed[30] as a replacement for Rahner's criterion: instead of a fully actualized humanity, one should look for signs of a Christo-formic existence, in particular, for a participation in the suffering of Christ as an indication that someone outside the Church may have been justified by grace.[31]

---

[30] Heinrich Ott, "Als Protestantischer Theologe unterwegs mit dem Theologoumenon von den 'anonymen Christen'" *Christentum innerhalb und ausserhalb der Kirche / Quastiones Disputatae*, 73. / ed. E. Klingher (Herder: Freiburg, 1976), 86-99.

[31] Justin's view on the universality of the Logos's operation in humankind is somewhat obscured by his preference for philosophers and other educated people. Even though he affirms that the Logos was and is present in every human being, he mentions only philosophers and other kinds of educated people who lived according to the Logos (A II 10).

NAME INDEX

A

Abelard 159
Abraham 30, 87, 88, 92, 93, 97, 103, 113, 115, 117, 207, 209, 210, 216, 218-221
Abu Bakr 89, 90
Adam 88, 93, 95, 97, 108
Akiba 106
Ali 89, 94, 191
Aristotle 90
Asoka 59
Augustine 11, 222
Augustine of Canterbury 142
Avicenna 90

B

Bandhu, V. 185
Bar Kochba 105
Berger, P. 181
Bernard 64, 166
Bodhidharma 67, 187
Bonhoeffer, D. 220
Brandon, S.G.F. 182
Buber, M. 110, 139
Buddha 51-68, 120, 121, 138, 151, 152, 168, 183, 186, 187, 188, 194
Burke, T.P. 35, 183

C

Cain 117
Chadwick, H. 201
Ching Hsiung Wu, J. 84
Chuang Tzu 76, 78, 189
Confucius 75, 76, 79-85, 137, 153, 189, 190
Cusanus, N. 141, 142

D

Dalai Lama 187
David 104, 148
Davies, B. 181
de Chergé, Fr. C. 101, 162, 192
de Foucauld, Charles 96, 161, 179
de Lubac, H. 13, 144, 167, 177, 178, 182, 188
Derrida, J. 2
Dumoulin, H. 56, 61, 62, 187
Dupuis, J. 144, 197, 198

E

Eliade, M. 24, 25, 28, 36, 183, 194, 195
Esposito, J.L. 183
Ezekiel 180

F

Feeney, Fr. L. 166
Foucault, M. 2
Francis Xavier 165, 179, 180, 200
Freud, S. 2

G

Gabriel 88, 91, 92
Gambhirananda, S. 185
Gandhi 153, 174, 175
Gilson, E. 201
Gregory the Great 142, 174
Griffiths, B. 185

H

Habito, R.L.F. 68, 187
Haight, R. 148
Hanh, Thich Nhat 187
Harvey, P. 188
Heraclitus 152, 206, 207, 209
Heschel, A.J. 110
Hick, J. 181, 198
Hilary 166
Hosea 116

I

Irenaeus 166, 204
Isaac 108, 110, 112, 177, 220
Isaac of Stella 177
Isaiah 106, 113, 189, 204, 216
Ishmael 87, 93

J

Jacob 108, 110, 112, 220
James 134, 140
Jeremias, J. 136
Jesus Christ 19, 33, 34, 47, 116, 117, 134, 137, 138, 140, 146, 147, 148, 149, 153, 154, 156, 159, 160, 170, 175, 178, 188, 192, 196, 198, 205-224
Job 153, 174
John 103, 117, 216, 217